barbecues
and salads

barbecues
and salads

Creative ideas for outdoor eating with more than
400 sizzling barbecue recipes and succulent salads

Christine France and
Steven Wheeler

HERMES
HOUSE

First published by Hermes House in 2002

© Anness Publishing Limited 2002, 2003

Hermes House is an imprint of Anness Publishing Limited
Hermes House, 88–89 Blackfriars Road, London SE1 8HA

Printed and bound in China

A CIP catalogue record for this book is available from the British Library.

Publisher: Joanna Lorenz
Managing Editor: Helen Sudell
Project Editor: Valerie Ferguson
Copy Editor: Linda Doeser
Designers: Bill Mason, Nigel Partridge and Ian Sandom
Jacket Illustration and Design: Katrina Dallaware
Illustrations: Madeleine David, Lucinda Ganderton and Anna Koska
Consultant Editors: Christine France and Steven Wheeler
Photographers: William Adams-Lingwood, Karl Adamson, Edward Allwright, Steve Baxter, James Duncan, John Freeman, Michelle Garrett, Amanda Heywood, David Jordan, Dave King, Don Last, Patrick McLeavey, Michael Michaels, Thomas Odulate, Debbie Patterson, Juliet Piddington, Craig Robertson and Simon Smith
Recipes contributed by: Michelle Berriedale Johnson, Angela Boggiano, Janet Brinkworth, Carla Capalbo, Kit Chan, Jacqueline Clark, Carole Clements, Roz Denny, Nicola Diggins, Matthew Drennan, Joanna Farrow, Rafi Fernandez, Christine France, Silvana Franco, Brian Glover, Rosamund Grant, Rebekah Hassan, Deh-Ta Hsiung, Christine Ingram, Judy Jackson, Soheila Kimberley, Lucy Knox, Elisabeth Lambert Ortiz, Ruby Le Bois, Lesley Mackley, Sue Maggs, Maggie Mayhew, Jane Milton, Sallie Morris, Annie Nichols, Maggie Pannell, Katherine Richmond, Keith Richmond, Anne Sheasby, Liz Trigg, Hilaire Walden, Steven Wheeler, Kate Whiteman, Elizabeth Wolf-Cohen and Jeni Wright

Previously published in two separate volumes, *The Ultimate Barbecue Cookbook* and *Best-Ever Salads*

3 5 7 9 10 8 6 4

NOTES
Bracketed terms are intended for American readers.
For all recipes, quantities are given in both metric and imperial measures and, where appropriate, measures are also given in standard cups and spoons. Follow one set, but not a mixture, because they are not interchangeable.
Standard spoon and cup measures are level. 1 tsp = 5ml, 1 tbsp = 15 ml, 1 cup = 250ml/8fl oz
Australian standard tablespooons are 20ml. Australian readers should use 3 tsp in place of 1 tbsp for measuring small quantities of gelatine, flour, salt, etc.
Medium (US large) eggs are used unless otherwise stated.

CONTENTS

INTRODUCTION

o o o

There is something special about eating outdoors – the appetite is sharpened, the aroma is more tempting, the flavour is enhanced and it is altogether more fun. Whether you are planning an *al fresco* family lunch in the garden, a barbecue for family and friends, a picnic at the coast or a sophisticated summer evening dinner party, you will find the perfect recipe for success here.

The first part of the book focuses on barbecues, offering a huge choice, from family favourites, such as home-made burgers and kebabs, to more exotic dishes inspired by cuisines from around the world. There are recipes for all occasions and every course, including delicious vegetable accompaniments, vegetarian dishes and fabulous grilled desserts. A chapter is dedicated to salsas, dips and marinades to inspire your creativity, and there is also advice on salad accompaniments and outdoor entertaining.

The second part concentrates on salads – from simple side dishes to luxurious special occasion menus and from quick and easy accompaniments to substantial main courses. You can mix and match with the recipes in the first part of the book, pick and choose delicious and healthy side salads to go with an ordinary family meal or plan an entire menu from the appetizer to a refreshing fruit salad dessert. Forget boring sandwiches – most of the salads featured can be transported in cool bags and plastic containers for a wonderful picnic, whether in the country, on the beach or simply in the local park. Make the best of both worlds and take a portable barbecue with you as well.

Both parts of the book include a wealth of practical information about ingredients, cooking and preparation techniques, types of barbecue and fuel, and dressings, marinades and other accompaniments to ensure success every time you cook.

Planning a Barbecue

A well-run barbecue is one of the most enjoyable ways to spend a warm afternoon or evening and it is not at all difficult to make sure that everything runs smoothly. In the following pages, you will find advice, hints and tips on how to do this.

Cooking on the barbecue is always fun and you will probably have plenty of volunteers who are willing to help. However, if too many cooks can spoil the broth, think of the havoc they can wreak with hot coals. You can make use of their enthusiasm by asking them to carry bowls of salad, dishes, cutlery and so on between the kitchen and the

garden. It is also sensible to have a designated adult to watch the barbecue if you need to leave it for any reason – once lit, it should never be left unattended, especially if there are children present.

One reason why barbecues are such a good way to entertain is that much of the work can be done in advance. Marinades, which not only tenderize ingredients but also give them flavour, need time to take effect, so you can often start the preparation the evening before. Meat and fish can be cut up for kebabs, and burgers can be made and stored, covered with clear film (plastic wrap) in the refrigerator.

Safety First

It is all too easy to get carried away with enthusiasm and invite half the neighbourhood to your barbecue. Be sensible about the numbers that can be safely contained at the venue and for whom you can cook without ending up limp and exhausted with scorched food. Serving large numbers of people increases the risk of not cooking the food sufficiently. While part of the charm of a barbecue is that instead of being hidden in the kitchen, you are at the centre of things and can chat to your guests, you won't want to spend the whole time slaving over a hot grill.

Although you don't have to be totally abstemious, remember that cooking on a barbecue is thirsty work and it is very easy to underestimate how much you are drinking. Too high an alcohol intake and hot charcoal could be a lethal combination. Keep an eye on the safety of drinking guests, too. Make sure that you have a good supply of soft drinks for children, drivers and those who prefer them. In the chapter on Outdoor Entertaining, you will find some delicious recipes for both alcoholic and non-alcoholic drinks.

Selecting the Food

Offering a choice of foods is part of the pleasure, but don't be over-ambitious. Depending on how many people you

will be serving, a good selection would include two or three different main ingredients, such as fish, meat and poultry, a vegetarian option and, perhaps, child-friendly food, such as burgers. However, you may be surprised to discover a toddler happily consuming a spicy chicken satay or a plateful of stuffed squid. There is nothing like a barbecue for bringing out just everyone's sense of adventure.

The one thing no one has any control over is the weather. Even when the forecast is promising and there have been weeks of clear blue skies, a sudden downpour or gusting wind can spoil the best-laid plans. It is therefore worth making some contingency arrangements. Before inviting your guests, think about the available space indoors if they need sudden shelter.

Most of the recipes in this book are easily adapted for cooking in the kitchen. Kebabs, drumsticks, steaks, chops and chunky fish fillets can all be cooked under a conventional grill (broiler) for the same length of time. Parcels can be cooked in a moderate oven, for about the same length of time as given in the recipe. Otherwise, if you have a barbecue with a lid, grab an umbrella, put a smile on your face and pass the plates through the nearest window into the house.

Salad for all Seasons

When the temperature soars and the evenings are long and light, no one wants to cook. Happily, this is just the time when baby vegetables are in season, salad leaves flourish and tomatoes, aubergines (eggplant) and courgettes (zucchini) ripen in the warm sunshine.

Nowadays, the range of salad ingredients is almost endless. Even the choice of salad leaves has expanded enormously. Supermarkets and other stores are packed with both familiar and exotic vegetables in a tempting array of colours, shapes and sizes.

While salads are, understandably, at their most popular in the summer, they are also a refreshing and healthy option all year round. All the chapters in the second half of this book include some winter specialities, based on seasonal produce, such as potatoes, fennel or celeriac, or on pasta and rice. However, with modern transportation, almost all vegetables are available at any time of year so that you can have greater variety of ingredients.

Side salads, whether made from raw or cooked ingredients, are versatile accompaniments to almost every main course dish, whether pasta, casseroles or grills. You can serve them as an appetizer, with the main course or, French-style, as a palate cleanser afterwards. They can range from a simple selection of salad leaves tossed in a vinaigrette to a colourful compilation of several different ingredients in a spicy or creamy dressing. You are sure to find a recipe whose flavours are the perfect complement to your chosen main course. Most can be prepared or partially prepared in advance, making entertaining easy.

Main Course Salads

It is during the summer months that main course salads reign supreme. They can be based around almost any ingredients from duck breast fillets to smoked trout and from mussels to steak. A quick and easy salad can provide an economical and filling midweek family supper, while a more elaborate and luxurious dish makes a wonderful centrepiece for a party

buffet or can play a starring role at an *al fresco* dinner. The chapter on Special Occasion Salads will be an eye-opener for those whose imagination has not stretched much beyond ham, hard-boiled eggs and lettuce. However, if these are your favourite salad

ingredients, you will be pleased to find them presented in new and ingenious ways in the chapter called Main Course Salads.

Perfect Picnics

Salads are an excellent choice for picnics and packed lunches. Make the dressing in a screw-top jar and transport it this way to your picnic site or workplace. Assemble the salad in advance or pack the separate ingredients in rigid plastic containers or plastic bags. Then all you have to do is toss it in the dressing and serve.

Use this book to plan an entire menu for a dinner party or special occasion or simply dip into it for ideas and suggestions for family meals. Whatever your taste, budget and level of culinary skill, you will find a recipe for every course and every kind of occasion to delight your family and friends.

SIZZLING BARBECUES

o o o

Just a glance through this mouthwatering selection of recipes, from seared scallops to glazed duck and from sirloin steaks to fruit kebabs, will give you an idea of just how versatile and tasty grilled food can be.

This section of the book begins with some practical guidance about cooking on a barbecue, including safety tips, cooking times and choosing the equipment and fuel. It also offers some handy hints on the magic of marinating.

The remaining chapters cover every aspect of the barbecue menu – from appetizers and snacks to desserts – and includes some unusual and delicious vegetable accompaniments, as well as an entire chapter on salsas, dips and marinades and a special section on outdoor entertaining that will inspire you to party throughout the summer.

While steaks, chicken drumsticks, chops and burgers are traditional barbecue fare, the range of suitable ingredients is far more extensive. Firm-textured fish, such as monkfish and tuna, can be cooked directly on the grill and respond beautifully to the smoky flavour imparted by the fire, while prawns (shrimp) make fabulous and colourful kebabs. More delicate fish can be wrapped in foil parcels to protect their texture from the fierce heat. Foil parcels are an ideal way of cooking vegetables, too, and this section of the book includes a chapter of succulent vegetable recipes, many of which are wonderful, main course vegetarian dishes.

Whatever your plan, from an impromptu midweek supper on a hot summer evening to a full-scale barbecue party at the weekend, you will find the recipes you want here. Accompany cold canapés with hot snacks straight from the grill, cook an entire meal, or even choose an unusual grilled dessert to follow an *al fresco* meal.

HERB POLENTA

*Golden polenta with fresh summer herbs makes a delicious appetizer or
light snack, served with barbecue-cooked tomatoes.*

INGREDIENTS

750ml/1¼ pints/3 cups stock
or water
5ml/1 tsp salt
175g/6oz/1 cup polenta
25g/1oz/2 tbsp butter
75ml/5 tbsp mixed chopped fresh
parsley, chives and basil, plus extra
to garnish
olive oil for brushing
4 large plum or beefsteak
tomatoes, halved
salt and freshly ground
black pepper

SERVES 4

1 Prepare the polenta in advance: place
the stock or water in a pan, with the
salt, and bring to the boil. Reduce the
heat and stir in the polenta.

2 Stir constantly over a moderate heat
for 5 minutes, until the polenta begins
to thicken and come away from the
sides of the pan.

Cook's Tip

Try using fresh basil or fresh chives
alone, for a distinctive flavour.

3 Remove from the heat and stir in the
butter, chopped herbs and pepper.

4 Lightly grease a wide dish and tip
the polenta into it, spreading it evenly.
Leave until cool and set.

5 Turn out the polenta and cut into
squares or stamp out rounds with a
large biscuit (cookie) cutter. Brush with
olive oil. Lightly brush the tomatoes
with olive oil and sprinkle with salt and
pepper to taste. Cook the tomatoes and
polenta on a medium-hot barbecue for
about 5 minutes, turning once. Serve
garnished with fresh herbs.

BRIE PARCELS WITH ALMONDS

· · ·

*Creamy French Brie makes a sophisticated appetizer or light meal, wrapped in
vine leaves and served hot with chunks of crusty bread.*

2 Cut the Brie into four chunks and
place each chunk on a vine leaf.

3 Mix together the chives, ground
almonds, peppercorns and olive oil, and
place a spoonful on top of each piece of
cheese. Sprinkle with flaked almonds.

4 Fold the vine leaves over tightly
to enclose the cheese completely. Brush
the parcels with olive oil and cook on
a hot barbecue for about 3–4 minutes,
until the cheese is hot and melting.
Serve immediately.

INGREDIENTS

*4 large vine (grape) leaves,
preserved in brine
200g/7oz piece Brie cheese
30ml/2 tbsp chopped fresh chives
30ml/2 tbsp ground almonds
5ml/1 tsp crushed
black peppercorns
15ml/1 tbsp olive oil
flaked (sliced) almonds*

SERVES 4

1 Rinse the vine leaves thoroughly
under cold running water and dry them
well. Spread the leaves out on a clean
work surface or chopping board.

TOFU STEAKS

° ° °

Vegetarians and meat-eaters alike will enjoy these grilled tofu steaks. The combination of ingredients in the marinade gives the steaks a distinctly Japanese flavour.

INGREDIENTS

*1 packet fresh tofu
(10 x 8 x 3cm/4 x 3¼ x 1¼in),
300g/11oz drained weight
2 spring onions (scallions), thinly
sliced, to garnish
mixed salad leaves, to garnish*

FOR THE MARINADE
*45ml/3 tbsp sake
30ml/2 tbsp soy sauce
5ml/1 tsp sesame oil
1 garlic clove, crushed
15ml/1 tbsp grated fresh
root ginger
1 spring onion (scallion), chopped*

SERVES 4

1 Wrap the tofu in a clean dishtowel and place it on a chopping board. Put a large plate on top and leave the beancurd for 30 minutes to remove any excess water.

2 Slice the tofu horizontally into three pieces, then cut the slices into quarters. Set aside. Combine all the ingredients for the marinade in a large bowl. Add the tofu to the bowl in a single layer and set aside to marinate for about 30 minutes. Drain the tofu steaks and reserve the marinade to use for basting while cooking.

3 Cook the steaks on the barbecue for 3 minutes on each side, basting regularly with the marinade, or fry them for 3 minutes in a large pan.

4 Arrange three tofu steaks on each plate. Any remaining marinade can be heated in a pan and then poured over the steaks. Sprinkle with the spring onions and garnish with mixed salad leaves. Serve immediately.

Cook's Tip
Firm tofu is easily obtainable from supermarkets and health food stores, and is an ideal alternative to meat.

GRILLED ASPARAGUS WITH SALT-CURED HAM

• • •

Barbecue-cooked asparagus has a wonderfully intense flavour that stands up well to the wrapping of crisp, salty ham. Serve this traditional tapas dish with drinks before a meal.

INGREDIENTS

6 slices of serrano ham
12 asparagus spears
15ml/1 tbsp olive oil
sea salt and coarsely ground black pepper

SERVES 4

1 Halve each slice of ham lengthways and wrap one half around each of the asparagus spears.

2 Brush the ham and asparagus lightly with olive oil and sprinkle with salt and pepper. Cook on a medium barbecue for about 4 minutes, turning frequently, until the asparagus is tender but still firm. Serve immediately.

Cook's Tip

If you can't find serrano ham, try using Italian prosciutto or Portuguese presunto.

GRILLED MUSSELS WITH PARSLEY AND PARMESAN

∘ ∘ ∘

Mussels release an irresistible aroma as they cook on the barbecue: don't be surprised
if they are devoured the moment they are ready.

INGREDIENTS

450g/1lb fresh mussels
45ml/3 tbsp water
15ml/1 tbsp melted butter
15ml/1 tbsp olive oil
45ml/3 tbsp freshly grated
Parmesan cheese
30ml/2 tbsp chopped fresh parsley
2 garlic cloves, finely chopped
2.5ml/½ tsp coarsely ground
black pepper

SERVES 4

2 Place the mussels with the water in a large pan. Cover with the lid and steam for 5 minutes, or until all of the mussels have opened.

4 In a large bowl, mix together the melted butter, olive oil, grated Parmesan cheese, chopped parsley, garlic and ground black pepper.

1 Scrub the mussels, scraping off any barnacles and pulling out the beards. Tap any open mussels sharply with a knife and discard any that fail to close.

3 Drain the mussels, discarding any that remain closed. Snap the top shell off each, leaving the mussel still attached to the bottom shell.

5 Using a teaspoon, place a small amount of the cheese mixture on top of each mussel.

6 Cook the mussels in a pan on a medium barbecue for 2–3 minutes or until the mussels are sizzling hot. Serve immediately, with crusty French bread.

QUICK SHELLFISH PIZZA

Make four mini pizzas or one large one with the same quantities of ingredients.
If you are short of time, use a pizza-base mix instead of making the dough.

INGREDIENTS

FOR THE PIZZA BASE
5ml/1 tsp easy-blend (rapid-rise)
dried yeast
450g/1lb/4 cups strong white
bread flour
15ml/1tbsp sugar
5ml/1tsp sea salt
300ml/¹⁄₂ pint/1¹⁄₄ cups
lukewarm water
30ml/2tbsp extra virgin olive oil

FOR THE FISH TOPPING
15ml/1 tbsp olive oil
1 onion, finely chopped
800g/1³⁄₄lb canned or fresh plum
tomatoes, chopped
salt and ground black pepper
15ml/1 tbsp chopped fresh thyme
100g/4oz cherry tomatoes, halved
12 fresh anchovy fillets, or 1 can
anchovy fillets, drained
8 fresh, peeled prawns (shrimp)
fresh thyme sprigs, to garnish

SERVES 4

2 Add the water and olive oil to the bowl, and stir to make a firm dough.

3 Knead the dough for 10 minutes. Cover and leave in a warm place until it has doubled in size.

4 Knock back (punch down) the dough and knead for 5 minutes, then cut the dough into four. Shape each of the four pieces of dough into 13m/5in rounds.

5 Cook the onions until soft. Add the canned tomatoes, seasoning and thyme and simmer for 15 minutes. Brush the pizza bases with olive oil and cook on a medium-hot barbecue, oiled-side down, for 6–8 minutes, until firm and golden underneath. Oil the uncooked side and turn the pizzas over.

6 Cut the cherry tomatoes in half. Assemble each of the pizzas with a spoonful of the sauce, a couple of anchovy fillets and prawns and the cherry tomatoes. Return the pizzas to the barbecue and cook for a further 8–10 minutes until golden and crispy. Sprinkle a few fresh sprigs of thyme on top of the pizzas to serve.

1 Stir the easy-blend yeast into the flour in a large bowl. Add the sugar and sea salt and mix together well.

Variation
Add your favourite shellfish, such as fresh or canned mussels, to the topping.

CIABATTA WITH MOZZARELLA AND ONIONS

. . .

Ciabatta bread is readily available and is even more delicious when made with spinach,
sun-dried tomatoes or olives: you can find these variations in most supermarkets.

INGREDIENTS

1 ciabatta loaf
60ml/4 tbsp red pesto
2 small onions
olive oil, for brushing
225g/8oz mozzarella cheese, sliced
8 black olives, halved and pitted

MAKES 4

1 Cut the bread in half horizontally and toast the cut sides lightly on the barbecue. Spread with the red pesto.

2 Peel the onions and then slice them horizontally. Brush with oil and cook on a hot barbecue for 4–5 minutes, until the edges are caramelized.

3 Arrange the cheese on the bread. Add the onion slices and sprinkle some olives over. Cut in half. Return to the barbecue to melt the cheese.

CROSTINI WITH TOMATO AND ANCHOVY

° ° °

Crostini are little rounds of bread cut from a baguette and crisply toasted, then covered with a topping, such as this savoury mixture of tomato and anchovy.

2 Cut the bread diagonally into eight slices about 1cm/½in thick and brush with the remaining oil. Toast on the barbecue until golden, turning once.

3 Spoon a little tomato mixture on to each slice of bread. Place an anchovy fillet on each one and dot with the halved olives. Serve the crostini garnished with a sprig of fresh basil.

INGREDIENTS

60ml/4 tbsp olive oil
2 garlic cloves
4 tomatoes, peeled and chopped
15ml/1 tbsp chopped fresh basil
15ml/1 tbsp tomato purée (paste)
1 small baguette (large enough to
give 8 slices)
8 canned anchovy fillets
12 black olives, halved and pitted
salt and freshly ground
black pepper
fresh basil, to garnish

MAKES 8

1 Heat half the olive oil in a frying pan and cook the whole garlic cloves with the chopped tomatoes for about 4 minutes. Stir in the chopped basil, tomato purée and season with plenty of salt and freshly ground black pepper.

Variation

CROSTINI WITH ONION AND OLIVE
Cook 2 large onions, sliced, in
30ml/2 tbsp olive oil until golden.
Stir in 8 chopped anchovy fillets,
12 halved, pitted black olives,
some seasoning and 5ml/1 tsp
dried thyme. Spread the bread with
15ml/1 tbsp black olive paste and
cover with the onion mixture.

Succulent grilled cuts of meat are often the starting point when

planning a barbecue, and chargrilling gives meat a unique

flavour. The recipes in this chapter draw on cuisines from all

over the world to offer an exciting range of dishes that are easy

to prepare and deliciously succulent.

MEAT
DISHES

MIXED GRILL SKEWERS WITH HORSERADISH SAUCE

This hearty selection of meats, cooked on a skewer and drizzled with horseradish sauce, makes a popular main course. Keep all the pieces of meat about the same thickness so they cook evenly.

INGREDIENTS

4 small lamb noisettes
4 lamb's kidneys
4 streaky (fatty) bacon
rashers (strips)
8 cherry tomatoes
8 chipolata sausages
12–16 bay leaves
salt and freshly ground
black pepper

FOR THE HORSERADISH SAUCE
30ml/2 tbsp horseradish relish
45ml/3 tbsp melted butter

SERVES 4

3 Thread the lamb noisettes, bacon-wrapped kidneys and cherry tomatoes, chipolatas and bay leaves on to four long metal skewers. Set aside while you prepare the sauce.

5 Brush a little of the horseradish sauce over the meat and sprinkle with salt and freshly ground black pepper.

1 Trim any excess fat from the lamb noisettes with a sharp knife. Halve the kidneys and remove the cores, using kitchen scissors.

4 Mix the horseradish relish with the melted butter in a small bowl and stir until thoroughly mixed.

6 Cook the skewers on a medium barbecue for 12 minutes, turning occasionally, until the meat is golden brown and thoroughly cooked. Serve hot, drizzled with the remaining sauce.

2 Cut each bacon rasher in half and wrap around the tomatoes or kidneys.

SAUSAGES WITH PRUNES AND BACON

• • •

Sausages are a perennial barbecue favourite and this is a delicious way to ring the changes.
Serve with crusty French bread or warmed ciabatta.

2 Spread the cut surface with the mustard and then place three prunes in each sausage, pressing them in firmly.

3 Stretch the bacon rashers out thinly, using a round-bladed knife.

INGREDIENTS

8 large, meaty sausages, such as Toulouse or other good-quality pork sausages
30ml/2 tbsp Dijon mustard, plus extra to serve
24 ready-to-eat prunes
8 smoked streaky (fatty) bacon rashers (strips)

SERVES 4

1 Use a sharp knife to cut a long slit down the length of each sausage, about three-quarters of the way through.

4 Wrap one bacon rasher tightly around each of the sausages, to hold them in shape. Cook on a hot barbecue for 15–18 minutes, turning occasionally, until evenly browned and thoroughly cooked. Serve immediately, with lots of fresh crusty bread and the additional mustard.

SHISH KEBAB

Many different kinds of kebab are eaten throughout the Middle East, and they are almost always cooked over an open wood or charcoal fire.

INGREDIENTS

450g/1lb boned leg of lamb, cubed
1 large green (bell) pepper, seeded and cut into squares
1 large yellow (bell) pepper, seeded and cut into squares
8 baby (pearl) onions, halved
225g/8oz button (white) mushrooms
4 tomatoes, halved
15ml/1 tbsp melted butter

FOR THE MARINADE
45ml/3 tbsp olive oil
juice of 1 lemon
2 garlic cloves, crushed
1 large onion, grated
15ml/1 tbsp fresh oregano
salt and freshly ground black pepper

SERVES 4

1 First make the marinade: blend together the olive oil, lemon juice, crushed garlic, onion, fresh oregano and seasoning. Place the cubed meat in a shallow dish and pour over the marinade. Cover with clear film (plastic wrap) and leave to marinate for several hours, or overnight, in the refrigerator.

2 Thread the lamb on to metal skewers, alternating with pieces of pepper, onions and mushrooms. Thread the tomatoes on to separate skewers.

3 Cook the kebabs and tomatoes on a hot barbecue for 10 minutes, turning occasionally and basting with butter. Serve with bulgur wheat.

51

BACON KOFTA KEBABS AND SALAD

. . .

*Kofta kebabs can be made with any type of minced meat, but bacon is very successful,
if you have a food processor.*

INGREDIENTS

250g/9oz lean bacon rashers
(strips), coarsely chopped
1 small onion, coarsely chopped
1 celery stick, coarsely chopped
75ml/5 tbsp fresh wholemeal
(whole-wheat) breadcrumbs
45ml/3 tbsp chopped fresh thyme
30ml/2 tbsp Worcestershire sauce
1 egg, beaten
salt and freshly ground
black pepper
olive oil, for brushing

FOR THE SALAD
115g/4oz/¾ cup bulgur wheat
60ml/4 tbsp toasted
sunflower seeds
15ml/1 tbsp olive oil
salt and freshly ground
black pepper
handful of celery leaves, chopped

SERVES 4

1 Place the bacon, onion, celery and
breadcrumbs in a food processor and
process until chopped. Add the thyme,
Worcestershire sauce and seasoning.
Bind to a firm mixture with the egg.

2 Divide the mixture into eight equal
portions and use your hands to shape
them around eight bamboo skewers.

3 For the salad, place the bulgur wheat
in a bowl and pour over boiling water
to cover. Leave to stand for 30 minutes,
until the grains are tender.

4 Drain well, then stir in the sunflower
seeds, olive oil, salt and pepper. Stir in
the celery leaves.

5 Cook the skewers on a medium-hot
barbecue for 8–10 minutes, turning
occasionally, until golden brown. Serve
with the salad.

PEPPERED STEAKS IN BEER AND GARLIC

The robust flavours of this dish will satisfy the heartiest appetites.
Serve the steaks with baked potatoes and a crisp mixed salad.

2 Remove the steaks from the dish and reserve the marinade. Sprinkle the peppercorns over the steaks and press them into the surface.

3 Cook the steaks on a hot barbecue, basting them occasionally with the reserved marinade during cooking. (Take care when basting, as the alcohol will tend to flare up: spoon or brush on just a small amount at a time.)

INGREDIENTS

4 beef sirloin or rump (round)
steaks, about 175g/6oz each
2 garlic cloves, crushed
120ml/4fl oz/1/2 cup stout
30ml/2 tbsp dark muscovado
(molasses) sugar
30ml/2 tbsp Worcestershire sauce
15ml/1 tbsp corn oil
15ml/1 tbsp crushed
black peppercorns

SERVES 4

1 Place the steaks in a dish and add the garlic, stout, sugar, Worcestershire sauce and oil. Turn to coat evenly, then leave to marinate in the refrigerator for 2–3 hours or overnight.

4 Turn the steaks once during cooking, and cook them for 3–6 minutes on each side, depending on whether you like them rare, medium or well done.

VEAL CHOPS WITH BASIL BUTTER

. . .

Veal chops from the loin are an expensive cut and are best cooked quickly and simply.
The flavour of basil goes well with veal, but other herbs can be used instead if you like.

INGREDIENTS

25g/1oz/2 tbsp butter, softened
15ml/1 tbsp Dijon mustard
15ml/1 tbsp chopped fresh basil
olive oil, for brushing
2 veal loin chops, 2.5cm/1in thick,
about 225g/8oz each
salt and freshly ground
black pepper
fresh basil sprigs, to garnish

SERVES 2

1 To make the basil butter, cream the softened butter with the Dijon mustard and chopped fresh basil in a large mixing bowl, then season with plenty of freshly ground black pepper.

2 Brush both sides of each chop with olive oil and season with a little salt.

3 Cook the chops on a hot barbecue for 7–10 minutes, basting with oil and turning once, until done to your liking. (Medium-rare meat will still be slightly soft when pressed, medium will be springy and well-done firm.) Top each chop with half the basil butter and serve immediately, garnished with basil.

PORK AND PINEAPPLE SATAY

• • •

*This variation on the classic satay has added pineapple, but keeps the traditional
coconut and peanut sauce.*

INGREDIENTS

500g/1¼lb pork fillet (tenderloin)
1 small onion, chopped
1 garlic clove, chopped
60ml/4 tbsp soy sauce
finely grated rind of ½ lemon
5ml/1 tsp ground cumin
5ml/1 tsp ground coriander
5ml/1 tsp ground turmeric
5ml/1 tsp dark muscovado
(molasses) sugar
225g/8oz can pineapple chunks, or
1 small pineapple, peeled and diced
salt and freshly ground
black pepper

FOR THE SATAY SAUCE
175ml/6fl oz/¾ cup coconut milk
90 ml/6 tbsp crunchy peanut butter
1 garlic clove, crushed
10ml/2 tsp soy sauce
5ml/1 tsp dark muscovado
(molasses) sugar

SERVES 4

1 Using a sharp kitchen knife, trim any
fat from the pork fillet and cut it
in 2.5cm/1in cubes. Place the meat in
a large mixing bowl and set aside.

2 Place the onion, garlic, soy sauce,
lemon rind, spices and sugar in a
blender or food processor. Add two
pieces of pineapple and process until
the mixture is almost smooth.

3 Add the paste to the pork, tossing
well to coat evenly. Thread the pieces
of pork on to bamboo skewers, with
the remaining pineapple pieces.

4 To make the sauce, pour the coconut
milk into a small pan and stir in the
peanut butter. Stir in the remaining
sauce ingredients and heat gently over
the barbecue, stirring until smooth and
hot. Cover and keep warm on the edge
of the barbecue.

5 Cook the pork and pineapple skewers
on a medium-hot barbecue, turning
occasionally, for 10–12 minutes, until
golden brown and thoroughly cooked.
Serve with the satay sauce.

Cook's Tip
If you cannot buy coconut milk,
use creamed coconut (coconut
cream). Dissolve a 50g/2oz piece in
150ml/¼ pint/⅔ cup boiling
water and use as above.

LEMON GRASS PORK CHOPS WITH MUSHROOMS

· · ·

Thai flavourings are used to make an aromatic marinade and a spicy sauce. The sauce can be put together in a pan on the barbecue while the chops and mushrooms are cooking.

INGREDIENTS

4 pork chops, about 225g/8oz each
4 large field (portabello)
mushrooms
45ml/3 tbsp vegetable oil
4 red chillies, seeded and sliced
45ml/3 tbsp Thai fish sauce
90ml/6 tbsp lime juice
4 shallots, chopped
5ml/1 tsp roasted ground rice
30ml/2 tbsp spring onions
(scallions), chopped
fresh coriander (cilantro) leaves
and 4 shredded spring onions,
to garnish

FOR THE MARINADE
2 garlic cloves, chopped
15ml/1 tbsp sugar
15ml/1 tbsp Thai fish sauce
30ml/2 tbsp soy sauce
15ml/1 tbsp sesame oil
15ml/1 tbsp whisky or dry sherry
2 lemon grass stalks,
finely chopped
2 spring onions (scallions), chopped

SERVES 4

2 Place the mushrooms and marinated pork chops on a rack and brush with 15ml/1 tbsp vegetable oil. Cook the pork chops on a medium-hot barbecue for 10–15 minutes and the mushrooms for about 2 minutes, turning once. Brush both with the marinade while they are cooking.

3 Meanwhile, heat the remaining oil in a small frying pan, then remove from the heat and mix in the remaining ingredients. Put the pork chops and mushrooms on a serving plate and spoon over the sauce. Garnish with the fresh coriander leaves and shredded spring onions.

1 To make the marinade, mix all the ingredients together. Arrange the pork chops in a shallow dish. Pour over the marinade and leave for 1–2 hours.

FARMHOUSE PIZZA

Pizza is not a dish usually associated with barbecue cooking, but in fact the open fire gives the base a wonderfully crisp texture. Shape the dough to fit the grill rack of your barbecue.

INGREDIENTS

90ml/6 tbsp olive oil
225g/8oz button (white) mushrooms, sliced
300g/11oz packet pizza-base mix
300ml/1/2 pint/1 1/4 cups tomato sauce
300g/11oz mozzarella cheese, thinly sliced
115g/4oz wafer-thin smoked ham slices
6 bottled artichoke hearts in oil, drained and sliced
50g/2oz can anchovy fillets, drained and halved lengthways
10 pitted black olives, halved
30ml/2 tbsp chopped fresh oregano
45ml/3 tbsp freshly grated Parmesan cheese
freshly ground black pepper

SERVES 8

1 Heat 30ml/2 tbsp oil in a pan, add the mushrooms and cook until all the juices have evaporated. Leave to cool.

2 Make up the pizza dough according to the directions on the packet. Roll it out on a lightly floured surface to a 30 x 25cm/12 x 10in rectangle. Brush with oil and place, oiled-side down, on a medium-hot barbecue. Cook for 6 minutes until firm.

3 Brush the uncooked side of the dough with oil and turn over. Spread with the tomato sauce and arrange the sliced mozzarella on top. Scrunch up the smoked ham and arrange on top with the artichoke hearts, anchovies and cooked mushrooms.

4 Dot with the halved olives, then sprinkle over the fresh oregano and Parmesan. Drizzle over the remaining olive oil and season with black pepper. Return to the barbecue and cook for a further 8–10 minutes, or until the dough is golden brown and crisp.

Chicken cooked on a barbecue is unfailingly popular with both
adults and children, and it can be as simple or sophisticated as
you choose. Don't forget other types of poultry, particularly
duck, which stays beautifully juicy and moist when prepared
in this way.

POULTRY AND
GAME

CHICKEN WITH PINEAPPLE

∘ ∘ ∘

The pineapple juice in this Indian recipe is used to tenderize the meat, but it also gives the chicken a deliciously tangy sweetness.

INGREDIENTS

225g/8oz can pineapple chunks
in juice
5ml/1 tsp ground cumin
5ml/1 tsp ground coriander
1 garlic clove, crushed
5ml/1 tsp chilli powder
5ml/1 tsp salt
30ml/2 tbsp natural (plain) yogurt
15ml/1 tbsp chopped fresh
coriander (cilantro)
few drops orange food
colouring (optional)
275g/10oz skinless, boneless
chicken breast and thigh meat
1/2 red (bell) pepper
1/2 yellow or green (bell) pepper
1 large onion
6 cherry tomatoes
15ml/1 tbsp vegetable oil

SERVES 6

2 In a large bowl, blend together the cumin, ground coriander, garlic, chilli powder, salt, yogurt, fresh coriander and food colouring, if using. Pour in the pineapple juice and mix together.

3 Cut the chicken into cubes, add to the yogurt and spice mixture and leave to marinate for about 1–1½ hours. Cut the peppers and onion into chunks.

4 Arrange the chicken pieces, vegetables and reserved pineapple chunks alternately on six skewers.

5 Brush the kebabs with oil and cook on a medium barbecue for about 10 minutes, turning and basting the chicken pieces regularly with the marinade, until cooked through. Serve with salad or plain boiled rice.

1 Drain the canned pineapple into a bowl. Reserve twelve large chunks of pineapple. Squeeze the juice from the remaining chunks into the bowl, then discard the chunks. You should be left with about 120ml/4fl oz/½ cup pineapple juice.

CITRUS KEBABS

Serve these succulent grilled chicken kebabs on a bed of lettuce leaves, garnished with sprigs of fresh mint and orange and lemon slices.

INGREDIENTS

4 skinless, boneless chicken
breast portions
fresh mint sprigs, to garnish
orange and lemon or lime slices,
to garnish

FOR THE MARINADE
finely grated rind and juice of
½ orange
finely grated rind and juice of
½ lemon or lime
30ml/2 tbsp olive oil
30ml/2 tbsp clear honey
30ml/2 tbsp chopped fresh mint
1.5ml/¼ tsp ground cumin
salt and freshly ground
black pepper

SERVES 4

1 Use a heavy knife to cut the chicken into 2.5cm/1in cubes.

2 Combine the marinade ingredients in a large bowl, add the chicken and cover with clear film (plastic wrap). Leave to marinate for at least 2 hours, or overnight in the refrigerator.

3 Thread the chicken on to metal skewers and cook on a medium barbecue for 10 minutes, basting with the marinade and turning frequently. Garnish with mint and citrus slices.

SWEET AND SOUR KEBABS

*This marinade contains sugar and will burn very easily, so cook the kebabs slowly
and turn them often. Serve these kebabs with harlequin rice.*

INGREDIENTS

2 skinless, boneless chicken
breast portions
8 pickling (pearl) onions or
2 medium onions
4 rindless streaky (fatty) bacon
rashers (strips)
3 firm bananas
1 red (bell) pepper, diced

FOR THE MARINADE
30ml/2 tbsp soft brown sugar
15ml/1 tbsp Worcestershire sauce
30ml/2 tbsp lemon juice
salt and freshly ground
black pepper

FOR THE HARLEQUIN RICE
30ml/2 tbsp olive oil
1 small red (bell) pepper, diced
225g/8oz/1⅓ cup cooked rice
115g/4oz/1 cup cooked peas

SERVES 4

1 Combine the marinade ingredients.
Cut each chicken portion into four
pieces, add to the marinade, cover and
leave for at least 4 hours, or preferably
overnight in the refrigerator.

2 Peel the pickling onions, blanch them
in boiling water for 5 minutes and
drain. If using medium onions, quarter
them after blanching.

3 Cut each rasher of bacon in half with
a sharp knife. Peel the bananas and cut
each one into three pieces. Wrap half a
bacon rasher around each of the
banana pieces.

4 Thread the bacon and bananas
on to metal skewers with the chicken
pieces, onions and pepper pieces. Brush
generously with the marinade.

5 Cook on a low barbecue for about
15 minutes, turning and basting
frequently with the marinade.

6 Meanwhile, heat the oil in a
frying pan and stir-fry the diced pepper
briefly. Add the rice and peas and stir
until heated through. Serve the
harlequin rice with the kebabs.

DUCK WITH RED PEPPER JELLY GLAZE

Sweet potatoes have pinkish skins and flesh varying from creamy white to deep orange.
Choose a long cylindrical tuber to make neat round slices for this Cajun dish.

INGREDIENTS

2 duck breast fillets
1 sweet potato, about 400g/14oz
30ml/2 tbsp red (bell) pepper jelly
15ml/1 tbsp sherry vinegar
50g/2oz/4 tbsp butter, melted
coarse sea salt and freshly ground
black pepper

SERVES 2

4 Meanwhile, warm the red pepper jelly and sherry vinegar together in a bowl set over a pan of hot water, stirring to mix them as the jelly melts. Brush the skin of the duck with this jelly glaze and return to the barbecue, skin-side down, for 2–3 minutes more to caramelize it.

5 Brush the sweet potato slices with melted butter and sprinkle with coarse sea salt. Cook on a hot barbecue for 8–10 minutes until soft, brushing with more butter and sprinkling with salt and pepper when you turn them. Serve the duck sliced with the sweet potatoes and accompany with a green salad.

1 Slash the skin of the duck diagonally at 2.5cm/1in intervals and rub plenty of salt and pepper over the skin and into the cuts.

2 Scrub the sweet potato and cut into 1cm/½in slices, discarding the ends.

3 Cook the duck on a medium barbecue, skin side down, for about 5 minutes. Turn them over and cook for 8–10 minutes more, according to how pink you like your duck.

DUCK WITH RED PLUMS

· · ·

The rich fruity sauce for this dish combines brandy and red plums with double cream and coriander. The sauce can be made in a pan on the barbecue while the duck is cooking.

INGREDIENTS

4 duck breast fillets, 175g/6oz each
10ml/2 tsp crushed cinnamon stick
50g/2oz/¼ cup butter
15ml/1 tbsp plum brandy
250ml/8fl oz/1 cup chicken stock
250ml/8fl oz/1 cup double
(heavy) cream
6 fresh red plums, stoned (pitted)
and sliced
6 sprigs fresh coriander (cilantro)
leaves, plus extra to garnish
salt and freshly ground
black pepper

SERVES 4

1 Skin the duck fillets, score them and sprinkle with salt. Press the crushed cinnamon on to both sides of the duck breasts. Brush with butter and cook on a medium barbecue for 15–20 minutes, turning once, until the duck is tender.

2 To make the sauce, melt half the remaining butter in a pan. Add the plum brandy and set it alight. When the flames have died down, add the stock and cream and simmer gently until reduced and thick. Season to taste with salt and pepper.

3 In a pan, melt the other half of the butter and cook the plums and coriander just enough to cook the fruit through. Slice the duck fillets and pour some sauce around each one, then garnish with the plum slices and the chopped fresh coriander.

JUNIPER-SPICED VENISON CHOPS

*Depending on the type of venison available, the chops will vary in size,
so you will need either one or two per person.*

INGREDIENTS

4–8 venison chops
250ml/8fl oz/1 cup red wine
2 medium red onions
6 juniper berries, crushed
1 cinnamon stick, crumbled
1 dried bay leaf, crumbled
thinly pared strip of orange rind
olive oil, for brushing
*salt and freshly ground black
pepper*

SERVES 4

2 Add the juniper berries, cinnamon, bay leaf and orange rind. Toss well to coat evenly and then cover the bowl and leave to marinate for at least an hour, or overnight in the refrigerator.

1 Place the venison chops in a large mixing bowl and pour over the red wine. Using a sharp knife, cut the red onions in half crossways and add them to the bowl.

3 Drain the venison and onions and reserve the marinade. Brush the venison and onions generously with the olive oil and sprinkle with plenty of salt and freshly ground black pepper.

4 Cook the venison and onions on a medium-hot barbecue for about 8–10 minutes on each side, basting regularly with the marinade. The venison should still be slightly pink inside even when fully cooked.

Cook's Tip

*Tender farmed venison
is now widely available from
supermarkets and good butchers
shops, but if venison is difficult
to find, beef steaks could be
used instead.*

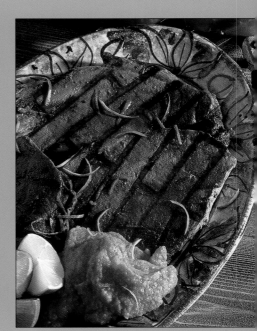

Oily fish, such as tuna, are perfectly suited to grilling and won't

dry out. Use plump prawns or shrimps or firm-textured fish,

such as monkfish, for kebabs, but marinate them first to keep

them moist. More delicate fish can be cooked wrapped in foil,

either on the rack or directly on the coals.

FISH AND
SHELLFISH

SPICED PRAWNS WITH VEGETABLES

* * *

This is a light and nutritious Indian dish, excellent served either on a bed of lettuce leaves,
or with plain boiled rice or chappatis.

INGREDIENTS

20 cooked king prawns (jumbo
shrimp), peeled
1 courgette (zucchini), sliced
1 medium onion, cut into 8 chunks
8 cherry tomatoes
8 baby corn cobs
mixed salad leaves, to serve

FOR THE MARINADE
30ml/2 tbsp chopped fresh
coriander (cilantro)
5ml/1 tsp salt
2 fresh green chillies, seeded
45ml/3 tbsp lemon juice
30ml/2 tbsp vegetable oil

SERVES 4

1 To make the marinade, process the coriander, salt, chillies, lemon juice and oil together in a food processor.

2 Empty the contents from the processor and transfer to a bowl.

3 Add the peeled king prawns to the mixture in the bowl and stir to make sure that all the prawns are thoroughly coated. Cover the bowl with clear film (plastic wrap) and set aside in a cool place, to marinate for 30 minutes.

4 Arrange the vegetables and prawns alternately on four long skewers. Cook on a medium barbecue for 5 minutes, turning frequently, until cooked and browned. Serve immediately, on a bed of mixed salad leaves.

TIGER PRAWN SKEWERS WITH WALNUT PESTO

This is an unusual appetizer or main course, which can be prepared in advance and kept in the refrigerator until you're ready to cook it.

INGREDIENTS

12–16 large, raw, unpeeled tiger
prawns (jumbo shrimp)
50g/2oz/¹⁄2 cup walnut pieces
60ml/4 tbsp chopped fresh flat
leaf parsley
60ml/4 tbsp chopped fresh basil
2 garlic cloves, chopped
45ml/3 tbsp freshly grated
Parmesan cheese
30ml/2 tbsp extra virgin olive oil
30ml/2 tbsp walnut oil
salt and freshly ground
black pepper

SERVES 4

3 Add half the pesto to the prawns, toss them well, then cover and chill in the refrigerator for a minimum of 1 hour, or leave them overnight.

4 Thread the prawns on to skewers and cook them on a hot barbecue for 3–4 minutes, turning once. Serve with the remaining pesto and a green salad.

1 Peel the prawns, removing the head but leaving the tail. Devein and then put the prawns in a large mixing bowl.

2 To make the pesto, place the walnuts, parsley, basil, garlic, cheese and oils in a food processor and process until finely chopped. Season to taste.

101

STUFFED SARDINES

∘ ∘ ∘

This Middle Eastern-inspired dish doesn't take much preparation and is a meal in itself.
Just serve with a crisp green salad tossed in a fresh lemon vinaigrette to make it complete.

INGREDIENTS

10g/¼ oz/¼ cup fresh parsley
3–4 garlic cloves, crushed
8–12 fresh or frozen
sardines, cleaned
30ml/2 tbsp lemon juice
50g/2oz/½ cup plain (all-purpose) flour
2.5ml/½ tsp ground cumin
olive oil, for brushing
salt and freshly ground
black pepper
naan bread and green salad,
to serve

SERVES 4

1 Finely chop the parsley and mix in a small bowl with the garlic. Pat the parsley and garlic mixture all over the outsides and insides of the prepared sardines. Sprinkle the sardines with lemon juice, then place them in a dish, cover and set aside in a cool place for up to 2 hours, to absorb the flavours.

2 Place the flour on a large plate and season with the cumin, salt and pepper. Roll the sardines in the flour.

3 Brush the sardines with olive oil and cook on a medium-hot barbecue for about 3 minutes each side. Serve with naan bread and a green salad.

111

MONKFISH WITH PEPPERED CITRUS MARINADE

. . .

Monkfish is a firm, meaty fish that cooks well on the barbecue and keeps its shape.
Serve with a green salad.

INGREDIENTS

2 monkfish tails, about
350g/12oz each
1 lime
1 lemon
2 oranges
handful of fresh thyme sprigs
30ml/2 tbsp olive oil
15ml/1 tbsp mixed peppercorns,
coarsely crushed
salt and freshly ground
black pepper

SERVES 4

2 Turn the fish and repeat on the other side, to remove the second fillet. Repeat on the second tail. (If you prefer, you can ask your fishmonger to do this for you.) Lay the four fillets out flat on a chopping board.

5 Squeeze the juice from the citrus fruits and mix it with the olive oil and more salt and pepper. Spoon over the fish. Cover with clear film (plastic wrap) and leave to marinate in the refrigerator for about 1 hour, turning the fish occasionally.

1 Using a sharp kitchen knife, remove any skin from the monkfish tails. Cut carefully down one side of the backbone, sliding the knife between the bone and flesh, to remove the fillet on one side.

3 Cut two slices from each of the citrus fruits and arrange them over two of the fillets. Add a few sprigs of fresh thyme and sprinkle with plenty of salt and freshly ground black pepper. Finely grate the rind from the remaining fruit and sprinkle it over the fish.

6 Drain the monkfish, reserving the marinade, and sprinkle evenly with the crushed peppercorns. Cook the fish on a medium-hot barbecue for about 15–20 minutes, turning occasionally and basting with the marinade, until the fish is evenly cooked.

4 Lay the other two fillets on top and tie them firmly at intervals.

SMOKED MACKEREL WITH BLUEBERRIES

*Fresh blueberries burst with flavour when cooked, and their sharpness complements
the rich flesh of mackerel very well.*

INGREDIENTS

30 ml/2 tbsp plain (all-
purpose) flour
4 hot-smoked mackerel fillets
50g/2oz/4 tbsp butter
juice of ½ lemon
salt and freshly ground
black pepper

FOR THE BLUEBERRY SAUCE
450g/1lb/4 cups blueberries
30ml/2 tbsp caster (superfine) sugar
15g/½oz/1 tbsp unsalted
(sweet) butter
SERVES 4

1 Season the flour with salt and freshly ground black pepper. Coat each fish fillet in the flour, covering it well.

2 Brush the fillets with butter and cook on a medium barbecue for a few minutes until heated through with a crisp coating.

3 To make the sauce, place the blueberries, sugar, butter and salt and pepper in a small roasting pan and cook on the barbecue, stirring occasionally, for about 10 minutes. Serve immediately, drizzling the lemon juice over the mackerel and with the blueberries on the side.

MACKEREL WITH TOMATOES, PESTO AND ONION

*Rich oily fish like mackerel needs a sharp, fresh-tasting sauce to go with it,
and this aromatic pesto is excellent drizzled over the top.*

INGREDIENTS

4 mackerel, cleaned and gutted
30ml/2 tbsp olive oil
115g/4oz onion, coarsely chopped
450g/1lb tomatoes,
coarsely chopped
salt and freshly ground
black pepper

FOR THE PESTO
50g/2oz/1/2 cup pine nuts
30ml/2 tbsp fresh basil leaves
2 garlic cloves, crushed
30ml/2 tbsp freshly grated
Parmesan cheese
150ml/1/4 pint/2/3 cup extra virgin
olive oil

SERVES 4

1 To make the pesto, place the pine
nuts, fresh basil leaves and garlic in a
food processor and blend to a coarse
paste. Add the Parmesan and, with the
motor running, gradually add the oil.

2 Season the mackerel well with plenty
of salt and freshly ground black pepper
and cook on a medium-hot barbecue
for about 12–15 minutes, turning the
fish once.

3 Meanwhile, heat the olive oil in
a large, heavy pan. Add the chopped
onions and sauté, stirring occasionally,
until soft and golden brown.

4 Stir the chopped tomatoes into the
contents of the pan and cook for about
5 minutes. Serve the fish on top of the
tomato mixture and top with a
generous spoonful of the pesto.

CHARGRILLED TUNA WITH FIERY PEPPER PURÉE

. . .

Tuna is an oily fish that barbecues well and is meaty enough to combine successfully with strong flavours – even hot chilli, as in this red pepper purée, which is excellent served with crusty bread.

INGREDIENTS

4 tuna steaks, about 175g/6oz each
finely grated rind and juice of 1 lime
30ml/2 tbsp olive oil
salt and freshly ground black pepper
lime wedges, to serve

FOR THE PEPPER PURÉE
2 red (bell) peppers, halved
45ml/3 tbsp olive oil, plus extra
for brushing
1 small onion
2 garlic cloves, crushed
2 red chillies
1 slice white bread without
crusts, diced
salt

SERVES 4

1 Trim any skin from the tuna and place the steaks in a single layer in a dish. Sprinkle over the lime rind and juice, olive oil, salt and pepper. Cover with clear film (plastic wrap) and chill in the refrigerator until required.

Cook's Tip
The (bell) pepper purée can be made in advance, cooking the peppers and onion under a hot grill (broiler); chill until required.

2 To make the pepper purée, brush the pepper halves with a little olive oil and cook them, skin-side down, on a hot barbecue, until the skin is charred and blackened. Place the onion in its skin on the barbecue and cook until browned, turning it occasionally.

3 Leave the peppers and onion until cool enough to handle, then remove the skins, using a sharp kitchen knife.

4 Place the cooked peppers and onion with the garlic, chillies, bread and olive oil in a food processor. Process until smooth. Add salt to taste.

5 Drain the tuna steaks from the marinade and cook them on a hot barbecue for 8–10 minutes, turning once, until golden brown. Serve with the pepper purée and lime wedges, with crusty bread if you like.

TROUT WITH BACON

∘ ∘ ∘

The smoky, savoury flavour of crispy grilled bacon perfectly complements
the delicate flesh of the trout in this simple dish.

INGREDIENTS

4 trout, cleaned and gutted
15ml/1 tbsp plain (all-purpose) flour
4 rashers (strips) smoked bacon
30ml/2 tbsp olive oil
juice of ½ lemon
salt and freshly ground
black pepper

SERVES 4

1 Place the trout on a chopping board and pat them dry with kitchen paper. Season the flour with the salt and freshly ground black pepper. Stretch the bacon rashers out thinly using the back of a heavy kitchen knife.

2 Roll the fish in the seasoned flour mixture and wrap them tightly in the bacon. Brush with olive oil and cook on a medium-hot barbecue for 10–15 minutes, turning once. Serve at once, drizzled with the lemon juice.

RED MULLET WITH BASIL AND CITRUS

° ° °

This Italian recipe is full of the warm, distinctive flavours of the Mediterranean.
Serve the dish with plain boiled rice and a green salad, or with lots of fresh crusty bread.

INGREDIENTS

4 red mullet or snapper, about
225g/8oz each, filleted
60ml/4 tbsp olive oil
10 peppercorns, crushed
2 oranges, one peeled and sliced
and one squeezed
1 lemon
15g/¹/₂ oz/1 tbsp butter
2 drained canned anchovy
fillets, chopped
60ml/4 tbsp shredded fresh basil
salt and freshly ground
black pepper

SERVES 4

1 Place the fish fillets in a shallow dish in a single layer. Pour over the olive oil and sprinkle with the crushed peppercorns. Lay the orange slices on top of the fish. Cover the dish with clear film (plastic wrap), and leave to marinate in the refrigerator for 4 hours.

2 Halve the lemon. Remove the skin and pith from one half using a small, sharp knife, and slice the flesh thinly. Squeeze the juice from the other half.

3 Drain the fish, reserving the marinade and orange slices, and cook on a medium-hot barbecue for about 10–12 minutes, turning once and basting with the marinade.

4 Melt the butter in a pan with any remaining marinade. Add the chopped anchovy fillets and cook until they are completely soft. Stir in the orange and lemon juice and allow to simmer on the edge of the barbecue until slightly reduced. Stir in the basil and check the seasoning. Pour over the fish and garnish with the reserved orange slices and the lemon slices.

FISH PARCELS

○ ○ ○

Sea bass is good for this recipe, but you could also use small whole trout or a white fish fillet, such as cod or haddock.

INGREDIENTS

4 pieces sea bass fillet, or 4 small
sea bass, about 450g/1lb each
olive oil for brushing
2 shallots, thinly sliced
1 garlic clove, chopped
15ml/1 tbsp capers
6 sun-dried tomatoes,
finely chopped
4 black olives, pitted and
thinly sliced
grated rind and juice of 1 lemon
5ml/1 tsp paprika
salt and freshly ground
black pepper

SERVES 4

1 Clean the fish if whole. Cut four squares of double-thickness baking foil, large enough to enclose the fish; brush lightly with a little olive oil.

2 Place a piece of fish in the centre of each piece of baking foil and season well with plenty of salt and pepper.

3 Sprinkle over the shallots, chopped garlic, capers, tomatoes, sliced olives and grated lemon rind. Sprinkle with the lemon juice and paprika.

4 Fold over the baking foil to enclose the fish loosely, sealing the edges firmly so that none of the juices can escape during cooking. Place the parcels on a moderately hot barbecue and cook for about 8–10 minutes. To serve, place each of the parcels on a plate and loosen the tops to open.

Cook's Tip

These parcels can also be baked in the oven: place them on a baking sheet and cook at 200°C/400°F/Gas 6 for about 15–20 minutes.

SPICED FISH BAKED THAI STYLE

· · ·

Banana leaves make a perfect, natural wrapping for barbecue-cooked foods, but if they are not available you can use baking foil instead.

INGREDIENTS

4 red snapper or mullet, about
350g/12oz each
banana leaves
1 lime
1 garlic clove, thinly sliced
2 spring onions (scallions), sliced
30ml/2 tbsp Thai red
curry paste
60ml/4 tbsp coconut milk

SERVES 4

1 Clean the fish, removing the scales, and make several deep slashes in the side of each with a sharp knife. Place each fish on a layer of banana leaves.

2 Thinly slice half the lime and tuck the slices into the slashes in the fish, with the slivers of garlic. Sprinkle the sliced spring onions over the fish.

3 Grate the rind and squeeze the juice from the remaining half-lime and mix with the curry paste and coconut milk. Spoon over the fish.

4 Wrap the leaves over the fish, to enclose them completely. Tie firmly with string and cook on a medium-hot barbecue for 15–20 minutes, turning occasionally. To serve, open up the parcels by cutting along the top edge with a knife and fanning out the leaves.

Sea Bream with Orange Butter Sauce

• • •

Sea bream is a revelation to anyone unfamiliar with its creamy rich flavour.
The fish has a firm white flesh that goes well with this rich butter sauce, sharpened with orange.

INGREDIENTS

2 sea bream, about 350g/12oz
each, scaled and gutted
10ml/2 tsp Dijon mustard
5ml/1 tsp fennel seeds
30ml/2 tbsp olive oil
50g/2oz watercress
175g/6oz mixed lettuce leaves,
such as escarole and frisée

FOR THE ORANGE BUTTER SAUCE
30ml/2 tbsp frozen orange
juice concentrate
175g/6oz/3/4 cup unsalted (sweet)
butter, diced
salt and cayenne pepper

SERVES 2

1 Slash the sea bream four times on either side. Combine the mustard and fennel seeds, then spread over both sides of the fish. Brush with olive oil and cook on a medium-hot barbecue for 10–12 minutes, turning once.

2 Place the orange juice concentrate in a bowl and heat over a pan of simmering water. Remove the pan from the heat and gradually whisk in the butter until creamy. Season well.

3 Dress the watercress and lettuce leaves with the remaining olive oil, and arrange with the fish on two plates. Spoon the sauce over the fish and serve with baked potatoes, if you like.

There are lots of ideas here for vegetable accompaniments to meat and fish dishes, as well as for substantial main dishes that everyone, vegetarian or not, will love. All vegetables can be cooked in foil parcels, but many are ideally suited to direct grilling on the barbecue.

VEGETARIAN DISHES AND VEGETABLES

RED BEAN AND MUSHROOM BURGERS

∘ ∘ ∘

Vegetarians, vegans and meat-eaters alike will enjoy these healthy, low-fat veggie burgers.
With salad, pitta bread and Greek-style yogurt, they make a substantial meal.

INGREDIENTS

15ml/1 tbsp olive oil
1 small onion, finely chopped
1 garlic clove, crushed
5ml/1 tsp ground cumin
5ml/1 tsp ground coriander
2.5ml/¹/₂ tsp ground turmeric
115g/4oz/1¹/₂ cups finely
chopped mushrooms
400g/14oz can red kidney beans
30ml/2 tbsp chopped fresh
coriander (cilantro)
wholemeal (whole-wheat) flour
olive oil, for brushing
salt and freshly ground
black pepper
Greek (US strained plain) yogurt

SERVES 4

2 Add the chopped mushrooms and cook, stirring, until softened and dry. Remove the pan from the heat and empty the contents into a large bowl.

5 Using floured hands, form the mixture into four flat burger shapes. If the mixture is too sticky to handle, mix in a little wholemeal flour.

3 Drain the beans thoroughly, place them in a bowl and mash with a fork.

6 Lightly brush the burgers with olive oil and cook on a hot barbecue for 8–10 minutes, turning once, until golden brown. Serve with a spoonful of yogurt and a green salad, if you like.

1 Heat the olive oil in a frying pan and cook the chopped onion and garlic over a moderate heat, stirring, until softened. Add the spices and cook for a further minute, stirring constantly.

4 Stir the kidney beans into the frying pan, with the chopped fresh coriander, and mix thoroughly. Season the mixture well with plenty of salt and freshly ground black pepper.

Cook's Tip

These burgers are not quite so firm as meat burgers, and will need careful handling on the barbecue.

GOAT'S CHEESE PIZZA

*Pizzas cooked on the barbecue have a beautifully crisp and golden base. The combination
of goat's cheese and red onion in this recipe makes for a flavoursome main course dish.*

2 Brush the dough round with olive oil
and place, oiled side down, on a
medium barbecue. Cook for about
6–8 minutes until firm and golden
underneath. Brush the uncooked side
with olive oil and turn the pizza over.

3 Mix together the passata and
red pesto and quickly spread over
the cooked side of the pizza, to within
about 1cm/½in of the edge. Arrange
the onion, tomatoes and cheese on top
and sprinkle with salt and pepper.

4 Cook the pizza for 10 minutes more,
until golden brown and crisp. Sprinkle
with fresh basil and serve.

INGREDIENTS

*150g/5oz packet pizza-base mix
olive oil, for brushing
150ml/¼ pint/⅔ cup passata
(bottled strained tomatoes)
30ml/2 tbsp red pesto
1 small red onion, thinly sliced
8 cherry tomatoes, halved
115g/4oz firm goat's cheese, sliced
handful shredded fresh basil leaves
salt and freshly ground black
pepper*

SERVES 4

1 Make up the pizza dough according
to the directions on the packet. Roll
out the dough on a lightly floured
surface to a round of about 25cm/
10in diameter.

RED ONION GALETTES

· · ·

If non-vegetarians are to eat these pretty puff pastry tarts, you can sprinkle some chopped anchovies over them before cooking them on the barbecue to add extra piquancy.

INGREDIENTS

60–75ml/4–5 tbsp olive oil
500g/1¼ lb red onions, sliced
1 garlic clove, crushed
30ml/2 tbsp chopped fresh mixed
herbs, such as thyme, parsley
and basil
225g/8oz ready-made puff pastry
15ml/1 tbsp sun-dried
tomato paste
freshly ground black pepper
fresh thyme sprigs, to garnish

SERVES 4

1 Heat 30ml/2 tbsp oil in a frying pan and add the onions and garlic. Cover and cook gently for 15–20 minutes, stirring occasionally, until soft but not browned. Stir in the herbs.

2 Divide the pastry into four and roll out each piece to a 15cm/6in round. Flute the edges, prick all over with a fork and place on baking sheets.

3 Chill the rounds, on the baking sheets, in the refrigerator for about 10 minutes. Mix 15ml/1 tbsp of the remaining oil with the tomato paste and spread over the pastry rounds, to within about 1cm/½in of the edge.

4 Spread the onion mixture over the pastry and season with pepper. Drizzle over a little oil, then place the baking sheets on a medium barbecue for 15 minutes, until the pastry is crisp. Serve hot, garnished with thyme sprigs.

141

TOFU SATAY

Grill cubes of tofu until crispy then serve with a Thai-style peanut sauce. Soak the satay sticks before use to prevent them from burning while on the barbecue.

INGREDIENTS

2 x 200g/7oz packs smoked tofu
45ml/3 tbsp light soy sauce
10ml/2 tsp sesame oil
1 garlic clove, crushed
1 yellow and 1 red (bell) pepper,
cut into squares
8–12 fresh bay leaves
sunflower oil, for brushing

FOR THE PEANUT SAUCE
2 spring onions (scallions), chopped
2 garlic cloves, crushed
good pinch of chilli powder, or a
few drops hot chilli sauce
5ml/1 tsp sugar
15ml/1 tbsp white wine vinegar
30ml/2 tbsp light soy sauce
45ml/3 tbsp crunchy peanut butter

SERVES 4–6

1 Cut the tofu into bitesize cubes and place in a large bowl. Add the soy sauce, sesame oil and crushed garlic and mix well. Cover and set aside to marinate for at least 20 minutes.

2 Beat all the peanut sauce ingredients together in a large bowl, using a wooden spoon, until well blended. Avoid using a food processor to blend the ingredients, as the texture should be slightly chunky.

3 Drain the tofu and thread the cubes on to 8–12 satay sticks, alternating with the pepper squares and bay leaves. Larger bay leaves may need to be halved before threading.

4 Brush the satays with sunflower oil and cook on a hot barbecue or grill (broiler), turning occasionally, until the tofu and peppers are browned and crisp. Serve hot with the peanut sauce.

SWEET AND SOUR VEGETABLES WITH PANEER

The Indian cheese used in this recipe, called paneer, can be bought from Asian stores, or you can use beancurd in its place. Paneer has a good firm texture and cooks very well on the barbecue.

INGREDIENTS

1 green and 1 yellow (bell) pepper,
cut into squares
8 cherry, or 4 medium, tomatoes
8 cauliflower florets
8 fresh or canned pineapple chunks
8 cubes paneer

FOR THE SEASONED OIL
15ml/1 tbsp soya oil
30ml/2 tbsp lemon juice
5ml/1 tsp salt
5ml/1 tsp freshly ground
black pepper
15ml/1 tbsp clear honey
30ml/2 tbsp chilli sauce

SERVES 4

1 Thread the prepared vegetables, pineapple and paneer cubes on to four skewers, alternating the ingredients.

2 Mix together all the ingredients for the seasoned oil. If the mixture is a little too thick, add 15ml/1 tbsp water to loosen it. Brush the vegetables with the seasoned oil, ready for cooking.

3 Cook on a hot barbecue or grill (broiler) for 10 minutes, until the vegetables begin to char slightly, turning the skewers often and basting with the seasoned oil.

STUFFED TOMATOES AND PEPPERS

Colourful peppers and tomatoes make perfect containers for meat and vegetable stuffings. The smoky flavours in this dish are simply superb.

INGREDIENTS

2 large ripe tomatoes
1 green (bell) pepper
1 yellow or orange (bell) pepper
60ml/4 tbsp olive oil, plus extra
for sprinkling
2 onions, chopped
2 garlic cloves, crushed
50g/2oz/½ cup blanched
almonds, chopped
75g/3oz/scant ½ cup long grain
rice, boiled and drained
30ml/2 tbsp fresh mint,
coarsely chopped
30ml/2 tbsp fresh parsley,
coarsely chopped
30ml/2 tbsp sultanas (golden raisins)
45ml/3 tbsp ground almonds
salt and freshly ground
black pepper
chopped mixed fresh herbs,
to garnish

SERVES 4

1 Cut the tomatoes in half and scoop out the pulp and seeds, using a teaspoon. Leave the tomatoes to drain on kitchen paper with the cut sides facing down. Roughly chop the tomato pulp and set it aside.

2 Halve the peppers, leaving the cores intact. Scoop out the seeds.
Brush the peppers with 15ml/1 tbsp olive oil and cook on a medium barbecue for 15 minutes. Place the peppers and tomatoes on a grill rack and season well with salt and pepper.

3 Cook the onions in the remaining olive oil for 5 minutes. Add the crushed garlic and chopped almonds to the pan and cook for a further minute.

4 Remove the pan from the heat and stir in the rice, chopped tomatoes, mint, parsley and sultanas. Season well with salt and pepper and spoon the mixture into the tomatoes and peppers.

5 Sprinkle with the ground almonds and drizzle with a little extra olive oil. Cook on a medium barbecue for about 15 minutes. Garnish with fresh herbs.

COUSCOUS STUFFED PEPPERS

· · ·

Couscous makes a good basis for a stuffing, and in this recipe it is studded with raisins and flavoured with fresh mint. Charred peppers make the combination of flavours truly special.

2 To cook the couscous, bring 250ml/8fl oz/1 cup water to the boil. Add the oil and salt, then remove from the heat and add the couscous. Stir and leave to stand, covered, for 5 minutes. Stir in the onion, raisins and mint. Season well and stir in the egg yolk.

3 Use a teaspoon to fill the peppers with the couscous mixture to about three-quarters full (the couscous will swell while cooking). Wrap each pepper in a piece of oiled baking foil.

4 Cook on a medium barbecue for 20 minutes, until tender. Serve hot or cold, garnished with fresh mint leaves.

INGREDIENTS

6 (bell) peppers
25g/1oz/2 tbsp butter
1 onion, finely chopped
5ml/1 tsp olive oil
2.5ml/½ tsp salt
175g/6oz/1 cup couscous
25g/1oz/2 tbsp raisins
30ml/2 tbsp chopped fresh mint
1 egg yolk
salt and freshly ground
black pepper
fresh mint leaves, to garnish

SERVES 4

1 Carefully slit each pepper with a sharp knife and remove the cores and seeds. Melt the butter in a small pan and add the chopped onion. Cook until soft but not browned.

CORN COBS IN A GARLIC BUTTER CRUST

Whether you are catering for vegetarians or serving this with meat dishes, it will disappear in a flash. The charred garlic butter crust adds a new dimension to the corn cobs.

INGREDIENTS

6 ripe corn cobs
225g/8oz/1 cup butter
30ml/2 tbsp olive oil
2 garlic cloves, crushed
115g/4oz/1 cup wholemeal (whole-wheat) breadcrumbs
15ml/1 tbsp chopped fresh parsley
salt and freshly ground black pepper

SERVES 6

1 Pull off the husks and silks and boil the corn cobs in a large pan of salted water until tender. Drain the corn cobs and leave to cool.

2 Melt the butter in a pan and add the olive oil, crushed garlic, salt and freshly ground black pepper, and stir to blend. Pour the mixture into a shallow dish. In another shallow dish blend the breadcrumbs and chopped fresh parsley. Roll the corn cobs in the melted butter mixture and then in the breadcrumbs until they are well coated.

3 Cook the corn cobs on a hot barbecue for about 10 minutes, turning frequently, until the breadcrumbs are golden brown.

STUFFED PARSLEYED ONIONS

These stuffed onions are a popular vegetarian dish served with fresh crusty bread and a crisp salad. They also make a very good accompaniment to meat dishes.

INGREDIENTS

4 large onions
60ml/4 tbsp cooked rice
20ml/4 tsp finely chopped fresh parsley, plus extra to garnish
60ml/4 tbsp strong Cheddar cheese, finely grated
30ml/2 tbsp olive oil
15ml/1 tbsp white wine
salt and freshly ground black pepper

SERVES 4

1 Cut a slice from the top of each onion and scoop out the centre to leave a fairly thick shell. Combine all the remaining ingredients in a large bowl and stir to mix, moistening with enough white wine to bind the ingredients together well.

2 Use a spoon to fill the onions, then wrap each one in a piece of oiled baking foil. Bake in the embers of the fire for 30–40 minutes, until tender, turning the parcels often so they cook evenly. Serve the onions garnished with chopped fresh parsley.

STUFFED ARTICHOKE BOTTOMS

The distinctive flavour of chargrilled globe artichokes is matched in this dish by an intensely savoury stuffing of mushrooms, cheese and walnuts.

INGREDIENTS

225g/8oz button (white) mushrooms
15g/½ oz/1 tbsp butter
2 shallots, finely chopped
50g/2oz/¼ cup soft cheese
30ml/2 tbsp chopped walnuts
45ml/3 tbsp grated Gruyère cheese
4 large or 6 small artichoke bottoms (from cooked artichokes, leaves and choke removed, or cooked frozen or canned artichoke hearts)
salt and freshly ground black pepper
fresh parsley sprigs, to garnish

SERVES 4

1 To make the duxelles for the stuffing, put the mushrooms in a food processor or blender and pulse until they are finely chopped.

2 Melt the butter in a frying pan and cook the shallots over a medium heat for about 2–3 minutes until just softened. Add the mushrooms, raise the heat slightly, and cook for 5–7 minutes more, stirring frequently, until all the liquid from the mushrooms has been driven off and they are almost dry. Season with plenty of salt and freshly ground black pepper.

3 In a large bowl, combine the soft cheese and cooked mushrooms. Add the chopped walnuts and half the grated Gruyère cheese, and stir well to combine the mixture.

4 Divide the mixture among the artichoke bottoms in an oiled baking tin (pan). Sprinkle over the remaining cheese. Cook on the barbecue for 12 minutes, garnish and serve.

SPINACH WITH RAISINS AND PINE NUTS

· · ·

Raisins and pine nuts are frequent partners in Spanish recipes. In this recipe they are tossed with wilted spinach and croûtons, and can be cooked quickly in a flameproof pan on the barbecue.

INGREDIENTS

50g/2oz/⅓ cup raisins
1 thick slice crusty white bread
45ml/3 tbsp olive oil
25g/1oz/¼ cup pine nuts
500g/1¼lb young spinach leaves, stalks removed
2 garlic cloves, crushed
salt and freshly ground black pepper

SERVES 4

1 Put the raisins in a bowl, cover with boiling water and leave to soak for 10 minutes. Drain and set aside.

2 Cut the bread into cubes and discard the crusts. Heat 30ml/2 tbsp of the olive oil in a large frying pan and fry the bread until golden brown.

3 Heat the remaining oil and fry the pine nuts, on the barbecue or hob, until beginning to colour. Add the spinach and garlic and cook quickly, turning the spinach until it has just wilted. Toss in the raisins and season lightly with salt and pepper. Transfer to a serving dish. Sprinkle with croûtons and serve.

GRILLED VEGETABLE TERRINE

A colourful terrine, using all the vegetables associated with the Mediterranean, makes an elegant dish for outdoor eating. Cooking them on the barbecue adds to the flavour.

INGREDIENTS

2 large red (bell) peppers,
quartered, cored and seeded
2 large yellow (bell) peppers,
quartered, cored and seeded
1 large aubergine (eggplant),
sliced lengthways
2 large courgettes (zucchini),
sliced lengthways
90ml/6 tbsp olive oil
1 large red onion, thinly sliced
75g/3oz/1/2 cup raisins
15ml/1 tbsp tomato purée (paste)
15ml/1 tbsp red wine vinegar
400ml/14fl oz/1 2/3 cups tomato juice
15g/1/2oz/2 tbsp powdered gelatine
fresh basil leaves, to garnish

FOR THE DRESSING
90ml/6 tbsp extra virgin olive oil
30ml/2 tbsp red wine vinegar
salt and freshly ground
black pepper

SERVES 6

1 Grill the peppers, skin-side down, on a hot barbecue or grill (broiler), until the skins are beginning to blacken. Using tongs, transfer to a bowl, cover and leave to cool.

2 Brush the aubergine and courgette slices with oil and cook until tender and golden, turning occasionally.

3 Heat the remaining oil in a pan and add the onion, raisins, tomato purée and red wine vinegar. Cook until soft and syrupy. Leave to cool in the pan.

4 Pour half the tomato juice into a pan and sprinkle with the gelatine. Dissolve gently over a very low heat, stirring.

5 Line an oiled 1.75 litre/3 pint/ 7 1/2 cup terrine with clear film (plastic wrap), leaving a little hanging over the sides. Place a layer of red peppers in the base and pour in enough of the tomato juice with gelatine to cover. Repeat with the aubergines, courgettes, yellow peppers and onion mixture, ending with another layer of red peppers and covering each layer with tomato juice and gelatine.

6 Add the remaining tomato juice to any left in the pan and pour into the terrine. Give it a sharp tap to eliminate air bubbles. Cover the terrine with clear film and chill until set.

7 To make the dressing, whisk the oil and vinegar, and season with salt and black pepper. Turn out the terrine and serve in thick slices, drizzled with the dressing. Garnish with the basil leaves.

SUMMER VEGETABLES WITH YOGURT PESTO

Chargrilled vegetables make a meal on their own, or are delicious served as a Mediterranean-style accompaniment to grilled meats and fish.

INGREDIENTS

2 small aubergines (eggplant)
2 large courgettes (zucchini)
1 red (bell) pepper
1 yellow (bell) pepper
1 fennel bulb
1 red onion
olive oil, for brushing
salt and freshly ground
black pepper

FOR THE YOGURT PESTO
150ml/¼ pint/⅔ cup Greek
(US plain strained) yogurt
45ml/3 tbsp pesto

SERVES 4

1 Cut the aubergines into 1cm/½in slices. Sprinkle with salt and leave to drain for about 30 minutes. Rinse well in cold running water and pat dry.

2 Use a sharp kitchen knife to cut the courgettes in half lengthways. Cut the peppers in half, removing the seeds but leaving the stalks in place.

3 Slice the fennel bulb and the red onion into thick wedges, using a sharp kitchen knife.

4 Stir the yogurt and pesto lightly together in a bowl, to make a marbled sauce. Spoon the yogurt pesto into a serving bowl and set aside.

5 Arrange the vegetables on the hot barbecue, brush generously with olive oil and sprinkle with plenty of salt and freshly ground black pepper.

6 Cook the vegetables until golden brown and tender, turning occasionally. The aubergines and peppers will take 6–8 minutes to cook, the courgettes, onion and fennel 4–5 minutes. Serve the vegetables as soon as they are cooked, with the yogurt pesto.

Cook's Tip

Baby vegetables make excellent candidates for grilling whole, so look out for baby aubergines and peppers, in particular. There's no need to salt the aubergines if they're small.

WILD RICE WITH VEGETABLES

Wild rice makes a special accompaniment to grilled vegetables in a simple vinaigrette dressing.
This recipe can be served as a side dish, but it also makes a tasty meal on its own.

INGREDIENTS

225g/8oz/1 cup wild and long
grain rice mixture
1 aubergine (eggplant), sliced
1 red, 1 yellow and 1 green (bell)
pepper, quartered, cored and seeded
2 red onions, sliced
225g/8oz shiitake mushrooms
2 small courgettes (zucchini), cut in
half lengthways
olive oil, for brushing
30ml/2 tbsp chopped fresh thyme

FOR THE DRESSING
90ml/6 tbsp extra virgin olive oil
30ml/2 tbsp balsamic vinegar
2 garlic cloves, crushed
salt and freshly ground
black pepper

SERVES 4

1 Put the wild and long grain rice mixture in a pan of cold salted water. Bring to the boil, then reduce the heat, cover and simmer for 30–40 minutes until the grains are tender (or follow the cooking instructions on the packet, if appropriate).

2 To make the dressing, mix together the olive oil, vinegar, crushed garlic and seasoning in a bowl or screw-topped jar until well blended.

3 Place the vegetables on a rack. Brush with oil and cook on a hot barbecue or grill (broiler) for 8–10 minutes, until tender and browned, turning them occasionally and basting with oil.

4 Drain the rice and toss in half the dressing. Tip into a serving dish and arrange the grilled vegetables on top. Pour over the remaining dressing and sprinkle over the chopped fresh thyme.

POTATO SKEWERS WITH MUSTARD DIP

Potatoes cooked on the barbecue have a tasty flavour and crisp skin.
These skewers are served with a thick, garlic-rich dip.

INGREDIENTS

1kg/2¼lb small new potatoes
200g/7oz/2 cups shallots, halved
30ml/2 tbsp olive oil
15ml/1 tbsp sea salt

FOR THE MUSTARD DIP
4 garlic cloves, crushed
2 egg yolks
30ml/2 tbsp lemon juice
300ml/½ pint/1¼ cups extra
virgin olive oil
10ml/2 tsp wholegrain mustard
salt and freshly ground
black pepper

SERVES 4

1 To make the mustard dip, place the garlic, egg yolks and lemon juice in a blender or food processor and process for a few seconds until smooth.

2 With the motor running, add the oil, until the mixture forms a thick cream. Add the mustard and season.

3 Par-boil the potatoes in salted boiling water for about 5 minutes. Drain thoroughly and then thread them on to metal skewers with the shallots.

4 Brush with olive oil and sprinkle with sea salt. Cook for 10–12 minutes over a hot barbecue, turning often, until tender. Serve with the mustard dip.

POTATO WEDGES WITH GARLIC AND ROSEMARY

* * *

Toss the potato wedges in fragrant, garlicky olive oil with chopped fresh rosemary before cooking them over the coals.

INGREDIENTS

675g/1½ lb medium old potatoes
15ml/1 tbsp olive oil
2 garlic cloves, thinly sliced
60ml/4 tbsp chopped
fresh rosemary
salt and freshly ground
black pepper

SERVES 4

1 Cut each potato into four wedges and par-boil in boiling salted water for 5 minutes. Drain well.

2 Toss the potatoes in the olive oil with the garlic, rosemary and black pepper. Arrange on a grill rack.

3 Cook the potatoes on a hot barbecue for about 15 minutes, turning occasionally, until the wedges are crisp and golden brown.

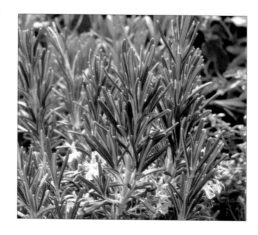

SPANISH POTATOES

. . .

This is an adaptation of a traditional recipe for peppery fried potatoes. Cook the potatoes in a flameproof dish on the barbecue or in a pan on the hob, and serve them with grilled meats.

INGREDIENTS

675g/1½ lb small new potatoes
75ml/5 tbsp olive oil
2 garlic cloves, sliced
2.5ml/½ tsp crushed chillies
2.5ml/½ tsp ground cumin
10ml/2 tsp paprika
30ml/2 tbsp red or white
wine vinegar
1 red or green (bell) pepper, sliced
coarse sea salt, to serve (optional)

SERVES 4

1 Cook the potatoes in a pan of boiling salted water until almost tender. Drain and cut into chunks.

2 Heat the olive oil in a large frying pan or sauté pan and fry the potatoes, turning them frequently, until golden.

3 Meanwhile, crush together the garlic, chillies and cumin using a mortar and pestle. Mix with the paprika and wine vinegar to form a thick paste.

4 Add the garlic mixture to the potatoes with the sliced pepper and cook, stirring, for 2 minutes. Serve warm, or leave until cold. Sprinkle with coarse sea salt, if you like, to serve.

The powerful flavours of food cooked on the barbecue call for chunky salsas and tangy barbecue sauces. This chapter also includes some appetizing dips to go with bread sticks and crudités, and a selection of delicious marinades suitable for a wide variety of meat and fish.

SALSAS, DIPS AND MARINADES

CLASSIC TOMATO SALSA

This is the traditional tomato-based salsa that most people associate with spicy Mexican-inspired food. There are innumerable recipes for it, but the basics of onion, tomato, chilli and coriander are common to every one of them. Serve this salsa as a condiment with a wide variety of dishes.

INGREDIENTS

3–6 fresh Serrano chillies
1 large white onion
grated rind and juice of 2 limes,
plus strips of lime rind, to garnish
8 ripe, firm tomatoes
large bunch of fresh
coriander (cilantro)
1.5ml/¼ tsp caster
(superfine) sugar
salt

SERVES 6

1 Use three chillies for a salsa of medium heat; up to six if you like it hot. To peel the chillies, spear them on a long-handled metal skewer and roast them over the flame of a gas burner until the skins blister and darken. Do not let the flesh burn. Alternatively, dry-fry them in a griddle pan until the skins are scorched.

Variations

Use spring onions (scallions) or mild red onions instead of the white onion. For a smoky flavour, use chipotle chillies instead of fresh Serrano chillies.

2 Place the roasted chillies in a strong plastic bag and tie the top of the bag to keep the steam in. Set aside for about 20 minutes.

3 Meanwhile, chop the onion finely and put it in a bowl with the strips of lime rind and juice. The lime juice will soften the onion.

4 Remove the chillies from the bag and peel off the skins wearing rubber gloves. Cut off the stalks, slit the chillies and scrape out the seeds with a knife. Chop the flesh coarsely and set aside.

5 Cut a small cross in the base of each tomato. Place the tomatoes in a heatproof bowl and pour in boiling water to cover.

6 Leave the tomatoes in the water for 30 seconds, then lift them out using a slotted spoon and plunge them into a bowl of cold water. Drain. The skins will have begun to peel back from the crosses. Remove the skins completely.

7 Dice the peeled tomatoes and put them in a bowl. Add the chopped onion and lime mixture. Chop the fresh coriander finely.

8 Add the coriander to the salsa, with the chillies, sugar and salt. Mix gently until the sugar has dissolved and all the ingredients are coated in lime juice. Cover and chill for 2–3 hours to allow the flavours to blend. The salsa will keep for 3–4 days in the refrigerator. Garnish with the strips of lime rind just before serving.

CHUNKY CHERRY TOMATO SALSA

*Succulent cherry tomatoes and refreshing cucumber form the base of this delicious dill-seasoned
salsa. Prepare up to 1 day in advance and store in the refrigerator until needed.*

INGREDIENTS

1 ridge cucumber
5ml/1 tsp sea salt
500g/1¼ lb cherry tomatoes
grated rind and juice of 1 lemon
45ml/3 tbsp chilli oil
2.5ml/½ tsp dried chilli flakes
30ml/2 tbsp chopped fresh dill
1 garlic clove, finely chopped
salt and freshly ground
black pepper

SERVES 4

1 Trim the ends off the cucumber and
cut it into 2.5cm/1in lengths, then cut
each piece lengthways into thin slices.
Place in a colander and sprinkle with
sea salt. Leave for 5 minutes.

2 Rinse the cucumber slices under cold
water and dry with kitchen paper.

3 Quarter the cherry tomatoes and
place in a bowl with the cucumber.

4 Whisk together the lemon rind
and juice, chilli oil, chilli flakes, dill
and garlic. Season, then pour over the
tomato and cucumber and toss well.
Marinate for 2 hours before serving.

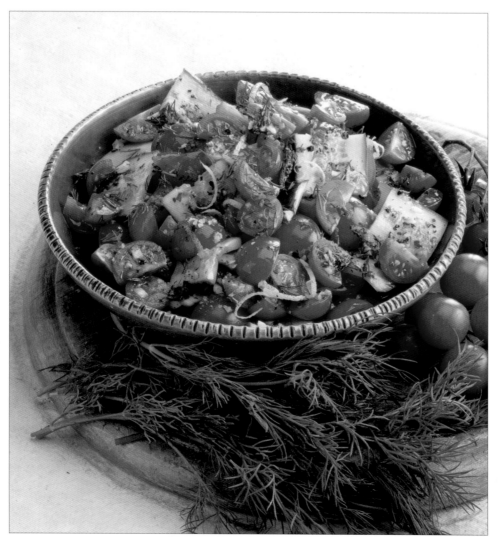

Cook's Tip

Try flavouring the salsa with other
herbs, such as tarragon or mint.

SALSA VERDE

· · ·

There are many versions of this classic green salsa. Try this one sprinkled over chargrilled squid, or with baked potatoes.

INGREDIENTS

2–4 green chillies, halved
8 spring onions (scallions)
2 garlic cloves
50g/2oz salted capers
sprig of fresh tarragon
bunch of fresh parsley
grated rind and juice of 1 lime
juice of 1 lemon
90ml/6 tbsp olive oil
about 15ml/1 tbsp green Tabasco
sauce, to taste
freshly ground black pepper

SERVES 4

1 Seed the chillies and trim the spring onions. Halve the garlic cloves. Place in a food processor and pulse briefly.

2 Use your fingers to rub the excess salt off the capers. Add them, with the tarragon and parsley, to the food processor and pulse again until the ingredients are quite finely chopped.

3 Transfer the mixture to a large bowl. Mix in the lime rind and juice, lemon juice and olive oil, stirring lightly so the citrus juice and oil do not emulsify.

4 Add green Tabasco sauce, a little at a time, and black pepper to taste. Chill the salsa in the refrigerator until ready to serve, but do not prepare it more than 8 hours in advance.

FAT-FREE SAFFRON DIP

*Serve this mild dip with fresh vegetable crudités – it is particularly good with
florets of cauliflower, asparagus tips and baby carrots and corn.*

INGREDIENTS

*15ml/1 tbsp boiling water
small pinch of saffron threads
200g/7oz/scant 1 cup fat-free
fromage frais or farmer's cheese
10 fresh chives
10 fresh basil leaves
salt and freshly ground
black pepper*

SERVES 4

1 Pour the boiling water into a bowl
and add the saffron threads. Leave to
infuse (steep) for 3 minutes.

2 Beat the fromage frais in a large bowl
until smooth. Stir in the saffron liquid
with a wooden spoon.

Cook's Tip

If you don't have any saffron, add
a squeeze of lemon or lime juice.

3 Snip the chives into the dip. Tear the
basil leaves into small pieces and stir
them in. Mix thoroughly.

4 Add salt and freshly ground black
pepper to taste. Serve the dip with fresh
vegetable crudités, if you like.

SPICY YOGURT MARINADE

Use this marinade for chicken, lamb or pork, and marinate the meat, covered and chilled, for 24–36 hours to develop a mellow spicy flavour.

INGREDIENTS

5ml/1 tsp coriander seeds
10ml/2 tsp cumin seeds
6 cloves
2 bay leaves
1 onion, quartered
2 garlic cloves
5ml/2in piece of fresh root ginger,
coarsely chopped
2.5ml/½ tsp chilli powder
5ml/1 tsp ground turmeric
150ml/¼ pint/⅔ cup natural
(plain) yogurt
juice of 1 lemon

SERVES 6

1 Spread the coriander and cumin seeds, cloves and bay leaves over the base of a large frying pan and dry-fry over a moderate heat until the bay leaves are crisp.

2 Leave the spices to cool, then grind coarsely with a mortar and pestle.

3 Finely chop the onion, garlic and ginger in a blender or food processor. Add the ground spices, chilli, turmeric, yogurt and lemon juice.

Cook's Tip
Garnish the finished dish with fresh coriander (cilantro) leaves and slices of lemon or lime.

4 If you are marinating cuts of chicken or large pieces of meat, make several deep slashes to allow the flavours to penetrate. Arrange the pieces in a single layer and pour over the marinade. Cover and leave in the refrigerator to marinate for at least 24 hours.

ORANGE AND GREEN PEPPERCORN MARINADE

This is an excellent light marinade for delicately flavoured whole fish, such as sea trout, bass or bream. The beauty of the fish is perfectly set off by the softly coloured marinade.

INGREDIENTS

1 red onion
2 small oranges
90ml/6 tbsp light olive oil
30ml/2 tbsp cider vinegar
30ml/2 tbsp green peppercorns in brine, drained
30ml/2 tbsp chopped fresh parsley
salt and sugar

FOR 1 MEDIUM-SIZE FISH

1 With a sharp knife, slash the fish 3–4 times on each side.

2 Cut a piece of foil big enough to wrap the fish and use to line a large dish. Peel and slice the onion and oranges. Lay half the slices on the foil, place the fish on top and cover with the remaining onion and orange.

3 Mix the remaining marinade ingredients and pour over the fish. Cover and leave to marinate for 4 hours, occasionally spooning the marinade over the fish.

4 Fold the foil loosely over the fish and seal the edges securely. Bake on a medium barbecue for 15 minutes for 450g/1lb, plus 15 minutes over.

GINGER AND LIME MARINADE

*This fragrant marinade will guarantee a mouth-watering aroma from the barbecue. Shown here
on prawn and monkfish kebabs, it is just as delicious with chicken or pork.*

INGREDIENTS

3 limes
15ml/1 tbsp green cardamom pods
1 onion, finely chopped
2.5cm/1in piece of fresh root
ginger, grated
1 large garlic clove, crushed
45ml/3 tbsp olive oil

SERVES 4–6

3 Mix all the marinade ingredients
together and pour over the meat or
fish. Stir in gently, cover and leave in
a cool place to marinate for 2–3 hours.

4 Drain the meat or fish when you are
ready to cook it on the barbecue. Baste
the meat occasionally with the
marinade, while cooking.

1 Finely grate the rind from one lime
and squeeze the juice from all of them.

2 Split the cardamom pods and remove
the seeds. Crush the seeds with a
mortar and pestle or the back of a
heavy-bladed knife.

SUMMER HERB MARINADE

Make the best use of summer herbs in this marinade. Try any combination of herbs, depending on what you have to hand, and use with veal, chicken, pork, lamb or salmon.

INGREDIENTS

*large handful of fresh herb sprigs,
e.g. chervil, thyme, parsley, sage,
chives, rosemary, oregano
90ml/6 tbsp olive oil
45ml/3 tbsp tarragon vinegar
1 garlic clove, crushed
2 spring onions (scallions), chopped
salt and freshly ground
black pepper*

SERVES 4

3 Place the meat or fish in a bowl and pour over the marinade. Cover and leave to marinate in a cool place for 4–6 hours.

4 Drain the meat or fish when you are ready to cook it on the barbecue. Use the marinade to baste the meat occasionally while cooking.

1 Discard any coarse stalks or damaged leaves from the herbs, then chop them very finely.

2 Add the chopped herbs to the remaining marinade ingredients in a large bowl. Stir to mix thoroughly.

At the end of a barbecue, it's a lovely idea to use the lingering

fire to make a delicious fruity dessert. Even those who thought

they couldn't eat another bite will be beguiled. Accompany

grilled fruit with a spicy sauce, crisp toasted brioche or freshly

made griddle cakes.

DESSERTS

CHARGRILLED APPLES ON CINNAMON TOASTS

. . .

This simple, scrumptious dessert is best made with an enriched bread such as brioche,
but any light sweet bread will do.

INGREDIENTS

4 sweet, eating apples
juice of ½ lemon
4 individual brioches or muffins
60ml/4 tbsp melted butter
30ml/2 tbsp golden caster
(superfine) sugar
5ml/1 tsp ground cinnamon
whipped cream, to serve

SERVES 4

2 Cut the brioches or muffins into thick slices. Brush the slices with melted butter on both sides.

4 Place the apple and brioche slices on a medium-hot barbecue and cook them for about 3–4 minutes, turning once, until they are beginning to turn golden brown. Do not allow to burn.

1 Core the apples and use a sharp knife to cut them into 3–4 thick slices. Sprinkle the apple slices with lemon juice and set them aside.

3 Mix together the caster sugar and ground cinnamon in a small bowl to make the cinnamon sugar. Set aside.

5 Sprinkle half the cinnamon sugar over the apple slices and brioche toasts and cook for a further minute on the barbecue, until the sugar is sizzling and the toasts are a rich golden brown.

6 To serve, arrange the apple slices over the toasts and sprinkle them with the remaining cinnamon sugar. Serve hot, with whipped cream.

PINEAPPLE WEDGES WITH RUM BUTTER GLAZE

· · ·

Fresh pineapple is even more full of flavour when barbecued, and this spiced rum glaze makes it into a very special dessert.

INGREDIENTS

1 medium pineapple
30ml/2 tbsp dark brown sugar
5ml/1 tsp ground ginger
60ml/4 tbsp melted butter
30ml/2 tbsp dark rum

SERVES 4

3 Soak 4 bamboo skewers in water for 15 minutes to prevent them from scorching on the barbecue. Push a skewer through each wedge, into the stalk, to hold the chunks in place.

4 Mix together the sugar, ginger, butter and rum and brush over the pineapple. Cook the wedges on the barbecue for 4 minutes; pour the remaining glaze over the top and serve.

1 With a large, sharp knife, cut the pineapple lengthways into four wedges. Cut out and discard the central core.

2 Cut between the flesh and skin, to release the skin, but leave the flesh in place. Slice the flesh across and lengthways to make thick chunks.

Cook's Tip

For an easier version, simply remove the skin and then cut the whole pineapple into thick slices and cook as above.

BAKED BANANAS WITH SPICY VANILLA FILLING

Bananas are ideal for barbecue cooking as they bake in their skins and need no preparation at all. This flavoured butter adds richness; children may prefer melted chocolate, jam or honey.

INGREDIENTS

4 bananas
6 green cardamom pods
1 vanilla pod (bean)
finely grated rind of 1 small orange
30ml/2 tbsp brandy or orange juice
60ml/4 tbsp light muscovado
(brown) sugar
45ml/3 tbsp butter
crème fraîche, to serve

SERVES 4

1 Place the bananas, in their skins, on a hot barbecue and leave for about 6–8 minutes, turning occasionally, until they are turning brownish-black.

2 Meanwhile, split the cardamom pods and remove the seeds. Crush lightly with a mortar and pestle.

3 Split the vanilla pod lengthways and scrape out the tiny seeds. Mix them with the cardamom seeds, orange rind, brandy or juice, muscovado sugar and butter into a thick paste.

4 Using a sharp knife, slit the skin of each banana, then open out the skin and spoon in a little of the paste. Serve the bananas immediately with a spoonful of crème fraîche.

195

ORANGES IN MAPLE AND COINTREAU SYRUP

• • •

*This is one of the most delicious ways to eat an orange, and a luxurious way to round off
a barbecue. For a children's or alcohol-free version, omit the liqueur.*

INGREDIENTS

*20ml/4 tsp butter, plus extra,
melted, for brushing
4 medium oranges
30 ml/2 tbsp maple syrup
30ml/2 tbsp Cointreau or Grand
Marnier liqueur
crème fraîche, fromage frais or
mascarpone cheese, to serve*

SERVES 4

1 Cut four double-thickness squares of baking foil, large enough to wrap each of the oranges. Brush the centre of each square of foil with plenty of melted butter.

2 Remove some shreds of orange rind, to decorate. Blanch these, dry them and set them aside. Peel the oranges, removing all the white pith and catching the juice in a bowl.

3 Slice the oranges crossways into thick slices. Reassemble them and place each orange on a square of baking foil.

4 Tuck the baking foil up securely around the oranges to keep them in shape, leaving the foil open at the top.

5 Mix together the reserved orange juice, maple syrup and liqueur and spoon the mixture over the oranges.

6 Add a knob (pat) of butter to each parcel and close the foil at the top to seal in the juices. Place the parcels on a hot barbecue for 10–12 minutes, until hot. Serve with crème fraîche, fromage frais or mascarpone cheese, topped with the shreds of orange rind.

NECTARINES WITH MARZIPAN AND MASCARPONE

. . .

A luscious dessert that no one can resist – dieters may prefer to use low-fat soft cheese or ricotta
instead of mascarpone.

INGREDIENTS

4 firm, ripe nectarines or peaches
75g/3oz/¹/₂ cup marzipan
75g/3oz/5 tbsp mascarpone cheese
3 macaroons, crushed

SERVES 4

1 Cut the nectarines or peaches in half
and remove the stones (pits).

2 Divide the marzipan into eight
pieces, roll into balls, using your
fingers, and press one piece of
marzipan into the stone cavity of each
nectarine half.

Cook's Tip

Either nectarines or peaches can be
used for this recipe. If the stone
(pit) does not pull out easily when
you halve the fruit, use a small,
sharp knife to cut around it.

3 Spoon the mascarpone cheese on top
of the fruit halves. Sprinkle the crushed
macaroon biscuits (cookies) over the
mascarpone cheese.

4 Place the half-fruits on a hot
barbecue for 3–5 minutes, until they
are hot and the mascarpone starts to
melt. Serve immediately.

GRILLED STRAWBERRY CROISSANTS

The combination of crisp croissants, ricotta cheese and sweet strawberry conserve makes for a deliciously simple, sinful dessert, which is like eating warm cream cakes!

INGREDIENTS

4 croissants
115g/4oz/½ cup ricotta cheese
115g/4oz/½ cup strawberry
conserve or jam

SERVES 4

1 On a chopping board, split the croissants in half and open them out.

2 Spread the bottom half of each croissant with a generous layer of the ricotta cheese.

3 Top the ricotta with a generous spoonful of strawberry conserve and replace the top half of the croissant.

4 Place the filled croissants on a hot barbecue and cook for 2–3 minutes, turning once. Serve immediately.

Cook's Tip

As an alternative to croissants, try scones (biscuits), brioches or muffins, toasted on the barbecue.

199

GRIDDLE CAKES WITH MULLED PLUMS

· · ·

*These delectably light little pancakes are fun to make on the barbecue. They are served with
a rich, spicy plum sauce, and you could offer cream or yogurt, too.*

INGREDIENTS
500g/1¼lb red plums
90ml/6 tbsp light muscovado
(brown) sugar
1 cinnamon stick
2 whole cloves
1 piece star anise
90ml/6 tbsp apple juice

FOR THE GRIDDLE CAKES
50g/2oz/½ cup plain (all-
purpose) flour
10ml/2 tsp baking powder
pinch of salt
50g/2oz/½ cup fine cornmeal
30ml/2 tbsp light muscovado sugar
1 egg, beaten
300ml/½ pint/1¼ cups milk
30ml/2 tbsp corn oil

SERVES 6

1 Halve, stone (pit) and quarter the
plums. Place them in a flameproof pan,
with the sugar, spices and apple juice.

Cook's Tip
If you prefer, make the griddle
cakes in advance, on the hob
(stovetop), and then simply heat
them for a few seconds on the
barbecue to serve with the plums.

2 Bring to the boil, then reduce the
heat, cover the pan and simmer gently
for 8–10 minutes, stirring occasionally,
until the plums are soft. Remove the
spices and keep the plums warm on
the side of the barbecue.

3 For the griddle cakes, sift the
plain flour, baking powder and salt
into a large mixing bowl and stir in
the cornmeal and muscovado sugar.

4 Make a well in the centre of
the ingredients and add the egg, then
beat in the milk. Beat thoroughly with
a whisk or wooden spoon to form a
smooth batter. Beat in half the oil.

5 Heat a griddle or a heavy frying pan
on a hot barbecue. Brush with the
remaining oil, then drop tablespoons
of batter on to it, allowing them to
spread. Cook the griddle cakes for
about a minute, until bubbles start
to appear on the surface and the
underside is golden brown.

6 Turn the cakes over and cook the
other side for a further minute, or until
golden. Serve the cakes hot from the
griddle with a spoonful of mulled
plums and cream or yogurt, if you like.

FRUIT KEBABS WITH CHOCOLATE FONDUE

Fondues are always lots of fun, and the delicious ingredients used here – fresh fruit, chocolate and marshmallow – mean that this recipe will be a popular choice with children and adults alike.

2 Mix together the butter, lemon juice and ground cinnamon and brush the mixture generously over the fruits.

3 For the fondue, place the chocolate, cream and marshmallows in a small pan and heat gently, without boiling, stirring constantly until the mixture has melted and is smooth.

INGREDIENTS

2 bananas and 2 kiwi fruit
12 strawberries
15ml/1 tbsp melted butter
15ml/1 tbsp lemon juice
5ml/1 tsp ground cinnamon
225g/8oz plain
(semisweet) chocolate
120ml/4fl oz/1/2 cup single
(light) cream
8 marshmallows
2.5ml/1/2 tsp vanilla
essence (extract)

SERVES 4

1 Peel the bananas and cut into thick chunks. Peel the kiwi fruit and quarter them. Thread the bananas, kiwi fruit and strawberries on to four wooden skewers. (Soak the skewers in water for 15 minutes beforehand to prevent them from scorching on the barbecue.)

4 Cook the kebabs on a medium-hot barbecue for about 2–3 minutes, turning once, or until the fruit is golden. Stir the vanilla essence into the fondue. Empty the fondue into a small bowl and serve immediately, with the fruit kebabs.

SPICED PEAR AND BLUEBERRY PARCELS

This fruity combination makes a delicious dessert for a hot summer's evening.
You could substitute other berry fruits for the blueberries if you like.

INGREDIENTS

4 firm, ripe pears
30ml/2 tbsp lemon juice
15ml/1 tbsp melted butter
150g/5oz/1¼ cups blueberries
60ml/4 tbsp light brown sugar
freshly ground black pepper

SERVES 4

3 Cut four squares of double-thickness foil, large enough to wrap the pears, and brush them with melted butter. Place two pear halves on each, cut sides upwards. Gather the foil up around them, to hold them level.

4 Mix the blueberries and sugar together and spoon them over the pears. Sprinkle with black pepper. Seal the edges of the foil over the pears and cook on a fairly hot barbecue for 20–25 minutes.

1 Peel the pears thinly. Cut them in half lengthways. Scoop out the core from each half, using a teaspoon and a sharp kitchen knife.

2 Brush the pears with lemon juice, to prevent them from discolouring.

Cook's Tip

To assemble in advance, line with a layer of greaseproof (waxed) paper, as the acid in the juice may react with the foil and taint the flavour.

PUMPKIN IN BROWN SUGAR

Rich, sticky and sweet, this warming dessert looks very attractive, tastes wonderful and is not at all difficult to prepare.

INGREDIENTS

butter, for greasing
1 small pumpkin, about 800g/1¾lb
350g/12oz/1½ cups soft dark brown sugar
90ml/6 tbsp water
5ml/1 tsp ground cloves
12 cinnamon sticks, each about 10cm/4in in length
fresh mint sprigs, to decorate
thick yogurt or crème fraîche, to serve

SERVES 6

1 Cut six large, double thickness squares of foil and lightly grease with butter. Using a sharp knife, halve the pumpkin, cut into wedges and remove the seeds and fibres. Divide the wedges among the foil squares, placing them in a single layer skin-side down. Fill the hollows with the sugar.

2 Carefully sprinkle the water over the wedges, taking care not to wash all the sugar out of the hollows. Sprinkle on the ground cloves and add two cinnamon sticks to each parcel. Fold up the sides of the foil, then tuck in and fold over the edges to make loosely wrapped, but secure, parcels.

3 Cook the parcels on a low barbecue turning them occasionally, for about 30 minutes, or until the pumpkin is tender and the sugar and water have formed a syrup.

4 Carefully unwrap the foil parcels and transfer the pumpkin to a warm platter and pour the hot syrup over. Decorate each portion with mint and the cinnamon sticks and serve with thick yogurt or crème fraîche.

BAKED APPLES IN HONEY AND LEMON

*Tender baked apples with a classic flavouring of lemon and honey make a simple dessert.
Serve with custard or a spoonful of whipped cream, if you like.*

INGREDIENTS

*4 medium cooking apples
15ml/1 tbsp clear honey
grated rind and juice of 1 lemon
15ml/1 tbsp butter, melted*

SERVES 4

1 Remove the cores from the apples, leaving them whole. Cut four squares of double-thickness baking foil, to wrap the apples, and brush with butter.

2 With a cannelle or sharp knife, cut lines through the apple skin at regular intervals.

3 Mix together the honey, lemon rind, juice and butter in a small bowl.

4 Spoon the mixture into the apples and wrap in foil, sealing the edges securely. Cook on a hot barbecue for 20 minutes, until the apples are tender.

POACHED PEARS IN MAPLE AND YOGURT SAUCE

This elegant dessert is easier to make than it looks – poach the pears on the hob or barbecue when you cook the main course, and have the cooled syrup ready to add just before serving.

INGREDIENTS

6 firm pears
15ml/1 tbsp lemon juice
250ml/8fl oz/1 cup sweet white
wine or cider
thinly pared rind of 1 lemon
1 cinnamon stick
30ml/2 tbsp maple syrup
2.5ml/½ tsp arrowroot
150ml/¼ pint/⅔ cup Greek
(US plain strained) yogurt

SERVES 6

1 Peel the pears, leaving them whole and with stalks. Brush with lemon juice to prevent them from discolouring. Use a potato peeler or small knife to scoop out the core from the base of each pear.

2 Place the pears in a wide, heavy pan and pour over the wine, with enough cold water almost to cover the fruit. Add the lemon rind and cinnamon stick, and bring to the boil on the hob (stovetop) or, using a flameproof pan, on the barbecue. Reduce the heat, cover and simmer for 30 minutes, or until tender. Lift out the pears carefully.

3 Boil the remaining liquid, uncovered, until reduced to about 120ml/4 fl oz/ ½ cup. Strain and add the maple syrup. Blend a little of the liquid with the arrowroot. Return to the pan and cook, stirring, until thick and clear. Leave to cool.

4 Slice each pear, leaving the slices attached at the stem end, and fan out on serving plates. Stir 30ml/2 tbsp of the cooled syrup into the yogurt and spoon around the pears. Drizzle the pears with the remaining syrup and serve immediately.

OYSTER AND BACON BROCHETTES

Six oysters per person make a good appetizer, served with the seasoned oyster liquor to trickle over the skewers. Alternatively, serve nine per person as a main course, accompanied by a salad.

INGREDIENTS

36 oysters
18 thin-cut rashers (strips) rindless
streaky (fatty) bacon
15ml/1 tbsp paprika
5ml/1 tsp cayenne pepper
freshly ground black pepper
celery leaves and fresh red chillies,
to garnish

FOR THE SAUCE
1/2 fresh red chilli, seeded and very
finely chopped
1 garlic clove, crushed
2 spring onions (scallions), very
finely chopped
30ml/2 tbsp finely chopped
fresh parsley
liquor from the oysters
juice of 1/4–1/2 lemon, to taste
salt and freshly ground
black pepper

SERVES 4–6

2 Push the knife in and cut the muscle, holding the shell closed. Tip the liquor into the bowl. Cut the oyster free. Discard the drained shells.

3 For the sauce, mix the chilli, garlic, spring onions and parsley into the oyster liquor and sharpen to taste with lemon juice. Season with salt and pepper and transfer to a serving dish.

4 Cut each bacon rasher across the middle. Season the oysters lightly with paprika, cayenne and freshly ground black pepper and wrap each one in half a bacon rasher, then thread them on to skewers. Cook on a hot barbecue for about 5 minutes, turning frequently, until the bacon is crisp and brown. Garnish with celery leaves and red chillies and serve with the sauce.

1 Open the oysters over a bowl to catch their liquor for the sauce. Wrap your left hand (if you are right-handed) in a clean dishtowel and cup the deep shell of each oyster in your wrapped hand. Work the point of a strong, short-bladed knife into the hinge between the shells and twist firmly.

TURKEY ROLLS WITH GAZPACHO SAUCE

This Spanish-style recipe uses quick-cooking turkey steaks, but you could also cook veal escalopes in the same way.

INGREDIENTS

4 turkey breast steaks
15ml/1 tbsp red pesto
4 chorizo sausages
15ml/1 tbsp olive oil
salt and freshly ground
black pepper

FOR THE GAZPACHO SAUCE
1 green (bell) pepper, chopped
1 red (bell) pepper, chopped
7.5cm/3in piece cucumber
1 medium tomato
1 garlic clove
45ml/3 tbsp olive oil
15ml/1 tbsp red wine vinegar

SERVES 4

1 To make the gazpacho sauce, place the peppers, cucumber, tomato, garlic, 30ml/2 tbsp of the olive oil and the vinegar in a food processor and process until almost smooth. Season to taste with salt and ground black pepper.

2 If the turkey breast steaks are quite thick, place them between two sheets of clear film (plastic wrap) and beat them with the side of a rolling pin or a meat mallet, to flatten them slightly.

3 Spread the red pesto over the turkey, place a chorizo sausage on each piece and roll up firmly.

4 Slice the rolls thickly and thread them on to skewers. Brush with olive oil and cook on a medium barbecue for about 10–12 minutes, turning once. Serve with the gazpacho sauce.

CHICKEN, MUSHROOM AND CORIANDER PIZZA

Shiitake mushrooms add an earthy flavour to this colourful pizza, while fresh chilli and chilli-flavoured olive oil give it a hint of spiciness. Cook the pizza on the barbecue or in the oven.

INGREDIENTS

45ml/3 tbsp olive oil
350g/12oz skinless chicken breast
fillets, cut into thin strips
8 spring onions (scallions), sliced
1 fresh red chilli, seeded
and chopped
1 red (bell) pepper, cut into strips
75g/3oz fresh shiitake
mushrooms, sliced
45–60ml/3–4 tbsp chopped fresh
coriander (cilantro)
1 pizza base, about
25–30cm/10–12in diameter
15ml/1 tbsp chilli oil
150g/5oz mozzarella cheese
salt and freshly ground
black pepper

SERVES 3–4

2 Pour off any excess oil, then set aside to let the chicken mixture cool.

3 Stir the fresh coriander into the cooled chicken mixture in the wok.

4 Brush all over the pizza base with the chilli oil.

5 Spoon over the chicken mixture and drizzle over the remaining olive oil.

1 Heat 30ml/2 tbsp olive oil in a wok or large frying pan. Add the chicken, spring onions, chilli, red pepper and mushrooms and stir-fry over a high heat for 2–3 minutes until the chicken is firm but still slightly pink inside. Season to taste.

6 Grate the mozzarella cheese and sprinkle it over the pizza base. Cook the pizza on a medium-hot barbecue for 15–20 minutes, until the base is crisp and golden and the cheese is bubbling. Serve the pizza immediately.

MEDITERRANEAN QUICHE

*This quiche forms the ideal base for a hearty picnic feast. The strong Mediterranean flavours of
tomatoes, peppers and anchovies complement the cheese pastry beautifully.*

INGREDIENTS

FOR THE PASTRY

225g/8oz/2 cups plain (all-
purpose) flour
pinch of salt
pinch of dry mustard
115g/4oz/½ cup butter, chilled
and diced
50g/2oz/½ cup grated
Gruyère cheese
salt

FOR THE FILLING

50g/2oz can anchovy fillets, drained
50ml/2fl oz/¼ cup milk
30ml/2 tbsp French mustard
45ml/3 tbsp olive oil
2 large Spanish onions, sliced
1 red (bell) pepper, very finely sliced
3 egg yolks
350ml/12fl oz/1½ cups double
(heavy) cream
1 garlic clove, crushed
175g/6oz/1½ cups grated mature
(sharp) Cheddar cheese
2 large tomatoes, thickly sliced
30ml/2 tbsp chopped fresh basil,
to garnish

SERVES 6–8

1 To make the pastry, place the flour,
salt and mustard in a food processor,
add the butter and process the mixture
until it resembles fine breadcrumbs.

2 Add the Gruyère cheese and process
again briefly. Add enough iced water to
make a stiff dough: the dough will be
ready when it forms a ball. Wrap the
dough in clear film (plastic wrap) and
chill in the refrigerator for 30 minutes.

3 Meanwhile, make the filling.
Soak the anchovies in the milk for
about 20 minutes to make them less
salty. Pour off the milk. Heat the olive
oil in a frying pan and cook the onions
and red pepper until they soften.

4 In a bowl, beat the egg yolks, double
cream, garlic and grated Cheddar
cheese together.

5 Preheat the oven to 200°C/400°F/
Gas 6. Roll out the chilled pastry and
line a 23cm/9in loose-based quiche tin
(pan). Spread the mustard over and
chill for a further 15 minutes.

6 Arrange the tomatoes in a layer in the
pastry crust. Top with the onion and
pepper mixture and the anchovy fillets.
Pour over the egg mixture. Bake for
30 minutes. Serve warm or at room
temperature, sprinkled with fresh basil.

Cook's Tip

Leave the quiche in its tin (pan) if
you are packing it for a picnic.

CHICKEN AND APRICOT FILO PIE

The filling for this pie has a Middle Eastern flavour – minced chicken combined with apricots, bulgur wheat, nuts and spices. It both looks and tastes spectacular.

INGREDIENTS

75g/3oz/½ cup bulgur wheat
75g/3oz/6 tbsp butter
1 onion, chopped
450g/1lb minced (ground) chicken
50g/2oz/¼ cup ready-to-eat dried apricots, finely chopped
25g/1oz/¼ cup blanched almonds, chopped
5ml/1 tsp ground cinnamon
2.5ml/½ tsp ground allspice
50ml/2fl oz/¼ cup Greek (US strained plain) yogurt
30ml/2 tbsp chopped fresh chives
30ml/2 tbsp chopped fresh parsley
6 large sheets filo pastry
salt and freshly ground black pepper

SERVES 6

1 Preheat the oven to 200°C/400°F/ Gas 6. Put the bulgur wheat in a large bowl with 120ml/4fl oz/½ cup boiling water. leave the wheat to soak for 5 minutes, until the water is absorbed.

2 Heat 25g/1oz/2 tbsp of the butter in a pan and cook the onion and chicken until pale golden. Stir in the apricots, almonds and bulgur wheat and cook for a further 2 minutes. Remove from the heat and stir in the cinnamon, allspice, yogurt, half the chives and the parsley. Season to taste.

3 Melt the remaining butter. Unroll the filo pastry and cut into 25cm/10in rounds. Keep the pastry rounds covered with a clean, damp dishtowel to prevent them from drying out.

4 Line a 23cm/9in loose-based flan tin (quiche pan) with three pastry rounds, brushing each with melted butter as you layer them. Spoon in the chicken mixture and cover with three more pastry rounds, brushed with melted butter as before.

5 Crumple the remaining rounds and place on top of the pie. Brush with any remaining butter. Bake the pie for 30 minutes, until the pastry is golden brown and crisp. Serve hot or cold, garnished with the remaining chives.

CHICKEN WITH FRESH HERBS AND GARLIC

A whole chicken can be roasted on a spit on the barbecue. This marinade keeps the flesh moist and delicious and the fresh herbs add summery flavours.

INGREDIENTS

*1.75kg/4½ lb free-range chicken
finely grated rind and juice of
1 lemon
1 garlic clove, crushed
30ml/2 tbsp olive oil
2 fresh thyme sprigs
2 fresh sage sprigs
90ml/6 tbsp unsalted (sweet)
butter, softened
salt and freshly ground
black pepper*

SERVES 4

1 Season the chicken well. Mix the lemon rind and juice, crushed garlic and olive oil together and pour them over the chicken. Leave to marinate in the refrigerator for at least 2 hours.

Cook's Tip

If roasting the chicken in the oven, preheat the oven to 230°C/450°F/ Gas 8 and reduce the heat to 190°C/375°F/Gas 5 after 10 minutes. If you are roasting a chicken to serve cold, cooking it in foil helps to keep it succulent – open the foil for the last 20 minutes to brown the skin, then close it as the chicken cools.

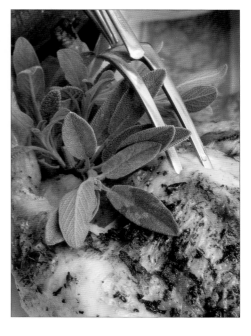

2 Place the herbs in the cavity of the bird and smear the butter over the skin. Season well. Cook the chicken on a spit on the barbecue for 1½–1¾ hours, basting with the marinade, until the juices run clear when the thigh is pierced with a skewer. Leave the bird to rest for 15 minutes before carving.

SENSATIONAL SALADS

° ° °

In these health-conscious days and with the increasing availability of exotic vegetables and produce from around the world, salads have become the fashion item in restaurants and on dining tables everywhere. This second part of the book is devoted to a mouthwatering selection of salads – from the subtle flavour combination of goat's cheese and figs to the flamboyant luxury of fresh lobster and from the charming simplicity of salad leaves combined with fresh herbs to the carnival colours of brown rice and tropical fruit.

This section starts with a detailed guide to ingredients – vegetables, fruit, salad leaves, herbs, spices, vinegars, oils and flavourings. The introductory pages also include step-by-step recipes for the most popular salad dressings and a time-saving selection of instant dressings and dips.

The recipes that follow cover all courses, occasions and seasons, from light meals and appetizers to glamorous dishes for special occasions and from raw and cooked side salads to main meals for a midweek family supper. The final chapter features fruit salads, and you may be surprised to discover how many different ways this popular dessert can be prepared.

Salads add a refreshing flavour and texture to any meal, as well as an appetizing splash of colour, but they are also a valuable source of vitamins, minerals and other nutrients – all year round. Nothing could make it easier to eat the five portions of vegetables and fruit a day that are recommended by nutritionists than this mouthwatering collection of recipes.

SALAD FRUIT
· · ·

The contents of the fruit bowl offer endless possibilities for sweet and savoury salads.

Apples
This versatile fruit offers a unique flavour and crunchy texture to both sweet and savoury salads.

Apricots
You can use apricots raw, dried or lightly poached.

Bananas
These bring a special richness to fruit salads, although their flavour can often interfere with more delicate fruit.

Blackberries
With a very short season, wild blackberries have more flavour than cultivated.

Blueberries
These tight-skinned berries combine well with the sharpness of fresh oranges.

Cherries
Cherries should be firm and glossy and are a deliciously sweet and colourful ingredient in many kinds of fruit salad.

Cranberries
Too sharp to eat raw but very good for cooking.

Dates
Fresh dates are sweet and juicy, dried ones have a more intense flavour. Both kinds work well in fresh fruit salads.

Figs
Green or purple skinned fruit, with sweet, pinkish-red flesh. Eat whole or peeled.

Gooseberries
Dessert types can be eaten raw, but cooking varieties are rather more widely available.

Grapefruit
These can have yellow, green or pink flesh; the pink-fleshed or ruby varieties are the sweetest.

Grapes
Large Muscat varieties, whose season runs from late summer to autumn, are the most coveted and also the most expensive.

Kiwi Fruit
Available all the year round.

Kumquats
Tiny relatives of the orange, they can be eaten raw or cooked.

Lemons and Limes
Both these indispensable citrus fruits are used for flavour, and to prevent fruit, such as apples, pears and avocados, from turning brown.

Lychees
A small fruit with a hard pink skin and sweet, juicy flesh.

Mangoes
Tropical fruit with an exotic flavour and golden-orange flesh that is wonderful in sweet or savoury salads.

Melons
These grow in abundance from mid to late summer and provide a resource of freshness and flavour. Melon is at its most delicious served icy cold.

Nectarines
A relative of the peach with a smoother skin.

Oranges
At their best during winter, they can be segmented and added to sweet and savoury salads.

Papaya
These fruits of the tropics have a distinctive, sweet flavour. When ripe they are yellow–green.

Peaches
Choose white peaches for the sweetest flavour, and yellow for a more aromatic taste.

Pears
Perfect for savoury salads, and with strong blue cheese and toasted pecan nuts.

Physalis
These small, fragrant, pleasantly tart orange berries, wrapped in a paper cape.

Pineapples
Ripe pineapples resist firm pressure in the hand and have a sweet smell.

Plums
There are many dessert and cooking varieties.

Raspberries
Much-coveted soft fruits that partner well with ripe mango, passion fruit and strawberries.

Rhubarb
Technically a vegetable, it is too tart to eat raw.

Star Fruit
When sliced, this makes a pretty shape perfect for garnishes.

Strawberries
A popular summer fruit, especially served with cream.

LETTUCES AND LEAVES

One particular aspect of lettuce that sets it apart from any other vegetable is that you can buy it in only one form – fresh.

Lettuce has been cultivated for thousands of years. In Egyptian times it was sacred to the fertility god Min. It was then considered a powerful aphrodisiac, yet for the Greeks and the Romans it was thought to have quite the opposite effect, making one sleepy and generally soporific. Chemists today confirm that lettuce contains a hypnotic similar to opium, and in herbal remedies lettuce is recommended for insomniacs.

There are hundreds of different varieties of lettuce. Today, an increasing choice is available in stores so that the salad bowl can become a riot of colour, taste and texture with no other ingredient than a selection of leaves.

Butterhead

These are the classic round lettuces. They have a pale heart and floppy, loosely packed leaves. They have a pleasant flavour as long as they are fresh. Choose the lettuce with the best heart by picking it up at the bottom and gently squeezing to check there is a firm centre. Many more varieties are now available.

Lollo Rosso

Both lollo rosso and lollo biondo are similar in shape but a paler green without any purple edges and are non-hearting lettuces. Although they do not have a lot of flavour, they look superb and are often used to form a nest of leaves on which to place the rest of a salad. They hold a lot of dressing.

Cos

The cos lettuce would have been known in antiquity. It has two names, cos, derived from the Greek island where it was found; and romaine, the name used by the French. Cos is considered to have the best flavour and is the correct lettuce for use in the famous American Caesar Salad.

Escarole

This is one of the more robust lettuces in terms of flavour and texture. Like the closely related frisée, escarole has a distinctive bitter flavour. Served with a judicious mixture of other leaves and a well-flavoured dressing, escarole and frisée will give your salad a pleasant "bite".

Oak Leaf Lettuce

Also known as feuille de chêne and salad bowl, oak leaf lettuce, together with lollo rosso and lollo biondo, is another member of the loosehead lettuce group. Oak leaf lettuce has a very gentle flavour. It is an extremely decorative leaf and makes a beautiful addition to any salad, and a lovely garnish.

Little Gem (Bibb)

These attractive little lettuces look like something between a baby cos and a tightly-furled butterhead. They have firm hearts and quite a distinct flavour. Their tight centres mean that they can be sliced whole and the quarters used for carrying slivers of smoked fish or anchovy as a simple appetizer.

Chinese Leaves (Chinese Cabbage)

This has pale green, crinkly leaves with long, wide, white ribs. Its shape is a little like a very fat head of celery, which gives rise to another of its names, celery cabbage. It has a crunchy texture, and since it is available all year round, it makes a useful winter salad component.

Radicchio

This is a variety developed from wild chicory (Belgian endive). It looks like a lettuce with deep wine-red leaves and cream ribs and owes its splendid foliage to careful shading from the light. If it is grown in the dark, the leaves are marbled pink. Its bitter flavour contrasts well with green salads.

Lamb's Lettuce

Also known as corn salad this is a popular winter leaf that does not actually belong to the lettuce family, but is terrific in salads. Called mâche in France, lamb's lettuce has small, attractive, dark green, delicate leaves and grows in pretty little sprigs. Its flavour is mild and nutty.

Watercress

Perhaps the most robustly flavoured of all the salad ingredients, a handful of watercress is all you need to perk up a dull or boring salad. It has a distinctive "raw" flavour, peppery and slightly pungent, and this, together with its shiny leaves, make it a popular and attractive garnish.

Rocket (Arugula)

This has a wonderful peppery flavour and is excellent in a mixed green salad. It was eaten by the Greeks and Romans as an aphrodisiac. Since it has such a striking flavour a little goes a long way; just a few leaves will transform a green salad and liven up a sandwich.

*For as long as salads have drawn
on the qualities of fresh produce,
sweet herbs have played an
important part in providing
individual character and flavour.
When herbs are used in a salad,
they should be as full of life as the
salad leaves they accompany. Dried
herbs are no substitute for fresh
ones and should be kept for cooked
dishes, such as casseroles. Salad
herbs are distinguished by their
ability to release flavour without
lengthy cooking.*

*Most salad herbs belong finely
chopped in salad dressings and
marinades, while the robust
flavours of rosemary, thyme and
fennel branches can be used on the
barbecue to impart a smoky herb
flavour. Ideally salad herbs should
be picked just before use, but if you
cannot use them immediately keep
them in water to retain their
freshness. Parsley, mint and
coriander (cilantro) will keep for
up to a week in this way if also
covered with a plastic bag and
placed in the refrigerator.*

Basil
Remarkable for its fresh, pungent
flavour unlike that of any other
herb, basil is widely used in
Mediterranean salads, especially
Italian recipes. It has a special
affinity with tomatoes. Basil leaves
are tender and delicate and should
be gently torn or snipped with
scissors, rather than chopped with
a knife, which will bruise them.

Chives
These belong to the onion family
and have a mild onion flavour. The
slender, green stems and soft mauve
flowers are both edible. Chives are
an indispensable flavouring for
potato salads.

Coriander (Cilantro)
The chopped leaves of this
pungent, distinctively flavoured
herb are popular in Middle Eastern
and Eastern salads.

Lavender
This soothingly fragrant herb is
edible and may be used in both
sweet and savoury salads as it
combines well with thyme, garlic,
honey and orange.

Mint
This much-loved, easy-to-grow
herb is widely used in Greek and
Middle Eastern salads, such as
Tzatziki and Tabbouleh. It is also
a popular addition to fruit salads.
Garden mint is the most common
variety; others include spearmint,
pineapple mint and the round-
leafed apple mint.

*Above: Clockwise from top left;
thyme, coriander, parsley, chives,
lavender, rose, mint and basil.*

Parsley
Flat leaf and curly parsley are both
used for their fresh, green flavour.
Flat leaf parsley is said to have a
stronger taste. Freshly chopped
parsley is used by the handful in
salads and dressings.

Rose
Although it is not technically a
herb, the sweet-scented rose can be
used to flavour fresh fruit salads. It
combines well with blackberries
and raspberries.

Thyme
An asset to salads featuring rich,
earthy flavours, this herb has a
penetrating flavour.

Spices are the aromatic seasonings found in the seed, bark, fruit and sometimes flowers of certain plants and trees. Spices are highly valued for their warm, inviting flavours, and thankfully their price is relatively low. The flavour of a spice is contained in the volatile oils of the seed, bark or fruit; so, like herbs, spices should be used as fresh as possible. Whole spices keep better than ground ones, which tend to lose their freshness within 3–4 months.

Not all spices are suitable for salad making, although many allow us to explore the flavours of other cultures. Some of the recipes in this book use curry spices, but only in moderation so as not to spoil the delicate salad flavours.

Caraway

These savoury-sweet-tasting seeds are widely used in German and Austrian cooking and feature strongly in many Jewish dishes. The small ribbed seeds are similar in appearance and taste to cumin. The flavour combines especially well with German mustard in a dressing for frankfurter salad.

Cayenne pepper

A type of chilli powder, this is the dried and finely ground fruit of a very hot chilli pepper. It is an important seasoning in South American cooking and is often used when seasoning fish and seafood. Cayenne pepper can be blended with paprika if it is too hot and should be used with care.

Celery salt

A combination of ground celery seed and salt, this is used for seasoning vegetables and has an especial affinity with carrots.

Cumin seeds

Often associated with Asian and North African cooking, cumin can be bought ground or as small, slender seeds. It combines well with coriander seeds.

Curry paste

Prepared curry paste consists of a blend of Indian spices preserved in oil. It may be added to dressings, and is particularly useful in this respect for showing off the sweet qualities of fish and shellfish.

Paprika

This spice is made from a variety of sweet red pepper. It is mild in flavour, and adds colour.

Pepper

Undoubtedly the most popular spice used in the West, pepper features in the cooking of almost every nation. Peppercorns can be

Above: Flavoursome additions to salads include (clockwise from top left) celery salt, caraway seeds, curry paste, saffron threads, peppercorns and cayenne pepper.

white, black, green or red and should always be freshly milled rather than bought already ground. Red or pink peppercorns are not actually a pepper, but a South American berry.

Saffron

The world's most expensive spice, made from the dried stigma of a crocus, real saffron has a tobacco-rich smell and gives a sweet yellow tint to liquids used for cooking. It can be used in creamy dressings and brings out the richness of fish and shellfish dishes. There are many powdered imitations which provide colour without the flavour of the real thing.

OILS, VINEGARS AND FLAVOURINGS
. . .

Oils

Oil is the main ingredient of most dressings and provides an important richness to salads. Neutral oils, such as sunflower, safflower or groundnut (peanut), are ideally used as a background for stronger oils. Sesame, walnut and hazelnut oils are the strongest and should be used sparingly. Olive oil is prized for its clarity of flavour and clean richness. The most significant producers of olive oil are Italy, France, Spain and Greece. These and other countries produce two main grades of olive oil: estate-grown extra-virgin olive oil; and semi-fine olive oil, which is of a good, basic standard.

Olive oils
Oils from different countries have distinctive characteristics.

French olive oils are subtly flavoured and provide a well-balanced lightness to dressings.

Greek olive oils are typically strong in character. They are often green with a thick texture and are unsuitable for mayonnaise.

Italian olive oils are noted for their vigorous Mediterranean flavours. Tuscan oils are noted for their well-rounded, spicy flavour. Sicilian oils tend to be lighter in texture, although they are often stronger in flavour.

Spanish olive oils are typically fruity and often have a nutty quality with a slight bitterness.

Nut oils
Hazelnut and walnut oils are valued for their strong, nutty flavour. Tasting richly of the nuts from which they are pressed, both are usually blended with neutral oils for salad dressings.

Seed oils
Groundnut oil, safflower and sunflower oil are valued for their clean, neutral flavour.

Salad Flavourings

Capers
These are the pickled flower buds of a bush native to the Mediterranean. Their strong, sharp flavour is well suited to richly flavoured salads.

Lemon and Lime Juice
The juice of lemons and limes is used to impart a clean acidity to oil dressings. They should be used in moderation.

Mustard
Mustard has a tendency to bring out the flavour of other ingredients. It also acts as an emulsifier in dressings and allows oil and vinegar to merge for a short period of time. The most popular mustards for use in salads are French, especially Dijon, German, English (hot) and wholegrain.

Above: Top left to right; Italian virgin olive oil, Spanish olive oil, Italian olive oil, safflower oil, hazelnut oil, walnut oil, groundnut oil, French olive oil, Italian olive oil, white wine vinegar. Left to right bottom; lemon, olives, limes, capers and mustard.

Olives
Black and green olives belong in salads with a Mediterranean flavour. Black olives are generally sweeter and juicier than green ones.

Vinegars

White wine vinegar
This should be used in moderation to balance the richness of an oil. A good-quality white wine vinegar will serve most purposes.

Balsamic vinegar
Sweeter than other vinegars, only a few drops of balsamic vinegar are necessary to enhance a salad or dressing. It is also a good substitute for lemon juice. The best types are more than 12 years old.

MAKING HERBED OILS AND VINEGARS

° ° °

Many herbed oils and vinegars are available commercially, but you can very easily make your own. Pour the oil or vinegar into a sterilized jar and add your flavouring. Allow to steep for 2 weeks, then strain and decant into an attractive bottle which has also been sterilized properly. Add a seal and an identifying label.

Flavoured vinegars should be used within 3 months, and herb-flavoured oils within 10 days. Fresh herbs for flavouring oils and vinegars should be rinsed clean and patted completely dry with kitchen paper before you use them.

Tarragon Vinegar

Steep tarragon in cider vinegar, then decant. Insert 2 or 3 long sprigs of tarragon into the bottle.

Rosemary Vinegar

Steep a sprig of fresh rosemary in red wine vinegar, then decant. Pour the vinegar into a sterilized, dry bottle and add a few long stems of rosemary as decoration.

Lemon and Lime Vinegar

Steep strips of lemon and lime rind in white wine vinegar, then decant. Pour into a sterilized, clean bottle and add fresh strips of rind for colour.

Raspberry Vinegar

Pour vinegar into a pan with 1 tablespoon of pickling spices and heat gently for 5 minutes. Pour the hot mixture over the raspberries in a bowl and then add 2 fresh sprigs of lemon thyme. Cover and leave the mixture to steep for two days in a cool, dark place. Strain the liquid and pour the flavoured vinegar into a sterilized bottle and seal.

Dill and Lemon Oil

Steep a handful of fresh dill and a large strip of lemon rind in virgin olive oil, then decant. Use for salads containing fish or shellfish.

Mediterranean Herb Oil

Steep fresh rosemary, thyme and marjoram in virgin or extra virgin olive oil, then decant.

Basil and Chilli Oil

Steep basil and 3 chillies in virgin olive oil, then decant. Add to tomato and mozzarella salads.

Warning

There is some evidence that oils containing fresh herbs and spices can grow harmful moulds, especially once the bottle has been opened and the contents are not fully covered by the oil. To protect against this, it is recommended that the herbs and spices are removed once their flavour has passed into the oil.

From left: Tarragon Vinegar, Rosemary Vinegar, Raspberry Vinegar, Lemon and Lime Vinegar.

VEGETABLE PREPARATION

Shredding Cabbage

Cabbage features in many salad recipes, such as coleslaw, and this method for shredding can be used for all varieties.

1 Use a large knife to cut the cabbage into quarters.

2 Cut the hard core from each quarter and discard; this part is not really edible when raw.

3 Slice each quarter to form fine shreds. Shredded cabbage will keep for several hours in the refrigerator, but do not dress it until you are ready to serve.

Chopping an Onion

Chopped onions are used in many recipes and, whether they are very finely or coarsely chopped, the method is the same; just vary the gap between cuts.

1 Cut off the stalk end of the onion and cut in half through the root, leaving the root intact. Remove the skin and place the halved onion, cut-side down, on the board. Make lengthways vertical cuts into the onion, taking care not to cut right through to the root.

2 Make two or three horizontal cuts from the stalk end through to the root, but without cutting all the way through. Space the cuts at about 5mm/¼in intervals.

3 Turn the onion on to its side. Cut the onion across from the stalk end to the root, again at about 5mm/¼in intervals. The onion will fall away in small squares. Cut further apart for larger squares.

Preparing Garlic

Don't worry if you don't have a garlic press: instead, try this method, which gives wonderful, juicy results.

1 Break off the clove of garlic, place the flat side of a large knife on top and strike with your fist. Remove all the papery outer skin. Begin by finely chopping the clove.

2 Sprinkle over a little table salt and, using the flat side of a large knife blade, work the salt into the garlic, until the clove softens and releases its juices. Use the garlic pulp as required.

Preparing Chillies

Chillies add a distinct flavour, but remove the fiery-hot seeds.

1 Always protect your hands, as chillies can irritate the skin; wear rubber gloves and never rub your eyes after handling chillies. Halve the chilli lengthways and remove and discard the seeds.

2 Slice, finely chop and use as required. Wash the knife and board thoroughly in hot, soapy water. Always wash your hands thoroughly after preparing chillies.

Peeling Tomatoes

If you have the time, peel tomatoes before adding them to dressings. This avoids including rolled-up, tough pieces of tomato skin.

1 Make a cross in each tomato with a sharp knife and place in a bowl.

2 Pour over enough boiling water to cover and leave to stand for about 30 seconds. The skins should start to come away. Slightly unripe tomatoes may take a little longer.

3 Drain the tomatoes and peel off the skin with a sharp knife. Don't leave the tomatoes in the boiling water for too long.

Chopping Herbs

Chop fresh herbs just before you use them.

1 Remove the leaves and place on a clean, dry board.

2 Chop the herbs, as finely or as coarsely as required, by holding the tip of the blade of a large, sharp knife on the board and rocking the handle up and down.

Cutting Julienne Strips

Julienne strips of carrots, celery, cucumber and other vegetables make attractive garnishes and salad ingredients.

1 Peel the vegetable and use a large knife to cut it into 5cm/2in lengths. Cut a thin sliver from one side of the first piece so that it sits flat on the board.

2 Cut each piece into thin slices lengthways. Stack the slices of vegetable and then cut through them again to make fine strips.

Preparing Spring Onions (Scallions)

Spring onions make such a crisp and tasty addition to salads that they are worth the bother.

1 Trim off the root of the spring onion with a sharp knife. Peel away any damaged or tough leaves.

2 For an intense flavour and an attractive green colour cut the dark green part into thin sticks.

3 For a milder flavour just use the white part of the spring onion, discard the root and slice thinly on a slight diagonal.

FRUIT PREPARATION

. . .

Citrus Fruit

1 To peel, cut a slice from the top and from the base. Set the fruit base down on a work surface.

2 Cut off the peel lengthways in thick strips. Remove the coloured rind and all the white pith (which has a bitter taste). Cut following the curve of the fruit.

1 To remove the thin, coloured rind, use a vegetable peeler to shave off the rind in wide strips, taking none of the white pith. Use these strips whole or cut them into fine shreds with a sharp knife.

2 Alternatively, rub the fruit against the fine holes of a metal grater, turning the fruit so that you take just the rind and not the white pith. Or use a special tool, called a citrus zester, to take fine threads of rind. The shallow angle of the blade cuts into the outer surface of the rind only. Finely chop the threads for tiny pieces.

1 For slices, cut across the fruit in slices with a serrated knife.

1 For segments, hold the fruit over a bowl to catch the juice. Working from the side of the fruit to the centre, slide the knife down first one side of a separating membrane and then the other. Continue cutting out all the segments.

Fresh Currants

1 Pull small bunches of fruit through the tines of a fork to remove red, black or white currants from the stalks. This prevents squashing them.

Apples and Pears

1 For whole fruit, use an apple corer to stamp out the whole core from stalk end to base.

1 For halves, use a melon baller to scoop out the core. Cut out the stalk and base with a sharp knife.

2 For rings, remove the core and seeds. Set the fruit on its side and cut across into rings, as required.

1 For slices, cut the fruit in half and remove the core and seeds. Set one half, cut side down, and cut it across into neat slices. Repeat with the other half.

Fresh Dates

1 Halve the fruit lengthways and lift out the stone (pit).

Papayas and Melons

1 Halve the fruit. Scoop out the seeds from the central hollow, then scrape away any fibres. For slices, follow the pear technique.

Kiwi Fruit, Star Fruit (Carambola)

1 Cut the fruit across into neat slices; discard the ends.

Pineapples

1 To peel the pineapple, set the pineapple on its base, hold it at the top and cut thick slices of skin from top to bottom. Dig out any "eyes" that remain with the point of the knife.

2 For chunks, halve the peeled fruit lengthways and then cut into quarters. Cut each quarter into spears and cut out the core. Cut each spear into chunks.

3 For rings, cut the peeled fruit across into slices and cut or stamp out the core.

Keeping Fresh Colour

If exposed to the air for long, the cut flesh of fruits such as apples, bananas and avocados starts to turn brown. So if cut fruit has to wait before being served, sprinkle the cut surfaces with lemon juice, or immerse hard fruits in water and lemon juice, but do not soak or the fruit may become soggy.

Mangoes

1 Cut lengthways on either side of the stone (pit). Then cut from the two thin ends of the stone.

2 Remove the skin and cut the flesh into slices or cubes.

Peaches, Nectarines, Apricots and Plums

1 Cut the fruit in half, cutting around the indentation. Twist the halves apart. Lift out the stone (pit), or lever it out with the tip of a knife. Or cut the unpeeled fruit into wedges, removing the stone. Set each wedge peel side down and slide the knife down to peel.

SALAD DRESSINGS

Although the ingredients of a salad are important, the true secret of a perfect salad is a good dressing.

A French dressing made from the very best olive oil and vinegar can rescue even the dullest selection of lettuce leaves, while a home-made mayonnaise is impressive.

If you are a confident and experienced salad dresser you might feel able simply to add olive oil and vinegar directly to your salad just before serving, but the safest way of creating a perfect dressing is to prepare it in advance. Home-made dressings can be stored in the refrigerator for up to a week and will improve in flavour. Here is a selection of favourites.

Thousand Islands Dressing

This creamy dressing is great with green salads and grated carrot, hot potato, pasta and rice salads.

INGREDIENTS
60ml/4 tbsp sunflower oil
15ml/1 tbsp orange juice
15ml/1 tbsp lemon juice
10ml/2 tsp grated lemon rind
15ml/1 tbsp finely chopped onion
5ml/1 tsp paprika
5ml/1 tsp Worcestershire sauce
15ml/1 tbsp finely chopped
fresh parsley
salt and ground black pepper

MAKES ABOUT
120ML/4FL OZ/1/2 CUP

Put all the ingredients into a screw-top jar and season to taste with salt and pepper. Replace the lid and shake well.

French Dressing

This is the most popular dressing.

INGREDIENTS
90ml/6 tbsp extra virgin olive oil
15ml/1 tbsp white wine vinegar
5ml/1 tsp French mustard
pinch of caster (superfine) sugar

MAKES ABOUT 120ML/
4FL OZ/1/2 CUP

1 Place the extra virgin olive oil and white wine vinegar in a clean screw-top jar.

2 Add the French mustard and caster sugar.

3 Replace the lid and shake the jar well to mix.

French Herb Dressing

The delicate scents and flavours of fresh herbs combine especially well in a French dressing. Use just one herb or a selection.

INGREDIENTS
60ml/4 tbsp extra virgin olive oil
30ml/2 tbsp sunflower oil
15ml/1 tbsp lemon juice
60ml/4 tbsp finely chopped fresh
herbs (parsley, chives, tarragon
and marjoram)
pinch of caster (superfine) sugar

MAKES ABOUT 120ML/
4FL OZ/1/2 CUP

1 Place the extra virgin olive oil and sunflower oil in a clean screw-top jar.

2 Add the lemon juice, chopped herbs and sugar.

3 Replace the lid and shake the jar well to mix.

Mayonnaise

For consistent results, make sure that both egg yolks and oil are at room temperature before combining. Home-made mayonnaise is made with raw egg yolks and may therefore be considered unsuitable for young children, pregnant mothers and the elderly.

INGREDIENTS

2 egg yolks
5ml/1 tsp French mustard
150ml/¼ pint/⅔ cup extra virgin olive oil
150 ml/¼ pint/⅔ cup groundnut or sunflower oil
10ml/2 tsp white wine vinegar
salt and ground black pepper

MAKES ABOUT 300ML/
½ PINT/1¼ CUPS

1 Place the egg yolks and mustard in a food processor and process until smoothly blended.

2 Add the olive oil through the feeder tube, a little at a time, while the processor is still running. When the mixture is thick, add the groundnut or sunflower oil in a slow, steady stream.

3 Add the vinegar and season to taste with salt and pepper.

Yogurt Dressing

This is a less rich version of a classic mayonnaise and is much easier to make. It can be used as a low-fat substitute. Change the herbs as you wish, or leave them out.

INGREDIENTS

150ml/¼ pint/⅔ cup natural (plain) yogurt
30ml/2 tbsp mayonnaise
30ml/2 tbsp milk
15ml/1 tbsp chopped fresh parsley
15ml/1 tbsp chopped fresh chives

MAKES ABOUT 200ML/
7FL OZ/SCANT 1 CUP

Put all the ingredients in a bowl. Season to taste and mix well.

Blue Cheese and Chive Dressing

Blue cheese dressings have a strong, robust flavour and are well suited to winter salad leaves such as escarole, chicory (Belgian endive) and radicchio.

INGREDIENTS

75 g/3 oz blue cheese (Stilton, Bleu d'Auvergne or Gorgonzola)
150 ml/¼ pint/⅔ cup medium-fat natural (plain) yogurt
45 ml/3 tbsp olive oil
30 ml/2 tbsp lemon juice
15 ml/1 tbsp chopped fresh chives
ground black pepper

MAKES ABOUT 350ML/
12FL OZ/1½ CUPS

1 Remove the rind from the cheese and combine the cheese with a third of the yogurt in a bowl.

2 Add the remainder of the yogurt, the olive oil and the lemon juice and mix well.

3 Stir in the chopped chives and season the dressing to taste with ground black pepper.

Basil and Lemon Mayonnaise

This luxurious dressing is flavoured with lemon juice and two types of fresh basil. It can be served with all kinds of leafy salads, crudités or coleslaws. The dressing will keep in an airtight jar for up to a week in the refrigerator.

INGREDIENTS

2 large (US extra large) egg yolks
15ml/1 tbsp lemon juice
150ml/¼ pint/⅔ cup extra virgin olive oil
150 ml/¼ pint/⅔ cup sunflower oil
4 garlic cloves
handful of fresh green basil
handful of fresh opal basil
salt and ground black pepper

MAKES ABOUT 300ML/
½ PINT/1¼ CUPS

1 Place the egg yolks and lemon juice in a blender or food processor and process briefly.

3 Once half of the oil mixture has been added and the dressing has successfully emulsified, the remaining oil can be incorporated more quickly in a continuous steady stream. Continue processing until a thick, creamy mayonnaise has formed.

4 Peel and crush the garlic cloves and add to the mayonnaise. Alternatively, place the cloves on a chopping board and sprinkle with salt, then flatten them with the heel of a heavy-bladed knife and chop the flesh. Flatten the garlic again to make a coarse purée, then add to the mayonnaise.

5 Remove the basil stalks and tear both types of leaves into small pieces. Stir into the mayonnaise.

6 Add salt and pepper to taste, then transfer the mayonnaise to a serving dish. Cover and chill until ready to serve.

2 In a jug (pitcher), stir together both oils. With the machine running, pour in the oil very slowly, a little at a time.

INSTANT DRESSINGS AND DIPS
∘ ∘ ∘

If you need an instant dressing or dip, try one of these quick recipes. Most of them use pantry ingredients.

Creamy Black Olive Dip

Stir a little black olive paste into a carton of extra-thick double (heavy) cream until smooth and well blended. Add salt, ground black pepper and a squeeze of lemon juice to taste. Serve chilled.

Crème Fraîche Dressing with Spring Onions

Finely chop a bunch of spring onions (scallions) and stir into a carton of crème fraîche. Add a dash of chilli sauce and a squeeze of lime juice and season with salt and ground black pepper.

Yogurt and Mustard Dip

Mix a small carton of creamy, Greek (US strained plain) yogurt with 5–10ml/1–2 tsp wholegrain mustard. Serve with crudités.

Herb Mayonnaise

Liven up ready-made French-style mayonnaise with a handful of chopped fresh herbs.

Passata and Horseradish Dip

Bring a little tang to a small carton or bottle of passata (bottled strained tomatoes) by adding some horseradish sauce or 5–10 ml/ 1–2 tsp creamed horseradish and salt and pepper to taste.

Pesto Dip

Stir 15ml/1 tbsp ready-made red or green pesto into a carton of soured cream. Serve with crisp crudités or wedges of oven-roasted Mediterranean vegetables.

Spiced Yogurt Dressing

Stir a little curry paste and chutney into a carton of yogurt.

Sun-dried Tomato Dip

Stir 15–30ml/1–2 tbsp sun-dried tomato paste into a carton of Greek (US strained plain) yogurt. Season with salt and black pepper.

Above: Top row; Creamy Black Olive Dip, Crème Fraîche Dressing with Spring Onions. Second row; Herb Mayonnaise, Sun-dried Tomato Dip. Third row; Yogurt and Mustard dip, Soft Cheese and Chive Dip, Spiced Yogurt Dressing. Fourth row; Pesto Dip, Passata and Horseradish Dip.

Soft Cheese and Chive Dip

Mix a tub of soft cheese with 30–45 ml/2–3 tbsp chopped fresh chives and season to taste with salt and ground black pepper. If the dip is too thick, stir in a little milk. Use as a dressing for all kinds of salads, especially winter coleslaws.

Salads are the most versatile accompaniments to hot and cold

dishes – in both summer and winter – and are ideal for serving

at a barbecue. They are perfect for picnics and make effortless

appetizers when you are entertaining.

LIGHT AND SIDE
SALADS

CRUDITÉS

∘ ∘ ∘

A colourful selection of raw vegetables, or crudités, may be served with drinks or as small appetizers. The term "crudités" is used both for small pieces of vegetables served with a tasty dip and for a selection of vegetable salads presented in separate dishes. By choosing contrasting colours, you can make a beautiful presentation of raw or lightly cooked vegetables, attractively arranged on a platter or in baskets and served with a tangy dip, such as aioli (garlic mayonnaise) or tapenade (olive paste). Allow 75–115g/3–4oz of each vegetable per person.

Aioli

Put four crushed garlic cloves (or more or less, to taste) in a small bowl with a pinch of salt and crush with the back of a spoon. Add two egg yolks and beat for 30 seconds with an electric mixer until creamy. Beat in 250ml/8fl oz/1 cup extra virgin olive oil, one drop at a time, until the mixture thickens. As it begins to thicken, the oil can be added in a thin, steady stream until the mixture is thick. Thin the sauce with a little lemon juice and season to taste with salt and pepper. Chill for up to 2 days; bring to room temperature and stir before serving.

Tapenade

Put 200g/7oz pitted black olives, 6 canned anchovy fillets, 30ml/ 2 tbsp rinsed capers, 1–2 garlic cloves, 5ml/1 tsp fresh thyme leaves, 15ml/1 tbsp Dijon mustard, the juice of ½ lemon, freshly ground black pepper and, if you like, 15ml/1 tbsp brandy in a food processor fitted with the metal blade. Process for 15–30 seconds until smooth, then scrape down the sides of the bowl. With the machine running, slowly add 60–90ml/4–6 tbsp extra virgin olive oil to make a smooth, firm paste. Store in an airtight container.

Raw Vegetable Platter

INGREDIENTS

2 red and 2 yellow (bell) peppers, seeded and sliced lengthways
225g/8oz fresh baby corn cobs, blanched
1 chicory (Belgian endive) head (red or white), trimmed and leaves separated
175–225g/6–8oz thin asparagus, trimmed and blanched
1 small bunch radishes with small leaves
175g/6oz cherry tomatoes
12 quail's eggs, boiled for 3 minutes, drained, refreshed and peeled
aioli or tapenade, to serve

SERVES 6–8

Arrange the prepared vegetables on a large serving plate together with the quail's eggs. Cover with a damp dishtowel until ready to serve. Serve with aioli or tapenade for dipping.

Tomato and Cucumber Salad

INGREDIENTS

1 medium cucumber, peeled and thinly sliced
5–6 ice cubes
30ml/2 tbsp white wine vinegar
90ml/6 tbsp crème fraîche or sour cream
30ml/2 tbsp chopped fresh mint
4 or 5 ripe tomatoes, sliced
salt and freshly ground black pepper

SERVES 4–6

Place the cucumber in a bowl, sprinkle with a little salt and 15ml/ 1 tbsp of the vinegar and toss with the ice cubes. Chill for 1 hour to crisp, then rinse, drain and pat dry. Return to the bowl, add the cream, pepper and mint and stir to mix well. Arrange the tomato slices on a serving plate, sprinkle with the remaining vinegar and spoon the cucumber slices into the centre.

Carrot and Parsley Salad

INGREDIENTS

1 garlic clove, crushed
grated rind and juice of 1 orange
30–45ml/2–3 tbsp groundnut (peanut) oil
450 g/1lb carrots, cut into very fine julienne strips
30–45ml/2–3 tbsp chopped fresh parsley
salt and freshly ground black pepper

SERVES 4–6

Rub a bowl with the garlic and leave in the bowl. Add the orange rind and juice and season. Whisk in the oil until blended, then remove the garlic. Add the carrots and half of the parsley and toss well. Garnish with the remaining parsley.

LETTUCE AND HERB SALAD

· · ∘

Stores now sell many different types of lettuce leaves all year, so try to use a mixture.

INGREDIENTS

½ cucumber
mixed lettuce leaves
1 bunch watercress, about 115g/4oz
1 chicory (Belgian endive)
head, sliced
45ml/3 tbsp chopped fresh herbs

FOR THE DRESSING
15ml/1 tbsp white wine vinegar
5ml/1 tsp prepared mustard
75ml/5 tbsp olive oil
salt and freshly ground
black pepper

SERVES 4

3 Either toss the cucumber, lettuce, watercress, chicory and herbs together in a bowl, or arrange them in the bowl in layers.

4 Stir the dressing, then pour over the salad and toss lightly to coat the salad vegetables and leaves. Serve immediately.

1 To make the dressing, mix the vinegar and mustard together, then whisk in the oil and seasoning.

2 Peel the cucumber, if you like, then halve it lengthways and scoop out the seeds. Thinly slice the flesh. Tear the lettuce leaves by hand into bitesize pieces.

MINTED MELON AND GRAPEFRUIT COCKTAIL
o · o ·

Melon is always a popular and refreshing appetizer.

INGREDIENTS

1 small Galia or charentais melon,
about 1kg/2¼lb
2 pink grapefruit
1 yellow grapefruit
5ml/1 tsp Dijon mustard
5ml/1 tsp raspberry or
sherry vinegar
5ml/1 tsp clear honey
15ml/1 tbsp chopped fresh mint
fresh mint sprigs, to garnish

SERVES 4

1 Halve the melon and remove the seeds with a teaspoon. With a melon baller, carefully scoop the flesh into balls.

2 With a sharp knife, peel the pink and yellow grapefruit and cut away all the white pith. Carefully remove the segments by cutting between the membranes, holding the fruit over a bowl to catch any juice.

3 Whisk the Dijon mustard, raspberry or sherry vinegar, honey, chopped mint and reserved grapefruit juice together in a mixing bowl. Add the melon balls and grapefruit segments and mix well. Cover and chill in the refrigerator for 30 minutes.

4 Ladle into four serving dishes, garnish each one with a sprig of fresh mint and serve.

BLACK AND ORANGE SALAD

This dramatically colourful salad, with its piquant, spicy dressing, is very unusual. It is a feast for the eyes as well as for the taste buds.

INGREDIENTS
3 oranges
115g/4oz/1 cup pitted black olives
15ml/1 tbsp chopped fresh coriander (cilantro)
15ml/1 tbsp chopped fresh parsley

FOR THE DRESSING
30ml/2 tbsp olive oil
15ml/1 tbsp lemon juice
2.5ml/½ tsp paprika
2.5ml/½ tsp ground cumin

SERVES 4

1 With a sharp knife, cut away the peel and pith from the oranges and divide the fruit into segments.

2 Place the oranges in a salad bowl and add the black olives, coriander and parsley.

3 Blend together the olive oil, lemon juice, paprika and cumin. Pour the dressing over the salad and toss gently. Chill for about 30 minutes and serve.

ROCKET AND CORIANDER SALAD

Unless you have a plentiful supply of rocket, you may well have to use extra spinach or another green leaf.

INGREDIENTS
115g/4oz or more rocket (arugula) leaves
115g/4oz young spinach leaves
1 large bunch fresh coriander (cilantro), about 25g/1oz
2–3 fresh parsley sprigs

FOR THE DRESSING
1 garlic clove, crushed
45ml/3 tbsp olive oil
10ml/2 tsp white wine vinegar
pinch of paprika
cayenne pepper
salt

SERVES 4

1 Place the rocket and spinach leaves in a salad bowl. Chop the coriander and parsley and sprinkle them over the top.

2 In a small jug (pitcher), blend together the garlic, olive oil, vinegar, paprika, cayenne pepper and salt to taste.

3 Pour the dressing over the salad and serve immediately.

CAESAR SALAD

∘ ∘ ∘

There are many stories about this salad's origin. The most likely is that it was invented by Caesar Cardini in his Mexican restaurant in the 1920s.

INGREDIENTS

3 slices day-old bread, 1cm/ ½in thick
60ml/4 tbsp garlic oil
50g/2oz piece Parmesan cheese
1 cos or romaine lettuce
salt and freshly ground black pepper

FOR THE DRESSING

2 egg yolks, as fresh as possible
25g/1oz canned anchovy fillets, drained and coarsely chopped
2.5ml/½ tsp French mustard
120ml/4fl oz/½ cup olive oil
15ml/1 tbsp white wine vinegar

SERVES 4

1 To make the dressing, combine the egg yolks, anchovies, mustard, oil and vinegar in a screw-top jar and shake well.

2 Remove the crusts from the bread with a serrated knife and cut into 2.5cm/1in fingers.

3 Heat the garlic oil in a large frying-pan, add the pieces of bread and fry until golden brown all over. Remove from the pan, sprinkle with salt and leave to drain on kitchen paper.

4 Cut thin shavings from the Parmesan cheese with a swivel-bade vegetable peeler.

5 Wash the lettuce leaves and spin dry or pat dry with kitchen paper or a clean dishtowel. Place in a salad bowl or on individual plates, smother with the dressing, and sprinkle with the garlic croûtons and Parmesan cheese shavings. Season to taste with salt and pepper and serve immediately.

> *Cook's Tip*
> The classic dressing for Caesar Salad is made with raw egg yolks. Make sure that you use only the freshest eggs, bought from a reputable supplier. Expectant mothers, young children and the elderly are not advised to eat raw egg yolks. You could omit them from the salad dressing and grate hard-boiled yolks on top of the salad instead.

TURKISH SALAD

This is a perfect combination of textures and flavours.

INGREDIENTS

1 cos or romaine lettuce heart
1 green (bell) pepper
1 red (bell) pepper
½ cucumber
4 tomatoes
1 red onion
225g/8oz feta cheese, crumbled
black olives, to garnish

FOR THE DRESSING

45ml/3 tbsp olive oil
45ml/3 tbsp lemon juice
1 garlic clove, crushed
15ml/1 tbsp chopped fresh parsley
15ml/1 tbsp chopped fresh mint
salt and freshly ground
black pepper

SERVES 4

1 Chop the lettuce into bitesize pieces. Seed the peppers, remove and discard the cores and cut the flesh into thin strips. Chop the cucumber and slice or chop the tomatoes. Cut the onion in half, then slice finely.

2 Place the chopped lettuce, peppers, cucumber, tomatoes and onion in a large salad bowl. Sprinkle the crumbled feta over the top and toss together lightly.

3 To make the dressing, blend together the olive oil, lemon juice and garlic in a small bowl. Stir in the chopped parsley and mint and season with salt and black pepper to taste. Alternatively, put all the ingredients in a screw-top jar and shake well.

4 Pour the dressing over the salad and toss lightly. Garnish with a handful of black olives and serve the salad immediately.

PERSIAN SALAD

This very simple salad can be served with almost any dish. Don't add the dressing until just before you are ready to serve.

INGREDIENTS

4 tomatoes
½ cucumber
1 onion
1 cos or romaine lettuce heart

FOR THE DRESSING

30ml/2 tbsp olive oil
juice of 1 lemon
1 garlic clove, crushed
salt and freshly ground
black pepper

SERVES 4

1 Cut the tomatoes and cucumber into small cubes. Finely chop the onion and tear the lettuce heart into pieces.

2 Place the prepared tomatoes, cucumber, onion and lettuce in a large salad bowl and mix them lightly together.

3 To make the dressing, pour the olive oil into a small bowl. Add the lemon juice, garlic and seasoning and blend together well.

4 Pour the dressing over the salad and toss lightly to mix. Sprinkle with extra black pepper to taste and serve immediately.

SPINACH AND MUSHROOM SALAD

· ◦ ◦ ◦

This nutritious salad goes well with strongly flavoured dishes. If served alone as a light lunch, it could be dressed with a French vinaigrette and served with warm French bread.

INGREDIENTS
*10 baby corn cobs
2 medium tomatoes
115g/4oz/1½ cups mushrooms
1 medium onion cut into rings
20 small spinach leaves
25g/1oz salad cress (optional)
salt and freshly ground
black pepper*

SERVES 4

1 Halve the baby corn cobs lengthways and slice the tomatoes.

2 Trim the mushrooms and cut them into thin slices.

3 Arrange the corn cobs, tomatoes, mushrooms, onions, spinach and cress, if using, attractively in a large bowl. Season with salt and pepper to taste and serve.

NUTTY SALAD

◦ ◦ ◦

A delicious salad with a tangy bite to it that can be served as an accompaniment to a main meal, or as an appetizer.

INGREDIENTS
*1 medium onion, cut into 12 rings
115g/4oz/¾ cup canned red kidney
beans, drained
1 medium green courgette
(zucchini), sliced
1 medium yellow courgette
(zucchini), sliced
50g/2oz pasta shells, cooked
50g/2oz/½ cup cashew nuts
25g/1oz/¼ cup peanuts
lime wedges and fresh coriander
(cilantro) sprigs, to garnish*

FOR THE DRESSING
*120ml/4fl oz/½ cup fromage frais
or farmer's cheese
30ml/2 tbsp natural (plain) yogurt
1 fresh green chilli, chopped*

*15ml/1 tbsp chopped fresh
coriander (cilantro)
2.5ml/½ tsp crushed
black peppercorns
2.5ml/½ tsp crushed dried
red chillies
15ml/1 tbsp lemon juice
2.5ml/½ tsp salt*

SERVES 4

1 Arrange the onion rings, red kidney beans, green and yellow courgette slices and pasta shells in a salad dish, ready for serving. Sprinkle the cashew nuts and peanuts over the top.

2 In a separate bowl, blend together the fromage frais, yogurt, green chilli, coriander and salt and beat well using a fork.

3 Sprinkle the crushed black pepper, red chillies and lemon juice over the dressing. Garnish the salad with the lime wedges and coriander sprigs and serve with the dressing in a separate bowl or poured over the salad.

FRESH CEPS SALAD

° · ○

To capture the just-picked flavour of a cep, this delicious salad is enriched with an egg yolk and walnut oil dressing.

INGREDIENTS
350g/12oz fresh ceps
175g/6oz mixed salad leaves,
including batavia, young spinach
and frisée
50g/2oz/¹/₂ cup broken walnut
pieces, toasted
50g/2oz piece Parmesan cheese
salt and freshly ground
black pepper

FOR THE DRESSING
2 egg yolks
2.5ml/¹/₂ tsp French mustard
75ml/5 tbsp groundnut (peanut) oil
45ml/3 tbsp walnut oil
30ml/2 tbsp lemon juice
30ml/2 tbsp chopped fresh parsley
pinch of caster (superfine) sugar

SERVES 4

1 To make the dressing, place the egg yolks in a screw-top jar with the mustard, groundnut and walnut oils, lemon juice, parsley and sugar. Shake well.

2 Trim the ceps and cut them into thin slices.

3 Place the ceps in a large salad bowl and combine with the dressing. Leave for 10–15 minutes for the flavours to mingle.

4 Wash and dry the salad leaves, then add them to the salad bowl and toss them with the ceps.

5 Turn the ceps out on to four large serving plates. Season well with salt and pepper, sprinkle with the toasted walnuts and shavings of Parmesan cheese, then serve.

CLASSIC GREEK SALAD
∘ ∘ ∘

If you have ever visited Greece, you'll know that this salad makes a delicious first course.

INGREDIENTS
1 cos or romaine lettuce
½ cucumber, halved lengthways
4 tomatoes
8 spring onions (scallions), sliced
black olives
115g/4oz feta cheese

FOR THE DRESSING
90ml/6 tbsp white wine vinegar
150ml/¼ pint/⅔ cup extra virgin
olive oil
salt and freshly ground
black pepper

SERVES 4

1 Tear the lettuce leaves into pieces and place in a large bowl. Slice the cucumber and add to the bowl.

2 Cut the tomatoes into wedges and put them into the bowl.

Cook's Tip
The salad can be assembled in advance and chilled, but should be dressed only just before serving. Keep the dressing at room temperature as chilling deadens the flavour.

3 Add the spring onions to the bowl together with the black olives, and toss well.

4 Cut the feta cheese into cubes and add to the salad.

5 Put the vinegar, olive oil and seasoning into a small bowl and whisk well. Pour the dressing over the salad and toss to combine. Serve with extra black olives and chunks of bread, if you like.

ORANGE AND RED ONION SALAD WITH CUMIN

Cumin and fresh mint give this refreshing salad a very Middle Eastern flavour. Small, seedless oranges are the most suitable type, if available.

INGREDIENTS

6 oranges
2 red onions
15ml/1 tbsp cumin seeds
5ml/1 tsp coarsely ground
black pepper
15ml/1 tbsp chopped fresh mint
90ml/6 tbsp olive oil
salt
fresh mint sprigs and black olives,
to serve

SERVES 6

1 Slice the oranges thinly, working over a bowl to catch any juice. Then, holding each orange slice in turn over the bowl, cut around with kitchen scissors to remove the peel and pith. Reserve the juice. Slice the onions thinly and separate out into rings.

2 Arrange the orange and onion slices in layers in a shallow dish, sprinkling each layer with cumin seeds, black pepper, chopped mint, olive oil and salt to taste. Pour over the reserved orange juice.

3 Leave the salad to marinate in a cool place for about 2 hours. Sprinkle over the mint sprigs and black olives and serve.

SPANISH SALAD WITH CAPERS AND OLIVES

Make this refreshing salad in the summer when tomatoes are at their sweetest.

INGREDIENTS

4 tomatoes
½ cucumber
1 bunch spring onions (scallions),
trimmed and chopped
1 bunch watercress
8 stuffed olives
30ml/2 tbsp drained capers

FOR THE DRESSING
30ml/2 tbsp red wine vinegar
5ml/1 tsp paprika
2.5ml/½ tsp ground cumin
1 garlic clove, crushed
75ml/5 tbsp olive oil
salt and freshly ground
black pepper

SERVES 4

1 Peel the skin from the tomatoes and finely dice the flesh. Put them in a salad bowl.

2 Peel the cucumber, dice the flesh finely and add it to the tomatoes. Add half the chopped spring onions to the salad bowl and mix lightly. Break the watercress into small sprigs. Add to the tomato mixture, with the stuffed olives and capers.

3 To make the dressing, mix the wine vinegar, paprika, cumin and garlic in a bowl. Whisk in the olive oil and season with salt and pepper to taste. Pour the dressing over the salad and toss lightly to combine. Serve the salad immediately with the remaining spring onions.

CARROT AND ORANGE SALAD

The ingredients of this fresh-tasting salad could have been made for each other.

INGREDIENTS

450g/1lb carrots
2 large oranges
15ml/1 tbsp olive oil
30ml/2 tbsp lemon juice
pinch of sugar (optional)
30ml/2 tbsp toasted pine nuts
salt and freshly ground
black pepper

SERVES 4

1 Peel the carrots and grate them into a large bowl.

2 Peel the oranges with a sharp knife and cut into segments, catching the juice in a small bowl.

Variation
Substitute shelled chopped pistachio nuts for the toasted pine nuts, if you like.

3 Blend together the olive oil, lemon juice and orange juice. Season with a little salt and pepper to taste and stir in a pinch of sugar if you like.

4 Toss the orange segments together with the carrots and pour the dressing over them. Sprinkle the salad with the pine nuts just before serving.

SPINACH AND ROAST GARLIC SALAD

Don't worry about the amount of garlic in this salad. During roasting, the garlic becomes sweet and subtle and loses its pungent taste.

INGREDIENTS

12 garlic cloves, unpeeled
60ml/4 tbsp extra virgin olive oil
450g/1lb baby spinach leaves
50g/2oz/½ cup pine nuts,
lightly toasted
juice of ½ lemon
salt and freshly ground
black pepper

SERVES 4

1 Preheat the oven to 190°C/ 375°F/Gas 5. Place the garlic cloves separately in a small roasting pan, add 30ml/2 tbsp of the olive oil and toss thoroughly to coat. Roast for about 15 minutes, until the garlic cloves are slightly charred around the edges.

2 While still warm, tip the garlic into a salad bowl. Add the spinach, pine nuts, lemon juice, remaining olive oil and a little salt. Toss well and add black pepper to taste. Serve immediately, inviting guests to squeeze the softened garlic purée out of the skin to eat.

MIXED GREEN SALAD

A good combination of leaves for this salad would be rocket, radicchio, lamb's lettuce and frisée, with herbs such as chervil, basil and parsley.

INGREDIENTS
1 garlic clove, peeled
30ml/2 tbsp red wine vinegar
5ml/1 tsp Dijon mustard (optional)
75–120ml/5–8 tbsp extra virgin olive oil
200–225 g/7–8oz mixed salad leaves and herbs
salt and freshly ground black pepper

SERVES 4–6

1 Rub a large salad bowl with the garlic clove. Leave the garlic clove in the bowl.

2 Add the vinegar, salt and pepper to taste and mustard, if using. Stir to mix the ingredients and dissolve the salt, then gradually whisk in the olive oil.

3 Remove the garlic clove and stir the vinaigrette to combine.

4 Add the salad leaves to the bowl and toss well. Serve the salad immediately before it starts to wilt.

Variation
Try young dandelion leaves when they are in season, but be sure to pick them well away from traffic routes and agricultural crop spraying.

APPLE AND CELERIAC SALAD

Celeriac, despite its coarse appearance, has a sweet and subtle flavour. In this salad it is served raw, allowing its unique taste and texture to emerge.

INGREDIENTS
675g/1½ lb celeriac, peeled
10–15ml/2–3 tsp lemon juice
5ml/1 tsp walnut oil (optional)
1 eating apple
45ml/3 tbsp mayonnaise
10ml/2 tsp Dijon mustard
15ml/1 tbsp chopped fresh parsley
salt and freshly ground black pepper

SERVES 3–4

1 Using a food processor or coarse cheese grater, shred the celeriac. Alternatively, cut it into very thin julienne strips.

2 Place the prepared celeriac in a bowl and sprinkle with the lemon juice and the walnut oil, if using. Stir well to mix.

3 Peel the apple if you like. Cut the apple into quarters and remove the core. Slice the apple quarters thinly crossways and toss together with the celeriac.

4 Mix together the mayonnaise, mustard and parsley and season with salt and pepper to taste. Add the dressing to the celeriac mixture and stir well. Chill for several hours until ready to serve.

Cook's Tip
The knobbly skin of celeriac is too tough for a vegetable peeler. Use a sharp knife.

CHICORY, FRUIT AND NUT SALAD

o o o

The mildly bitter taste of the chicory combines well with the sweetness of the fruit and the creamy curry sauce.

INGREDIENTS

45ml/3 tbsp mayonnaise
15ml/1 tbsp Greek (US strained plain) yogurt
15ml/1 tbsp mild curry paste
90ml/6 tbsp single (light) cream
½ iceberg lettuce
2 chicory (Belgian endive) heads
50g/2oz/½ cup cashew nuts
50g/2oz/1¼ cups flaked coconut
2 red eating apples
75g/3oz/⅓ cup currants

SERVES 4

1 Mix the mayonnaise, yogurt, curry paste and single cream in a small bowl. Cover with clear film (plastic wrap) and chill in the refrigerator until required.

2 Tear the lettuce into pieces and put into a mixing bowl.

3 Cut the root end off each head of chicory, separate the leaves and add them to the lettuce. Preheat the grill (broiler).

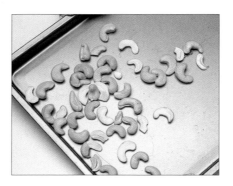

4 Spread out the cashew nuts on a baking sheet and grill (broil) for 2 minutes, until golden. Tip into a bowl and set aside. Spread out the coconut on a baking sheet. Grill for 1 minute, until golden.

5 Quarter the apples and cut out the cores. Thinly slice the apples and add them to the lettuce with the toasted coconut and cashew nuts and the currants.

6 Spoon the dressing over the salad, toss lightly and serve.

Variation

For an even more colourful salad, use 1 head chicory (Belgian endive) and 1 head radicchio, and substitute 1 green eating apple for 1 of the red ones.

Cook's Tip

Watch the coconut flakes and cashew nuts with great care when they are under the grill (broiler), as they brown very fast and can burn easily.

FENNEL, ORANGE AND ROCKET SALAD

° ° °

This light and refreshing salad is an ideal accompaniment to serve with spicy or rich foods.

INGREDIENTS

*2 oranges
1 fennel bulb
115g/4oz rocket (arugula) leaves
50g/2oz/½ cup black olives*

FOR THE DRESSING

*30ml/2 tbsp extra virgin olive oil
15ml/1 tbsp balsamic vinegar
1 small garlic clove, crushed
salt and freshly ground
black pepper*

SERVES 4

1 With a vegetable peeler, cut thin strips of rind from the oranges, making sure that you leave the pith behind. Cut the rind into thin julienne strips. Cook in a small pan of boiling water for a few minutes, then drain.

2 Peel the oranges, removing all the white pith. Slice them into thin rounds and discard any seeds.

3 Cut the fennel bulb in half lengthways with a sharp knife. Slice across the bulb as thinly as possible, using a food processor fitted with a slicing disc. Alternatively, use a mandolin.

4 Combine the oranges and fennel in a serving bowl and toss with the rocket leaves. Mix together the oil, vinegar and garlic and season to taste with salt and pepper. Pour over the salad, toss well and leave to stand for a few minutes. Sprinkle with the olives and strips of orange and serve.

AUBERGINE, LEMON AND CAPER SALAD

° ° °

This cooked vegetable relish is delicious served as an accompaniment to cold meats, with pasta, or simply on its own with some good, crusty bread. Make sure the aubergine is well cooked until it is meltingly soft.

INGREDIENTS

*1 large aubergine (eggplant), about
675g/1½lb
60ml/4 tbsp olive oil
grated rind and juice of 1 lemon
30ml/2 tbsp capers, rinsed
12 pitted green olives
30ml/2 tbsp chopped fresh
flat leaf parsley
salt and freshly ground
black pepper*

SERVES 4

1 Cut the aubergine into 2.5cm/ 1in cubes. Heat the olive oil in a large, heavy frying pan and cook the aubergine cubes over a medium heat for about 10 minutes, tossing regularly, until golden and softened. You may need to do this in two batches. Drain on kitchen paper and sprinkle with a little salt.

2 Place the aubergine cubes in a large serving bowl. Toss with the lemon rind and juice, capers, olives and chopped parsley, and season well with salt and pepper. Serve at room temperature.

Cook's Tip

This will taste even better when made the day before. It will store, covered, in the refrigerator for up to 4 days.

APPLE COLESLAW

There are many variations of this Dutch salad; this recipe combines the sweet flavours of apple and carrot with celery salt. Coleslaw is traditionally served with ham.

INGREDIENTS

450g/1lb white cabbage
1 medium onion
2 eating apples, peeled and cored
175g/6oz carrots, peeled
150ml/¼ pint/⅔ cup mayonnaise
5ml/1 tsp celery salt
freshly ground black pepper

SERVES 4

1 Discard the outside leaves of the white cabbage if they are dirty or damaged. Cut the cabbage into 5cm/2in wedges, then remove the stem sections.

2 Feed the cabbage wedges and the onion through a food processor fitted with a slicing blade. Change to a grating blade and grate the apples and carrots. Alternatively use a vegetable slicer and a hand grater for the apples and carrots.

3 Combine all the salad ingredients in a large serving bowl. Fold in the mayonnaise and season with the celery salt and black pepper.

Variation

For a richer coleslaw, add 115g/4oz/½ cup grated Cheddar cheese. You may find you will need smaller portions, as the cheese makes a more filling dish.

CARROT, RAISIN AND APRICOT COLESLAW

° ° °

This colourful salad combines cabbage, carrots and dried fruit.

INGREDIENTS

350g/12oz white cabbage, finely shredded
225g/8oz carrots, grated
1 red onion, thinly sliced
3 celery sticks, sliced
175g/6oz/generous 1 cup raisins
75g/3oz/³/₄ cup dried apricots, chopped

FOR THE DRESSING

120ml/4fl oz/¹/₂ cup mayonnaise
90ml/6 tbsp natural (plain) yogurt
30ml/2 tbsp chopped fresh herbs
salt and freshly ground black pepper

SERVES 6

1 Put the cabbage and carrots in a large bowl.

2 Add the sliced onion, sliced celery, raisins and chopped apricots and mix well.

3 In a small bowl, mix together the mayonnaise, yogurt and chopped herbs and season to taste with salt and black pepper.

4 Add the mayonnaise dressing to the coleslaw ingredients and toss together to mix. Cover with clear film (plastic wrap) and chill in the refrigerator before serving.

Variation

Substitute other dried fruit, such as sultanas (golden raisins) and ready-to-eat dried pears or peaches.

283

FENNEL COLESLAW

The flavour of fennel plays a major role in this coleslaw.

INGREDIENTS
175g/6oz fennel
2 spring onions (scallions), plus extra to garnish
175g/6oz white cabbage
115g/4oz celery
175g/6oz carrots
50g/2oz/scant ½ cup sultanas (golden raisins)
2.5ml/½ tsp caraway seeds
15ml/1 tbsp chopped fresh parsley
45ml/3 tbsp extra virgin olive oil
5ml/1 tsp lemon juice

SERVES 4

3 Stir in the chopped parsley, olive oil and lemon juice and mix all the ingredients very thoroughly. Cover and chill for 3 hours to allow the flavours to mingle. Shred the spring onion for the garnish and sprinkle it over the coleslaw before serving.

Cook's Tip
Use sour cream instead of olive oil for a creamier dressing.

1 Using a sharp knife, cut the fennel bulb and spring onions into thin slices.

2 Slice the cabbage and celery thinly and cut the carrots into fine strips. Place them in a serving bowl together with the sliced fennel and spring onions. Add the sultanas and caraway seeds and toss lightly to mix.

BEANSPROUT AND MOOLI SALAD
∘ ∘ ∘

Ribbon-thin slices of fresh, crisp vegetables and beansprouts are served with an Asian dressing.

INGREDIENTS
225g/8oz/1 cup beansprouts
1 cucumber
2 carrots
1 small mooli (daikon)
1 small red onion, thinly sliced
2.5cm/1in fresh root ginger, cut into thin matchsticks
1 red chilli, seeded and thinly sliced
1 bunch fresh coriander (cilantro)

FOR THE ASIAN DRESSING
15ml/1 tbsp rice wine vinegar
15ml/1 tbsp light soy sauce
15ml/1 tbsp Thai fish sauce
1 garlic clove, finely chopped
15ml/1 tbsp sesame oil
45ml/3 tbsp groundnut (peanut) oil
30ml/2 tbsp sesame seeds, lightly toasted

SERVES 4

1 First make the dressing. Place all the dressing ingredients in a bottle or screw-top jar and shake well.

Cook's Tip
The dressing may be made in advance and will keep well for a couple of days if stored in the refrigerator or a cool place.

2 Wash the beansprouts and drain thoroughly in a colander. If you like, blanch them in boiling water for 1 minute, drain refresh under cold water and drain again.

3 Peel the cucumber, cut in half lengthways and scoop out the seeds. Peel the cucumber flesh into long ribbon strips using a vegetable peeler or mandolin.

4 Peel the carrots and mooli into long strips in the same way as for the cucumber.

5 Place the carrots, radish and cucumber in a large, shallow serving dish, add the onion, ginger, chilli and coriander and toss to mix. Pour the dressing over the salad just before serving and toss lightly again.

TZATZIKI

Tzatziki is a Greek cucumber salad dressed with yogurt, mint and garlic. It is typically served with grilled lamb and chicken, but is also good with salmon and trout.

INGREDIENTS

*1 cucumber
5ml/1 tsp salt
45ml/3 tbsp finely chopped fresh mint, plus a few sprigs to garnish
1 garlic clove, crushed
5ml/1 tsp caster (superfine) sugar
200ml/7fl oz/scant 1 cup Greek (US strained plain) yogurt
paprika, to garnish (optional)*

SERVES 4

1 Peel the cucumber. Reserve a little to use as a garnish, if you like, and cut the remainder in half, lengthways. Remove the seeds with a teaspoon and discard. Slice the cucumber thinly and combine with the salt. Set aside for about 15–20 minutes. The salt will soften the cucumber and draw out any bitter juices.

2 Place the chopped mint, garlic, sugar and yogurt in a bowl. Stir well to combine.

3 Rinse the cucumber in a sieve under cold running water to wash away the salt. Drain well and combine with the yogurt mixture in a serving bowl. Decorate with sprigs of mint. Garnish with paprika, if you like.

Cook's Tip

If preparing tzatziki in a hurry, do not salt the cucumber. The cucumber will have a more crunchy texture, and will be slightly less sweet.

MARINATED CUCUMBER SALAD

A lovely cooling salad, with the distinctive flavour of fresh dill.

INGREDIENTS

2 medium cucumbers
15ml/1 tbsp salt
90g/3¹/₂oz/¹/₂ cup sugar
175ml/6fl oz/³/₄ cup dry (hard) cider
15ml/1 tbsp cider vinegar
45ml/3 tbsp chopped fresh dill
freshly ground black pepper

SERVES 4–6

1 Slice the cucumbers thinly and place them in a colander, sprinkling salt between each layer. Put the colander over a bowl and leave to drain for 1 hour.

2 Thoroughly rinse the cucumber under cold running water to remove excess salt, then pat dry with kitchen paper.

3 Gently heat the sugar, cider and vinegar in a pan, until the sugar has dissolved. Remove from the heat and leave to cool. Put the cucumber slices in a bowl, pour over the cider mixture and leave to marinate for 2 hours.

4 Drain the cucumber well and discard the marinade. Sprinkle the cucumber with the dill and pepper to taste. Mix well and transfer to a serving dish. Cover with clear film (plastic wrap) and chill in the refrigerator until ready to serve.

Cook's Tip

The salad would be a perfect accompaniment for poached fresh salmon.

FLOWER GARDEN SALAD

° ° °

Dress a colourful mixture of salad leaves with olive oil and lemon juice, then top it with crispy bread crostini.

INGREDIENTS

*3 thick slices day-old bread
120ml/4fl oz/¹/₂ cup extra virgin
olive oil
1 garlic clove, halved
¹/₂ small cos or romaine lettuce
¹/₂ small oak-leaf lettuce
25g/1oz rocket (arugula) leaves
25g/1oz fresh flat leaf parsley
a small handful of young
dandelion leaves
juice of 1 lemon
a few nasturtium leaves
and flowers
pansy and pot marigold flowers
sea salt flakes and freshly ground
black pepper*

SERVES 4–6

3 Tear all the salad leaves into bitesize pieces and pile them into the bowl with the oil. Season to taste with salt and pepper. Cover and keep chilled until you are ready to serve the salad.

4 To serve, toss the leaves in the oil in the base of the bowl, then sprinkle with the lemon juice and toss again. Scatter the crostini and the leaves and flowers over the top and serve immediately.

1 Cut the slices of bread into 1cm/¹/₂in cubes. Heat half the olive oil in a heavy frying pan and fry the bread cubes over a medium-low heat, tossing and turning them until they are well coated and lightly browned. Remove and cool.

2 Rub the inside of a large salad bowl with the cut sides of the garlic clove, then discard the clove. Pour the remaining olive oil into the base of the bowl.

FRESH SPINACH AND AVOCADO SALAD
o o o

Young spinach leaves make a change from lettuce. They are delicious served with avocado, cherry tomatoes and radishes in an unusual tofu sauce.

INGREDIENTS
1 large avocado
juice of 1 lime
225g/8oz baby spinach leaves
115g/4oz cherry tomatoes
4 spring onions (scallions), sliced
1/2 cucumber
50g/2oz radishes, sliced

FOR THE DRESSING
115g/4oz soft silken tofu
45ml/3 tbsp milk
10ml/2 tsp mustard
2.5ml/1/2 tsp white wine vinegar
cayenne pepper
salt and freshly ground
black pepper
radish roses and fresh herb sprigs,
to garnish

SERVES 2–3

1 Cut the avocado in half, remove the stone (pit) and peel. Cut the flesh into slices. Transfer to a plate, and drizzle over the lime juice.

2 Wash and dry the baby spinach leaves. Put them in a mixing bowl.

3 Cut the larger cherry tomatoes in half and add all the tomatoes to the mixing bowl with the spring onions. Cut the cucumber into chunks and add to the bowl with the sliced radishes.

Cook's Tip
Use soft silken tofu rather than the firm block variety. It can be found in most supermarkets in small long-life cartons.

4 To make the dressing, put the tofu, milk, mustard, white wine vinegar and a pinch of cayenne pepper in a blender or food processor. Season with salt and pepper to taste. Process for 30 seconds, until smooth.

5 Scrape the dressing into a bowl and add a little extra milk if you like a thinner dressing. Sprinkle with a little extra cayenne, garnish with radish roses and herb sprigs and serve separately. Place the avocado slices with the spinach salad on a serving dish and serve with the tofu dressing.

Radish, Mango and Apple Salad

Radish is a year-round vegetable and this salad, with its clean, crisp tastes and mellow flavours, can be served at any time of year.

INGREDIENTS
10–15 radishes
1 apple, peeled, cored and thinly sliced
2 celery sticks, thinly sliced
1 small ripe mango
fresh dill sprigs, to garnish

FOR THE DRESSING
120ml/4fl oz/½ cup sour cream
10ml/2 tsp creamed horseradish
15ml/1 tbsp chopped fresh dill
salt and freshly ground black pepper

SERVES 4

1 To prepare the dressing, blend together the sour cream, creamed horseradish and dill in a small bowl and season to taste with a little salt and pepper.

2 Trim the radishes and slice them thinly. Put in a medium serving bowl together with the apple and celery slices.

3 Halve the mango lengthways, cutting either side of the stone (pit). Make even, criss-cross cuts through the flesh of each side section, without cutting through the skin, and bend it back to separate the cubes. Remove the cubes with a small knife and add to the bowl.

4 Pour the dressing over the vegetables and fruit and stir gently so that all the ingredients are well coated. Garnish with dill sprigs and serve immediately.

MANGO, TOMATO AND RED ONION SALAD

*This salad makes a flavoursome
appetizer or accompaniment.*

INGREDIENTS

*1 firm under-ripe mango
½ cucumber
2 large tomatoes, sliced
½ red onion, sliced into rings*

FOR THE DRESSING
*30ml/2 tbsp sunflower oil
15ml/1 tbsp lemon juice
1 garlic clove, crushed
2.5ml/½ tsp hot pepper sauce
salt and freshly ground
black pepper
chopped chives, to garnish*

SERVES 4

1 Halve the mango lengthways,
cutting either side of the stone (pit).
Cut the flesh into slices and peel off
the skin.

2 Peel and slice the cucumber very
thinly with a sharp knife. Arrange
the slices of mango, tomato, red
onion and cucumber decoratively
on a large serving plate.

3 Blend the sunflower oil, lemon
juice, garlic and pepper sauce in a
blender or food processor, or place
in a small screw-top jar and shake
vigorously. Season to taste with salt
and pepper.

4 Pour the dressing over the salad
and serve immediately garnished
with chopped chives.

ORANGE AND WATER CHESTNUT SALAD

° ° °

Crunchy water chestnuts combine with radicchio and oranges in this unusual salad.

INGREDIENTS

1 red onion, thinly sliced into rings
2 oranges, peeled and cut into segments
1 can drained water chestnuts, peeled and cut into strips
2 radicchio heads, cored
45ml/3 tbsp chopped fresh parsley
45ml/3 tbsp chopped fresh basil
15ml/1 tbsp white wine vinegar
50ml/2fl oz/¹⁄₄ cup walnut oil
salt and freshly ground black pepper
1 fresh basil sprig, to garnish

SERVES 4

1 Put the onion in a colander and sprinkle with 5ml/1 tsp salt. Leave to drain for 15 minutes.

2 In a large mixing bowl combine the oranges and water chestnuts.

3 Spread out the radicchio leaves in a large, shallow bowl or on a serving platter to make a bed for the salad.

4 Rinse the onion to remove excess salt and dry on kitchen paper. Add to the mixing bowl and toss it with the water chestnuts and oranges.

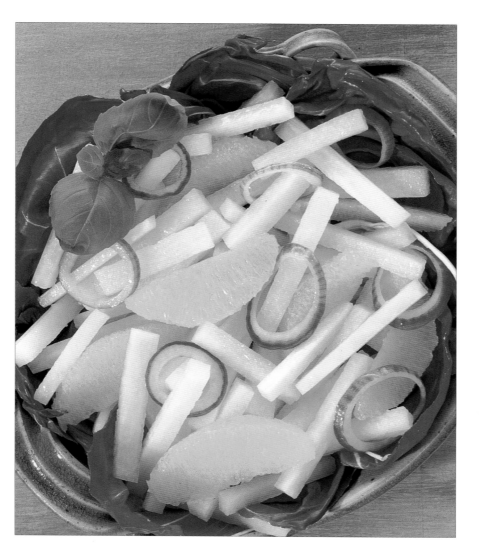

5 Arrange the water chestnut, orange and onion mixture on top of the radicchio leaves. Sprinkle with the chopped parsley and basil.

6 Put the white wine vinegar, walnut oil and salt and pepper to taste in a screw-top jar and shake vigorously to combine. Pour the dressing over the salad and serve immediately, garnished with a sprig of basil.

COLESLAW WITH PESTO MAYONNAISE

Both the pesto and the mayonnaise can be made for this dish, but if time is short, buy them ready-prepared.

INGREDIENTS
1 small white cabbage
3–4 carrots, grated
4 spring onions (scallions), sliced
25–40 g/1–1½oz/¼–⅓ cup pine nuts
15ml/1 tbsp chopped fresh mixed herbs such as parsley, basil, chervil

FOR THE PESTO MAYONNAISE
1 egg yolk
about 10ml/2 tsp lemon juice
200ml/7fl oz/scant 1 cup sunflower oil
10ml/2 tsp pesto
60ml/4 tbsp natural (plain) yogurt
salt and freshly ground black pepper

SERVES 4–6

1 To make the mayonnaise, place the egg yolk in a blender or food processor and process with the lemon juice. With the machine running, gradually add the oil. As the mayonnaise emulsifies, add it more quickly in a steady stream.

2 Season to taste with salt and pepper and a little more lemon juice if necessary. Alternatively, make the mayonnaise by hand using a balloon whisk and adding the oil drop by drop.

3 Spoon 75ml/5 tbsp of the mayonnaise into a bowl and stir in the pesto and yogurt, beating well until thoroughly combined into a fairly thin dressing.

4 Remove the outer leaves of the cabbage and discard. Using a food processor or a sharp knife, thinly slice the cabbage and place in a large salad bowl.

5 Add the carrots and spring onions, together with the pine nuts and herbs, mixing thoroughly with your hands. Stir the pesto dressing into the salad or serve separately in a small dish.

Variation
You can also make the dressing with sun-dried tomato pesto.

293

PEPPER AND CUCUMBER SALAD

○ ○ ○

INGREDIENTS

1 yellow or red (bell) pepper
1 large cucumber
4–5 tomatoes
1 bunch spring
onions (scallions)
30ml/2 tbsp fresh parsley
30ml/2 tbsp fresh mint
30ml/2 tbsp fresh
coriander (cilantro)
2 pitta breads, to serve

FOR THE DRESSING
2 garlic cloves, crushed
75ml/5 tbsp olive oil
juice of 2 lemons
salt and freshly ground
black pepper

SERVES 4

1 Slice the pepper and discard the seeds and core. Coarsely chop the cucumber and tomatoes. Place in a large salad bowl.

2 Trim and slice the spring onions. Add to the cucumber, tomatoes and pepper. Finely chop the parsley, mint and coriander and add to the bowl. If you have plenty of herbs, you can add as much as you like.

3 To make the dressing, blend the garlic with the olive oil and lemon juice in a jug (pitcher), then season to taste with salt and pepper. Pour the dressing over the salad and toss lightly to mix.

4 Toast the pitta breads in a toaster or under a hot grill (broiler) until crisp and serve them with the pepper and cucumber salad.

Variation
If you like, make this eastern salad in the traditional way. After toasting the pitta breads, crush them in your hand and then sprinkle over the salad before serving.

294

GUACAMOLE SALSA IN RED LEAVES

This is a lovely, light, summery and attractive appetizer.

INGREDIENTS

2 tomatoes
15ml/1 tbsp grated onion
1 garlic clove, crushed
1 fresh green chilli, halved, seeded
and chopped
2 ripe avocados
30ml/2 tbsp olive oil
2.5ml/$\frac{1}{2}$ tsp ground cumin
30ml/2 tbsp chopped fresh
coriander (cilantro) or parsley
juice of 1 lime
radicchio leaves
salt and freshly ground
black pepper
fresh coriander (cilantro) sprigs,
to garnish
crusty garlic bread and lime
wedges, to serve

SERVES 4

2 Put the tomato flesh into a bowl together with the onion, garlic and chilli. Halve the avocados, remove the stones (pits), then scoop the flesh into the bowl, mashing it coarsely with a fork.

3 Add the oil, cumin, coriander or parsley and lime juice. Mix well and season to taste.

4 Lay the radicchio leaves on a platter and spoon in the salsa. Serve garnished with coriander sprigs and accompanied by garlic bread and lime wedges.

1 Using a sharp knife, slash a small cross on the top of the tomatoes, then place them in a bowl of boiling water for 30 seconds. The skins will slip off easily. Remove the core of each tomato and roughly chop the flesh.

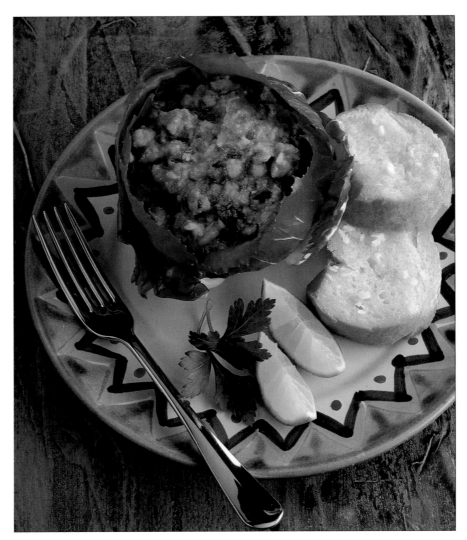

THAI FRUIT AND VEGETABLE SALAD

○ ○ ○

A cooling, refreshing salad served with a coconut dipping sauce that has a slight kick.

INGREDIENTS
1 small pineapple
1 small mango, peeled and sliced
1 green apple, cored and sliced
6 lychees, peeled and stoned (pitted)
115g/4oz green beans, trimmed and halved
1 medium red onion, sliced
1 small cucumber, cut into short fingers
115g/4oz/½ cup beansprouts
2 spring onions (scallions), sliced
1 ripe tomato, quartered
225g/8oz cos, romaine or iceberg lettuce leaves

FOR THE COCONUT DIPPING SAUCE
30ml/2 tbsp coconut cream
30ml/2 tbsp sugar
75ml/5 tbsp/⅓ cup boiling water
1.5ml/¼ tsp chilli sauce
15ml/1 tbsp Thai fish sauce
juice of 1 lime

SERVES 4–6

1 To make the coconut dipping sauce, put the coconut cream, sugar and boiling water in a screw-top jar. Add the chilli and fish sauces and lime juice and shake.

2 Trim both ends of the pineapple with a serrated knife, then cut away the outer skin. Remove the

central core with an apple corer. Alternatively, cut the pineapple into quarters down the middle and remove the core with a knife. Roughly chop the pineapple and set aside with the other fruits.

3 Bring a small pan of salted water to the boil and cook the beans for 3–4 minutes. Refresh under cold running water and set aside. To serve, arrange the fruits and vegetables in small heaps in a wide, shallow bowl. Serve the coconut sauce separately as a dip.

SWEET CUCUMBER COOLER

○ ○ ○

Sweet dipping sauces such as this bring instant relief to the hot chilli flavours of Thai food.

INGREDIENTS
5 tbsp water
2 tbsp sugar
½ tsp salt
1 tbsp rice or white wine vinegar
¼ small cucumber
2 shallots, or 1 small red onion

MAKES 120ML/4FL OZ/½ CUP

1 With a small sharp knife, thinly slice the cucumber and cut into quarters. Thinly slice the shallots or red onion.

2 Measure the water, sugar, salt and vinegar into a stainless steel or enamel pan, bring to the boil and simmer, stirring constantly, until the sugar has dissolved, for less than 1 minute.

3 Remove the pan from the heat and set aside to cool. Add the cucumber and shallots or onion and serve at room temperature.

TRICOLOUR SALAD

This can be a simple appetizer if served on individual salad plates, or part of a light buffet meal laid out on a platter.

INGREDIENTS

1 small red onion, thinly sliced
6 large full-flavoured tomatoes
extra virgin olive oil, to sprinkle
50g/2oz rocket (arugula) or
watercress leaves,
coarsely chopped
175g/6oz mozzarella cheese, thinly
sliced or grated
30ml/2 tbsp pine nuts (optional)
salt and freshly ground
black pepper

SERVES 4–6

1 Soak the onion slices in a bowl of cold water for 30 minutes, then drain well and pat thoroughly dry with kitchen paper.

2 Peel the tomatoes by cutting a cross in the skin and plunging into boiling water for 30 seconds: the skins can then be easily slipped off.

3 Slice the tomatoes and arrange half on a large platter, or divide them among small plates.

4 Sprinkle liberally with olive oil, then layer with the chopped rocket or watercress, onion slices and cheese, sprinkling over more olive oil and seasoning well with salt and pepper between the layers.

5 Season well with more salt and pepper to finish and complete with a drizzle of oil and a good sprinkling of pine nuts, if you like. Cover the salad with clear film (plastic wrap) and chill in the refrigerator for at least 2 hours before serving.

TUSCAN TUNA AND BEAN SALAD

° ° °

A great pantry dish which can be put together in very little time. Served with fresh bread, it is a meal in itself.

INGREDIENTS

1 red onion
30ml/2 tbsp French mustard
300ml/½ pint/1¼ cups olive oil
60ml/4 tbsp white wine vinegar
30ml/2 tbsp chopped fresh parsley
30ml/2 tbsp chopped fresh chives
30ml/2 tbsp chopped fresh
tarragon or chervil
400g/14oz can haricot (navy) beans
400g/14oz can kidney beans
225g/8oz canned tuna in oil,
drained and lightly flaked
fresh chives and tarragon sprigs,
to garnish

SERVES 4

1 Chop the red onion finely, using a sharp knife.

2 To make the dressing, whisk together the mustard, olive oil, wine vinegar, parsley, chives and tarragon or chervil.

3 Drain the canned haricot and kidney beans through a colander, then rinse well under cold running water and drain again.

4 Mix the chopped onion, beans and dressing together thoroughly, then carefully fold in the flaked tuna. Garnish with chives and tarragon and serve immediately.

ROCKET, PEAR AND PARMESAN SALAD

∘ ∘ ∘

For a sophisticated start to an elaborate meal, try this simple, but delicious salad.

INGREDIENTS

3 ripe pears
10ml/2 tsp lemon juice
45ml/3 tbsp hazelnut or walnut oil
115g/4oz rocket (arugula) leaves
75g/3oz piece Parmesan cheese
freshly ground black pepper

SERVES 4

2 Combine the hazelnut or walnut oil with the pears in a large bowl. Add the rocket leaves and toss lightly to mix.

3 Turn the salad out on to four individual plates and top with shavings of Parmesan cheese. Season to taste with black pepper and serve immediately.

1 Peel and core the pears and slice thickly. Brush all over with lemon juice to keep the flesh white.

Cook's Tip

Parmesan cheese is a delicious main ingredient in a salad. Buy a chunk of fresh Parmesan and shave strips off the side, using a vegetable peeler. The distinctive flavour is quite strong. Store the rest of the Parmesan uncovered in the refrigerator.

TOMATO AND FETA CHEESE SALAD
∘ ∘ ∘

Sweet, sun-ripened tomatoes are rarely more delicious than when served with feta cheese.

INGREDIENTS

900g/2lb tomatoes
200g/7oz feta cheese
120ml/4fl oz/½ cup olive oil
12 black olives
4 fresh basil sprigs
freshly ground black pepper

SERVES 4

2 Slice the tomatoes thickly and arrange them attractively in a shallow serving dish.

3 Crumble the feta over the tomatoes, sprinkle with oil, then strew with the olives and basil sprigs. Season to taste with pepper and serve at room temperature.

1 Carefully remove the tough cores from the tomatoes, using a small, sharp knife.

Cook's Tip

Feta cheese has a strong flavour and can be salty. The least salty variety is imported from Greece and Turkey, and is available from specialist delicatessens.

Using cooked ingredients, such as roasted peppers, grilled cheese, hard-boiled eggs or crispy bacon vastly increases your repertoire of side salads. This chapter is packed with delicious accompaniments to serve at dinner parties, barbecues, picnics and family suppers.

COOKED SIDE SALADS

SIMPLE COOKED SALAD

○ ○ ○

This is a version of a popular Mediterranean recipe.

INGREDIENTS

2 tomatoes, quartered
2 onions, chopped
½ cucumber, halved lengthways,
seeded and sliced
1 green (bell) pepper, halved,
seeded and chopped

FOR THE DRESSING
30ml/2 tbsp lemon juice
45ml/3 tbsp olive oil
2 garlic cloves, crushed
30ml/2 tbsp chopped fresh
coriander (cilantro)
salt and freshly ground
black pepper

SERVES 4

1 Put the tomato quarters, onions, cucumber and green pepper into a large pan, add 60ml/4 tbsp water and bring to the boil. Lower the heat and simmer for 5 minutes. Remove the pan from the heat and leave to cool.

2 For the dressing, mix together the lemon juice, olive oil and garlic.

3 Strain the cooled vegetables, then transfer them to a serving bowl. Pour over the dressing, season to taste with salt and pepper and stir in the chopped coriander. Serve the salad immediately, garnished with coriander sprigs.

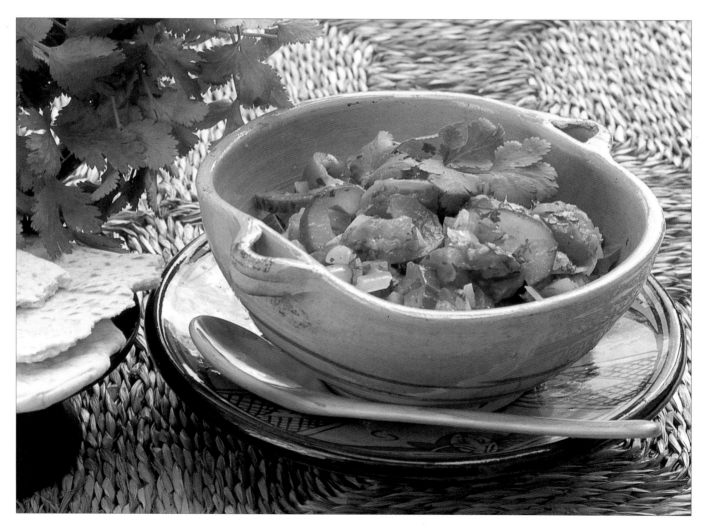

SWEET-AND-SOUR ARTICHOKE SALAD

° ° °

A sweet-and-sour sauce is poured over lightly cooked summer vegetables.

INGREDIENTS
6 small globe artichokes
juice of 1 lemon
30ml/2 tbsp olive oil
2 medium onions, chopped
175g/6oz/1½ cups fresh or frozen broad (fava) beans (shelled weight)
175g/6oz/1½ cups fresh or frozen peas (shelled weight)
salt and freshly ground black pepper
fresh mint leaves, to garnish

FOR THE SWEET-AND-SOUR SAUCE
120ml/4fl oz/½ cup white wine vinegar
15ml/1 tbsp sugar
a handful of fresh mint leaves, roughly torn

SERVES 4

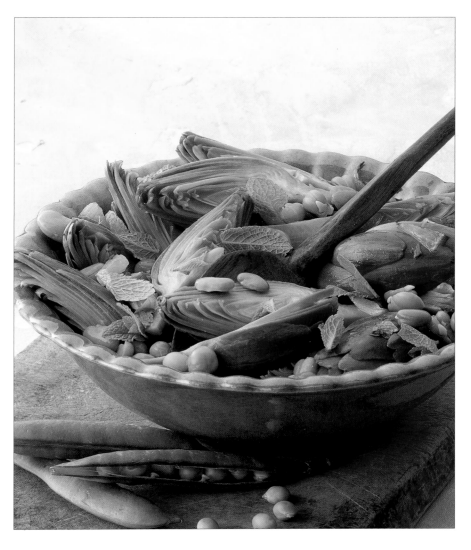

1 Cut off the outer leaves of the artichokes. Cut the artichokes into quarters and place them in a bowl of water with the lemon juice.

2 Heat the olive oil in a large, heavy pan and add the onions. Cook, stirring occasionally, for 10 minutes until the onions are golden. Add the beans and stir, then drain the artichokes and add to the pan. Pour in 300ml/½ pint/1¼ cups water and cook, covered, for a further 10–15 minutes.

3 Add the peas, season to taste with salt and pepper and cook, stirring occasionally, for a further 5 minutes, until the vegetables are tender. Strain through a sieve or colander and place all the vegetables in a bowl. Leave to cool, then cover with clear film (plastic wrap) and chill.

4 To make the sweet-and-sour sauce, mix all the ingredients in a small pan. Heat gently for about 2–3 minutes, until the sugar has dissolved. Simmer gently for about 5 minutes, stirring occasionally. Leave to cool. To serve, drizzle the sauce over the vegetables and garnish with mint leaves.

PEPPERS WITH TOMATOES AND ANCHOVIES

This is a Sicilian-style salad full of warm Mediterranean flavours. The salad improves if it is made and dressed an hour or two before serving.

INGREDIENTS

1 red (bell) pepper
1 yellow (bell) pepper
4 ripe plum tomatoes, sliced
2 canned anchovies, drained
and chopped
4 sun-dried tomatoes in oil,
drained and sliced
15ml/1 tbsp capers, drained
15ml/1 tbsp pine nuts
1 garlic clove, very finely sliced

FOR THE DRESSING
75ml/5 tbsp extra virgin olive oil
15ml/1 tbsp balsamic vinegar
5ml/1 tsp lemon juice
chopped fresh mixed herbs
salt and freshly ground
black pepper

SERVES 4

1 Preheat the grill (broiler). Cut the peppers in half and remove the seeds and stalks. Cut into quarters and grill (broil), skin-side up, until the skin chars. Transfer to a bowl, cover with kitchen paper and leave to cool. Peel the peppers and cut into strips.

2 Arrange the peppers and fresh tomatoes on a serving dish. Sprinkle over the anchovies, sun-dried tomatoes, capers, pine nuts and garlic.

3 To make the dressing, mix together the olive oil, vinegar, lemon juice and chopped fresh herbs and season with plenty of salt and pepper. Pour the dressing over the salad before serving.

SWEET AND SOUR ONION SALAD

This recipe for tangy, glazed onions in the Provençal style makes an unusual and flavourful accompaniment to steaks cooked on the barbecue.

INGREDIENTS

450g/1lb baby (pearl) onions
50ml/2fl oz/¼ cup wine vinegar
45ml/3 tbsp olive oil
45ml/3 tbsp caster (superfine) sugar
45ml/3 tbsp tomato purée (paste)
1 bay leaf
2 fresh parsley sprigs
65g/2½ oz/½ cup raisins
salt and freshly ground
black pepper

SERVES 6

1 Put all the ingredients in a pan with 300ml/½ pint/1¼ cups water. Bring to the boil and simmer gently, uncovered, for 45 minutes, or until the onions are tender and the liquid has evaporated.

2 Remove the bay leaf and parsley, from the pan and check the seasoning. Transfer the contents of the pan to a large serving dish. Serve the salad at room temperature.

SPICED AUBERGINE SALAD

∘ ∘ ∘

Serve this Middle-Eastern influenced salad with warm pitta bread as an appetizer, or as an accompaniment to any number of main course dishes.

INGREDIENTS

*2 small aubergines
(eggplant), sliced
75ml/5 tbsp olive oil
50ml/2fl oz/¼ cup red
wine vinegar
2 garlic cloves, crushed
15ml/1 tbsp lemon juice
2.5ml/½ tsp ground cumin
2.5ml/½ tsp ground coriander
½ cucumber, thinly sliced
2 tomatoes, thinly sliced
30ml/2 tbsp natural (plain) yogurt
salt and freshly ground
black pepper
chopped flat leaf parsley, to garnish*

SERVES 4

1 Preheat the grill (broiler). Brush the aubergine slices lightly with some of the olive oil and grill (broil) or cook over a hot barbecue until golden and tender, turning once to cook evenly. Allow the slices to cool slightly, then cut them into quarters.

2 Mix the remaining olive oil with the vinegar, crushed garlic, lemon juice, cumin and ground coriander. Season with plenty of salt and pepper and mix thoroughly. Add the warm aubergines, stir well and chill for at least 2 hours. Add the cucumber and tomatoes. Transfer the salad to a serving dish and spoon the yogurt on top. Garnish with chopped parsley to serve.

BABY AUBERGINES WITH RAISINS AND PINE NUTS

This is a recipe with an Italian influence, in a style that would have been familiar in Renaissance times. If possible, make it a day in advance, to allow the sweet and sour flavours to develop.

INGREDIENTS

*12 baby aubergines
(eggplant), halved
250ml/8fl oz/1 cup olive oil
juice of 1 lemon
30ml/2 tbsp balsamic vinegar
3 cloves
25g/1oz/1/3 cup pine nuts
25g/1oz/2 tbsp raisins
15ml/1 tbsp sugar
1 bay leaf
large pinch of dried chilli flakes
salt and freshly ground
black pepper*

SERVES 4

1 Preheat the grill (broiler). Brush the aubergines with olive oil and grill (broil), turning once, for 10 minutes.

2 To make the dressing, combine the remaining olive oil with the lemon juice, vinegar, cloves, pine nuts, raisins, sugar and bay leaf. Add the chilli flakes and salt and pepper and mix well.

3 Place the hot aubergines in an earthenware or glass bowl, and pour over the dressing. Leave to cool, turning the aubergines once or twice. Serve the salad cold.

ROASTED PEPPER AND TOMATO SALAD

° ° °

A lovely, colourful recipe that perfectly combines several red ingredients. Eat this dish at room temperature.

INGREDIENTS

3 red (bell) peppers
6 large plum tomatoes
2.5ml/¹/₂ tsp dried red chilli flakes
1 red onion, thinly sliced
3 garlic cloves, finely chopped
grated rind and juice of 1 lemon
45ml/3 tbsp chopped fresh
flat leaf parsley
30ml/2 tbsp extra virgin olive oil
salt and freshly ground
black pepper
black and green olives and extra
chopped flat leaf parsley, to garnish

SERVES 4

1 Preheat the oven to 220°C/ 425°F/Gas 7. Place the peppers on a baking sheet and roast, turning occasionally, for 10 minutes or until the skins are charred and almost blackened. Add the plum tomatoes to the baking sheet and bake for 5 minutes more.

2 Place the peppers in a strong plastic bag, close the top loosely, trapping in the steam. Set aside, with the tomatoes, until cool enough to handle.

3 Carefully pull the skin off the peppers. Remove the core and seeds, then chop the peppers and tomatoes coarsely and place in a mixing bowl.

4 Add the chilli flakes, onion, garlic, lemon rind and juice. Sprinkle over the parsley. Mix well, then transfer to a serving dish. Season with salt and pepper, drizzle over the olive oil and sprinkle the olives and extra parsley over the top. Serve at room temperature.

MARINATED COURGETTES

° ° °

This is a simple vegetable dish that uses the best of the season's courgettes. It can be eaten either hot or cold.

INGREDIENTS

4 courgettes (zucchini)
60ml/4 tbsp extra virgin olive oil
30ml/2 tbsp chopped fresh mint
30ml/2 tbsp white wine vinegar
salt and freshly ground
black pepper
fresh mint leaves, to garnish
wholemeal (whole-wheat) Italian
bread and green olives, to serve

SERVES 4

1 Cut the courgettes into thin slices. Heat 30ml/2 tbsp of the olive oil in a wide, heavy pan. Add the courgette slices in batches, and cook, stirring and turning occasionally, for 4–6 minutes, until tender and brown around the edges. Transfer the courgettes to a bowl. Season to taste with salt and black pepper.

2 Heat the remaining oil in the pan, then add the chopped mint and vinegar and let it bubble for a few seconds.

3 Pour the mint dressing over the courgettes. Cover and marinate for 1 hour, then serve garnished with mint leaves and accompanied by bread and olives.

GREEN BEAN AND SWEET RED PEPPER SALAD

o o o

INGREDIENTS

*350g/12oz cooked green
beans, quartered
2 red (bell) peppers, seeded
and chopped
2 spring onions (scallions), both
white and green parts chopped
1 or more drained pickled serrano
chillies, well rinsed, seeded
and chopped
1 iceberg lettuce, shredded, or
mixed salad leaves
green olives, to garnish*

FOR THE DRESSING
*45ml/3 tbsp red wine vinegar
135ml/9 tbsp olive oil
salt and freshly ground
black pepper*

SERVES 4

1 Place the cooked green beans,
peppers, spring onions and pickled
chilli(es) in a salad bowl and toss
lightly to mix.

2 To make the dressing, pour
the vinegar into a bowl or jug
(pitcher). Add salt and pepper to
taste, then gradually whisk in the
olive oil until well combined.

3 Pour the dressing over the
prepared vegetables and toss lightly
together to mix well and coat them
all thoroughly.

4 Line a large serving platter with the
shredded lettuce or mixed salad
leaves and arrange the vegetable
mixture attractively on top. Garnish
with the olives and serve.

GREEN GREEN SALAD

Even with frozen vegetables you would still get a pretty salad.

INGREDIENTS

175g/6oz shelled broad (fava) beans
115g/4oz green beans, quartered
115 g/4oz mangetouts (snow peas)
8–10 small fresh mint leaves
3 spring onions (scallions), chopped

FOR THE DRESSING
60ml/4 tbsp green olive oil
15ml/1 tbsp cider vinegar
15ml/1 tbsp chopped fresh mint
1 garlic clove, crushed
salt and freshly ground
black pepper

SERVES 4

1 Plunge the broad beans into a pan of boiling water and bring back to the boil. Remove from the heat immediately and plunge into cold water. Drain. Repeat with the green beans.

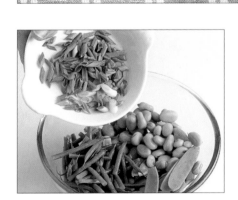

2 In a large bowl, combine the blanched broad beans and green beans with the raw mangetouts, mint leaves and spring onions.

3 In another bowl, mix together the olive oil, cider vinegar, chopped or dried mint, garlic and seasoning. Pour over the salad and toss well. Cover with clear film (plastic wrap) and chill until ready to serve.

Cook's Tip

Frozen broad (fava) beans are a good stand-by, but for this salad it is worth shelling fresh beans for the extra flavour.

LEEK AND EGG SALAD

° ° °

Smooth-textured leeks are especially delicious warm when partnered with an earthy sauce of parsley, olive oil and walnuts.

INGREDIENTS
675g/1½ lb young leeks
1 egg
fresh parsley sprigs, to garnish

FOR THE DRESSING
25g/1oz/1 cup fresh parsley
30ml/2 tbsp olive oil
juice of ½ lemon
50g/2oz/½ cup broken walnuts, toasted
5ml/1 tsp caster (superfine) sugar
salt and freshly ground black pepper

SERVES 4

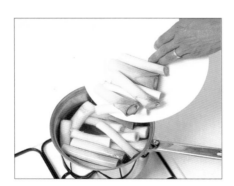

1 Bring a pan of salted water to the boil. Cut the leeks into 10cm/4in lengths and rinse well to flush out any grit or soil. Cook the leeks for 8 minutes. Drain and partially cool under cold running water.

2 Lower the egg into boiling water and cook for 12 minutes. Cool under cold running water, shell and set aside.

3 Meanwhile, to make the salad dressing, finely chop the parsley in a food processor. Alternatively, use a sharp knife or mezzaluna.

4 If you have chopped the parsley by hand, transfer it to a food processor. Add the olive oil, lemon juice and toasted walnuts to the food processor. Process for about 1–2 minutes, until smooth.

5 Adjust the consistency with about 90ml/6 tbsp water. Add the sugar and season to taste with salt and pepper.

6 Place the leeks on an attractive plate, then spoon on the sauce. Finely grate the hard-boiled egg and sprinkle it over the sauce. Garnish with the reserved parsley sprigs and serve immediately.

Cook's Tip
While raw and lightly cooked eggs increase the risk of salmonella and may be inadvisable for vulnerable people, such as the young, the elderly, pregnant women and invalids, to eat, hard-boiled eggs are quite safe.

WINTER VEGETABLE SALAD

· · ◦ ·

Mixed vegetables are flavoured with white wine and herbs.

INGREDIENTS

175ml/6fl oz/¾ cup white wine
5ml/1 tsp olive oil
30ml/2 tbsp lemon juice
2 bay leaves
1 fresh thyme sprig
4 juniper berries
450g/1 lb leeks, trimmed and cut into 2.5cm/1in lengths
1 small cauliflower, broken into florets
4 celery sticks, sliced diagonally
30ml/2 tbsp chopped fresh parsley
salt and freshly ground black pepper

SERVES 4

1 Put the white wine, olive oil, lemon juice, bay leaves, thyme and juniper berries into a large, heavy pan and bring to the boil. Lower the heat, cover and simmer for 20 minutes.

2 Add the leeks, cauliflower and celery. Simmer very gently for 5–6 minutes, or until just tender.

3 Remove the vegetables with a slotted spoon and transfer them to a serving dish. Briskly boil the cooking liquid for 15–20 minutes, or until reduced by half. Strain through a sieve.

4 Stir the parsley into the liquid and season to taste with salt and pepper. Pour over the vegetables and leave to cool. Chill in the refrigerator for at least 1 hour before serving.

> *Cook's Tip*
> Vary the vegetables for this salad according to the season.

AVOCADO AND SMOKED FISH SALAD

Avocado and smoked fish make a good combination.

INGREDIENTS
2 avocados
½ cucumber
15ml/1 tbsp lemon juice
2 firm tomatoes
1 fresh green chilli
salt and freshly ground
black pepper

FOR THE FISH
15g/½oz/1 tbsp butter
½ onion, thinly sliced
5ml/1 tsp mustard seeds
225g/8oz smoked mackerel, flaked
30ml/2 tbsp fresh chopped
coriander (cilantro) leaves
2 firm tomatoes, peeled
and chopped
15ml/1 tbsp lemon juice

SERVES 4

1 For the fish, melt the butter in a frying pan, add the onion and mustard seeds and cook for about 5 minutes, until the onion is soft.

2 Add the mackerel, chopped coriander, tomatoes and lemon juice and cook over a low heat for 2–3 minutes. Remove from the heat and leave to cool.

3 To make the salad, cut the avocados in half and remove the stones (pits). Peel and slice the flesh thinly. Peel the cucumber thinly. Place together in a bowl and sprinkle with the lemon juice.Slice the tomatoes and seed them. Finely chop the chilli.

4 Place the fish mixture in the centre of a serving plate.

5 Arrange the avocados, cucumber and tomatoes decoratively around the outside. Alternatively, spoon a quarter of the fish mixture on to each of four serving plates and divide the avocados, cucumber and tomatoes equally among them. Sprinkle with the chopped chilli, season to taste with a little salt and pepper and serve.

> ### Variation
> Smoked haddock or cod can also be used in this salad, or a mixture of smoked mackerel and haddock.

325

TOMATO AND BREAD SALAD

∘ ∘ ∘

This salad, which conveniently uses up stale bread, is best made with sun-ripened tomatoes.

INGREDIENTS
400g/14oz stale white bread
4 large tomatoes
1 large red onion or
6 spring onions (scallions)
a few fresh basil leaves, to garnish

FOR THE DRESSING
60ml/4 tbsp extra virgin olive oil
30ml/2 tbsp white wine vinegar
salt and freshly ground `
black pepper

SERVES 4

1 Thickly slice the bread. Place in a shallow bowl, cover with cold water and set aside for 30 minutes.

2 Cut the tomatoes into chunks and place in a serving bowl. Thinly slice the onion or spring onions and add them to the tomatoes. Squeeze as much water out of the bread as possible and add it to the bowl of vegetables.

3 To make the dressing, mix the oil and vinegar. Season to taste with salt and pepper, pour over the salad and mix well. Garnish with the basil leaves. Leave to stand in a cool place for at least 2 hours before serving.

GRILLED PEPPER SALAD

∘ ∘ ∘

Ideally, this salad should be made with a combination of red and yellow peppers for the most jewel-like, colourful effect and the sweetest flavour.

INGREDIENTS
4 large (bell) peppers, red or yellow or a combination of both
30ml/2 tbsp capers, rinsed
18–20 black or green olives

FOR THE DRESSING
90ml/6 tbsp extra virgin olive oil
2 garlic cloves, finely chopped
30ml/2 tbsp balsamic or red wine vinegar
salt and freshly ground black pepper

SERVES 6

1 Place the peppers under a hot grill and turn occasionally until they are black and blistered on all sides. Remove from the heat, place in a strong plastic bag and close the top loosely. Set aside until they are cool enough to handle. Carefully peel the peppers, then cut them into quarters. Remove and discard the stems and seeds.

2 Cut the peppers into strips, and arrange them on a serving dish. Distribute the capers and olives evenly over the peppers.

3 For the dressing, mix the oil and garlic in a small bowl, crushing the garlic with a spoon to release the flavour. Mix in the vinegar and season to taste with salt and pepper. Pour over the salad, mix well and leave to stand for at least 30 minutes before serving.

FRISÉE LETTUCE SALAD WITH BACON

° ° °

INGREDIENTS

50g/2oz white bread
225g/8oz frisée lettuce or
escarole leaves
75–90ml/5–6 tbsp extra virgin
olive oil
175g/6oz piece smoked bacon,
diced, or
6 thick-cut smoked bacon rashers
(strips), cut crossways into
thin strips
1 small garlic clove, finely chopped
15ml/1 tbsp red wine vinegar
10ml/2 tsp Dijon mustard
salt and freshly ground
black pepper

SERVES 4

1 Remove and discard the crusts, then cut the bread into small cubes. Tear the frisée lettuce or escarole into bitesize pieces and put into a salad bowl.

2 Heat 15ml/1 tbsp of the oil in a medium, non-stick frying pan over a medium-low heat and add the bacon. Fry gently until well browned, stirring occasionally. Remove the bacon with a slotted spoon and drain on kitchen paper.

3 Add another 30ml/2 tbsp of the oil to the pan and fry the bread cubes over a medium-high heat, turning frequently, until evenly browned. Remove the bread cubes with a slotted spoon and drain well on kitchen paper. Discard any remaining fat.

4 Stir the garlic, vinegar and mustard into the pan with the remaining oil and heat until just warm, whisking to combine. Season to taste with salt and pepper, then pour the dressing over the salad and sprinkle with the fried bacon and croûtons. Serve immediately while still warm.

ASPARAGUS AND ORANGE SALAD

· · ·

A slightly unusual combination of ingredients with a simple olive oil dressing.

INGREDIENTS

225g/8oz asparagus, trimmed and cut into 5cm/2in lengths
2 large oranges
2 well-flavoured tomatoes, cut into eighths
50g/2oz cos or romaine lettuce leaves
30ml/2 tbsp extra virgin olive oil
2.5ml/¹/₂ tsp sherry vinegar
salt and freshly ground black pepper

SERVES 4

1 Cook the asparagus in lightly salted boiling water for about 3–4 minutes, until just tender. Drain and refresh under cold water, then leave on one side to cool.

2 Grate the rind from half an orange and reserve. Working over a bowl to catch the juice, peel both the oranges and cut them into segments by slicing between the membranes with a small, sharp knife. Squeeze the juice from the membrane and reserve.

3 Put the asparagus, orange segments, tomatoes and lettuce into a salad bowl.

4 Mix together the olive oil and sherry vinegar, and add 15ml/ 1 tbsp of the reserved orange juice.

5 Add 5ml/1 tsp of the grated rind. Season to taste with salt and pepper. Just before serving, pour the dressing over the salad and mix gently to coat all the ingredients.

Cook's Tip

The cooking time for the asparagus will vary depending on the thickness of the stems. Thick stems can take as long as 10 minutes.

329

HARD-BOILED EGGS WITH TUNA SAUCE

A tasty tuna mayonnaise poured over hard-boiled eggs makes a nourishing first course that is quick to prepare.

INGREDIENTS
6 extra large eggs
200g/7oz can tuna in olive oil
3 canned anchovy fillets
15ml/1 tbsp capers, drained
30ml/2 tbsp lemon juice
60ml/4 tbsp olive oil
salt and freshly ground
black pepper
capers and anchovy fillets,
to garnish

FOR THE MAYONNAISE
1 egg yolk
5ml/1 tsp Dijon mustard
5ml/1 tsp white wine vinegar or
lemon juice
150ml/¹/₄ pint/²/₃ cup olive oil

SERVES 6

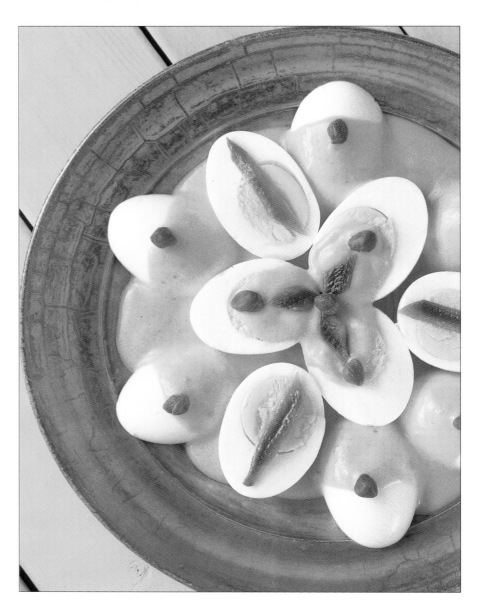

1 Boil the eggs for 12–14 minutes. Cool them under cold water. Shell the eggs carefully and set aside.

2 Make the mayonnaise by whisking the egg yolk, mustard and vinegar or lemon juice together.

3 Whisk in the olive oil, a few drops at a time to begin with, until 3–4 tablespoons have been fully incorporated. Then pour in the remaining oil in a slow, steady stream, whisking constantly.

4 Place the tuna with the oil from the can, the anchovies, capers, lemon juice and olive oil in a blender or food processor. Process until the mixture is smooth.

5 Fold the tuna mixture carefully into the mayonnaise. Season to taste with black pepper, and salt if necessary. Cover with clear film (plastic wrap) and chill in the refrigerator for at least 1 hour.

6 Cut the hard-boiled eggs in half lengthways. Arrange on a serving platter. Spoon on the mayonnaise and garnish with capers and anchovy fillets. Serve chilled.

ARTICHOKE AND EGG SALAD

* ° °

Artichoke hearts are best when cut from fresh artichokes, but can also be bought frozen.

INGREDIENTS
4 large artichokes or 4 frozen artichoke hearts, thawed
½ lemon
4 eggs, hard-boiled
fresh parsley sprigs, to garnish

FOR THE MAYONNAISE
1 egg yolk
10ml/2 tsp Dijon mustard
15ml/1 tbsp white wine vinegar
250ml/8fl oz/1 cup olive oil
30ml/2 tbsp chopped fresh parsley
salt and freshly ground
black pepper

SERVES 4

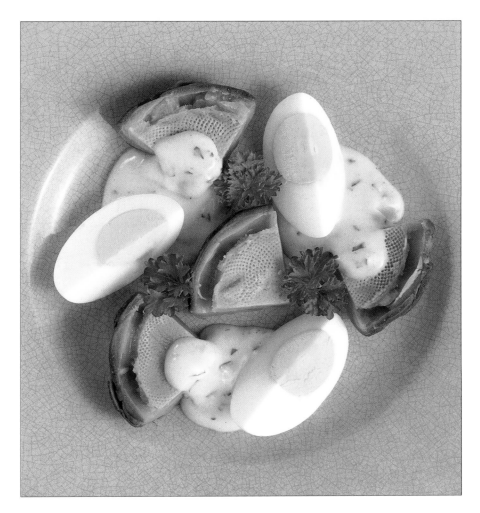

1 If using fresh artichokes, wash them. Squeeze the lemon and put the juice and the squeezed half in a bowl of cold water.

2 Prepare the artichokes one at a time. Cut off only the tip from the stem. Peel the stem with a small knife, pulling upwards towards the leaves. Pull off the small leaves around the stem and continue snapping off the upper part of the dark outer leaves until you reach the taller inner leaves. Cut the tops off the leaves with a sharp knife. Place the artichoke in the acidulated water to prevent it from discolouring. Repeat the process with the other artichokes.

3 Boil or steam fresh artichokes until just tender (when a leaf comes away quite easily when pulled). Cook frozen artichoke hearts according to the packet instructions. Remove the pan from the heat and set aside to cool.

4 To make the mayonnaise, combine the egg yolk, mustard and vinegar in a mixing bowl. Season with salt and pepper to taste. Add the oil, a few drops at a time, beating constantly with a wire whisk. When 3–4 tablespoons have been fully incorporated, add the oil in a slow, steady stream, beating constantly. When the mixture is thick and smooth, stir in the chopped parsley. Blend well. Cover and chill until needed.

5 If using fresh artichokes, pull off the leaves. Cut the stems off level with the base. Scrape off the hairy "choke" with a knife or the side of a spoon.

6 Shell the eggs and cut them and the artichokes into wedges. Place on a serving plate, spoon the mayonnaise over the top, garnish with parsley sprigs and serve.

PANZANELLA

. . .

Tomato juice, olive oil and wine vinegar dresses a colourful mixture of roasted peppers, anchovies and toasted ciabatta.

INGREDIENTS
225g/8oz ciabatta (about 2/3 loaf)
150ml/1/4 pint/2/3 cup olive oil
3 red (bell) peppers
3 yellow (bell) peppers
50g/2oz can anchovy
fillets, drained
675g/11/2lb ripe plum tomatoes
4 garlic cloves, crushed
60ml/4 tbsp red wine vinegar
50g/2oz capers
115g/4oz/1 cup pitted black olives
salt and freshly ground
black pepper
fresh basil leaves, to garnish

SERVES 4–6

1 Preheat the oven to 200°C/ 400°F/Gas 6. Cut the ciabatta into 2cm/3/4in chunks and drizzle with 50ml/2fl oz/1/4 cup of the oil. Grill (broil) lightly until just golden.

2 Place the peppers on a foil-lined baking sheet and bake for about 45 minutes, until the skins begin to char and blacken. Remove the peppers from the oven, place in a strong plastic bag, close the end and set aside to cool slightly.

3 Pull the skins off the peppers and cut the flesh into quarters, discarding the stalk ends and seeds. Coarsely chop the anchovies and set aside.

4 To make the tomato dressing, peel and halve the tomatoes. Scoop the seeds and pulp into a sieve set over a bowl. Using the back of a spoon, press the tomato pulp in the sieve to extract as much juice as possible. Discard the pulp and add the remaining oil, the garlic and vinegar to the juices.

5 Layer the toasted ciabatta, peppers, tomatoes, anchovies, capers and olives in a large salad bowl. Season the tomato dressing with salt and black pepper to taste and pour it over the salad. Leave to stand in a cool place for about 30 minutes. Serve garnished with plenty of fresh basil leaves.

RADICCHIO, ARTICHOKE AND WALNUT SALAD

. . .

The distinctive, earthy taste of Jerusalem artichokes makes a lovely contrast to the sharp freshness of radicchio and lemon. Serve the salad warm or cold as an accompaniment to grilled steak or meats cooked on the barbecue.

INGREDIENTS
1 large radicchio or 150g/5oz
radicchio leaves
40g/11/2oz/1/3 cup walnut pieces
45ml/3 tbsp walnut oil
500 g/11/4 lb Jerusalem artichokes
thinly pared rind and juice of
1 lemon
coarse sea salt and freshly ground
black pepper
fresh flat leaf parsley, to
garnish (optional)

SERVES 4

1 If using a whole radicchio, cut it into 8–10 wedges. Put the wedges or leaves in a flameproof dish. Sprinkle over the walnuts, then spoon over the oil and season to taste with salt and pepper. Grill (broil) for 2–3 minutes.

2 Peel the artichokes and cut up any large ones so that the pieces are all roughly the same size. Add the artichokes to a pan of boiling salted water with half the lemon juice and cook for 5–7 minutes, until tender. Drain well. Preheat the grill (broiler) to high.

3 Toss the artichokes into the salad with the remaining lemon juice and the pared lemon rind. Season with coarse sea salt and pepper. Grill until beginning to brown. Serve immediately garnished with torn pieces of parsley, if you like.

> ### Cook's Tip
> Look for Treviso radicchio, which has long, pointed leaves with thick white ribs. It is said to have the best flavour.

Egg, Bacon and Avocado Salad

○ ○ ○

INGREDIENTS

1 large cos or romaine lettuce
8 bacon rashers (strips), fried
until crisp
2 large avocados, peeled and diced
6 hard-boiled eggs, shelled
and chopped
2 beefsteak tomatoes, peeled,
seeded and chopped
175g/6oz blue cheese, crumbled

FOR THE DRESSING
1 garlic clove, crushed
5ml/1 tsp sugar
7.5ml/1½ tsp lemon juice
25ml/1½ tbsp red wine vinegar
120ml/4fl oz/½ cup groundnut
(peanut) oil
salt and freshly ground
black pepper

SERVES 4

1 Slice the lettuce into thin strips across the leaves. Crumble the fried bacon rashers.

2 To make the dressing, combine all the ingredients in a screw-top jar, season to taste and shake well. Spread out the strips of lettuce to make a bed on a large rectangular or oval platter.

3 Arrange the diced avocados, hard-boiled eggs, tomatoes and crumbled blue cheese neatly in rows on top of the lettuce. Sprinkle the bacon on top.

4 Pour the dressing carefully and evenly all over the salad just before serving.

Spicy Corn Salad

○ ○ ○

INGREDIENTS

30ml/2 tbsp vegetable oil
450g/1 lb drained canned
corn, or frozen corn, thawed
1 green (bell) pepper, seeded
and diced
1 small fresh red chilli, seeded
and finely diced
4 spring onions (scallions), sliced
45ml/3 tbsp chopped fresh parsley
225g/8oz cherry tomatoes, halved
salt and freshly ground
black pepper

FOR THE DRESSING
2.5ml/½ tsp sugar
30ml/2 tbsp white wine vinegar
2.5ml/½ tsp Dijon mustard
15ml/1 tbsp chopped
fresh basil
15ml/1 tbsp mayonnaise
1.5ml/¼ tsp chilli sauce

SERVES 4

1 Heat the oil in a large, heavy frying pan. Add the corn, green pepper, chilli and spring onions. Cook over a medium heat for about 5 minutes, until softened, stirring frequently.

2 Transfer the vegetables to a salad bowl. Stir in the parsley and the cherry tomatoes.

3 To make the dressing, combine all the ingredients in a small bowl and whisk together.

4 Pour the dressing over the corn mixture. Season to taste with salt and pepper. Toss well to combine, then serve immediately, while the salad is still warm.

CHORIZO IN OLIVE OIL
· · ·

*Spanish chorizo sausage has a deliciously pungent taste. Frying chorizo with onions and olive oil
is one of the best ways of using it; you can also cook it on the barbecue, brushed with olive oil.*

INGREDIENTS
75ml/5 tbsp extra virgin olive oil
350g/12oz chorizo, sliced
1 large onion, thinly sliced
flat leaf parsley, coarsely chopped,
to garnish

SERVES 4

3 Tip the mixture into a shallow
serving dish and sprinkle with the
coarsely chopped flat leaf parsley.
Serve the chorizo on its own or as
a side dish, with warm crusty bread.

Variation
Chorizo is usually available
in large supermarkets and
delicatessens, but any other
similar spicy sausage can be
used as a substitute.

1 Heat the olive oil in a frying pan and
fry the chorizo over a high heat until
beginning to colour. Remove from the
pan with a slotted spoon.

2 Add the onion slices to the pan and
cook until golden. Return the sausage
slices to the pan to heat through for
about 1 minute.

BROAD BEAN, MUSHROOM AND CHORIZO SALAD

. . .

*This salad can be served as a first course or as part of a buffet menu. Prepare it a day
in advance and store it in the refrigerator until needed.*

INGREDIENTS

*225g/8oz shelled broad (fava) beans
175g/6oz chorizo
60ml/4 tbsp extra virgin olive oil
225g/8oz brown cap
mushrooms, sliced
handful of fresh chives
salt and freshly ground
black pepper*

SERVES 4

1 Cook the broad beans in a large pan
of lightly salted boiling water until just
tender. Drain and refresh under cold
running water. If the beans are large,
peel away the tough outer skins.

2 Remove the skin from the chorizo
and cut it into small chunks. Heat the
olive oil in a heavy frying pan, add the
chorizo and cook over a low heat for
2 minutes. Transfer to a bowl with
the mushrooms, mix well and set aside
to cool.

3 Chop half the chives and stir the
beans and chopped chives into the
mushroom mixture. Season to taste.
Serve the salad at room temperature,
garnished with the remaining chives.

LEEK AND GRILLED RED PEPPER SALAD WITH GOAT'S CHEESE

. . .

The contrasting textures of silky, grilled peppers, soft cheese and slightly crisp leeks makes this salad extra-specially delicious. This would be a sophisticated first course served with plenty of fresh, crusty bread.

INGREDIENTS

4 x 1cm/¹/₂in thick slices French goat's cheese log (chèvre)
65g/2¹/₂oz/1 cup fine dry white breadcrumbs
675g/1¹/₂lb young slender leeks, trimmed
15ml/1 tbsp olive oil
2 large red (bell) peppers
few fresh thyme sprigs, chopped
vegetable oil, for shallow frying
45ml/3 tbsp chopped fresh flat leaf parsley
salt and freshly ground black pepper

FOR THE DRESSING
75ml/5 tbsp extra virgin olive oil
1 small garlic clove, finely chopped
5ml/1 tsp Dijon mustard, plain or flavoured with herbes de Provence
15ml/1 tbsp red wine vinegar

SERVES 6

1 Remove any skin from the cheese. Spread out the breadcrumbs on a plate and roll the cheese slices in them, pressing them in so that the cheese is well coated. Chill the coated cheese for 1 hour.

2 Cook the leeks in lightly salted boiling water for 3–4 minutes. Drain and cut into 7.5–10cm/3–4in lengths and toss in the olive oil and season to taste. Grill (broil) the leeks for 3–4 minutes on each side.

3 Halve and seed the peppers, then grill them, skin side uppermost, until the skin is blackened and blistered. Place them in a bowl, cover and leave to stand for about 10 minutes, so that they soften in their own steam. Remove the skin and cut the flesh into strips, then mix with the leeks and thyme, adding pepper to taste.

4 Make the dressing by shaking all the ingredients together in a screw-top jar, adding seasoning to taste. Pour the dressing over the salad and chill it for several hours. Bring the salad back to room temperature before serving.

5 When ready to serve, heat a shallow layer of vegetable oil in a non-stick frying pan and fry the goat's cheeses quickly until golden brown on each side. Drain them on kitchen paper and cool slightly, then cut into bitesize pieces. Toss the cheese and parsley into the salad and serve immediately.

ROASTED CHERRY TOMATO AND ROCKET SALAD

Little cherry tomatoes are sweet and juicy, and roasting them in the oven makes the flavour wonderfully rich and intense. Together with the pungent, fresh taste of rocket, they make an excitingly different salad.

INGREDIENTS

225g/8oz/2 cups dried chifferini or pipe pasta
450g/1lb ripe baby Italian plum tomatoes, halved lengthways
75ml/5 tbsp extra virgin olive oil
2 garlic cloves, cut into thin slivers
30ml/2 tbsp balsamic vinegar
2 pieces sun-dried tomato in olive oil, drained and chopped
large pinch of sugar
1 handful rocket (arugula), about 65g/2½oz
salt and ground black pepper

SERVES 4

1 Preheat the oven to 190°C/375°F/ Gas 5. Meanwhile, cook the pasta in lightly salted boiling water for about 10 minutes, or according to the instructions on the packet.

2 Arrange the halved tomatoes cut side up in a roasting pan, drizzle 30ml/2 tbsp of the olive oil over them and sprinkle with the slivers of garlic. Season to taste with salt and pepper. Roast in the oven for 20 minutes, turning once.

3 Put the remaining olive oil in a large bowl with the vinegar, sun-dried tomato pieces, sugar and a little salt and pepper to taste. Stir well to mix. Drain the pasta, add it to the bowl of dressing and toss to combine. Add the roasted tomatoes and mix gently.

4 Before serving, add the rocket, toss lightly and taste for seasoning. Serve either at room temperature or chilled.

TOFU AND CUCUMBER SALAD

∘ ∘ ∘

This refreshing salad has a hot, sweet-and-sour dressing.

INGREDIENTS
1 small cucumber
115g/4oz square tofu
vegetable oil, for frying
115g/4oz/¹/₂ cup beansprouts
salt
celery leaves, to garnish

FOR THE DRESSING
1 small onion, grated
2 garlic cloves, crushed
5–7.5ml/1–1¹/₂ tsp chilli sauce
30–45ml/2–3 tbsp dark soy sauce
15–30ml/1–2 tbsp rice
wine vinegar
10ml/2 tsp dark brown sugar

SERVES 4–6

1 Cut the cucumber into neat cubes and place on a plate. Sprinkle with salt to extract the excess liquid. Set aside, while you are preparing the remaining ingredients.

2 Cut the tofu into cubes. Heat a little oil in a pan and cook on both sides until golden brown. Drain on kitchen paper.

3 To make the dressing, put the onion, garlic and chilli sauce in a screw-top jar and shake well. Stir in the soy sauce, vinegar, sugar and salt to taste.

4 Just before serving, rinse the cucumber under cold running water. Drain and dry thoroughly. Toss the cucumber, tofu and beansprouts together in a serving bowl and pour over the dressing. Garnish with the celery leaves and serve the salad immediately.

PLANTAIN AND GREEN BANANA SALAD

Cook the plantains and bananas in their skins. Their soft texture will then absorb the dressing.

INGREDIENTS
2 firm yellow plantains
3 green bananas
1 garlic clove, crushed
1 red onion
15–30ml/1–2 tbsp chopped fresh
coriander (cilantro)
45ml/3 tbsp sunflower oil
25ml/1½ tbsp malt vinegar
salt and freshly ground
black pepper

SERVES 4

1 Slit the plantains and bananas lengthways along their natural ridges, then cut in half and place in a large pan.

2 Cover the plantains and bananas with water, add a little salt and bring to the boil. Boil gently for 20 minutes, until tender, then remove from the water. When they are cool enough to handle, peel and cut into medium-size slices.

3 Put the plantain and banana slices into a large bowl and add the garlic, turning the mixture with a wooden spoon to distribute the garlic evenly.

4 Cut the onion in half and slice thinly. Add it to the bowl with the chopped coriander, oil and vinegar. Season to taste with salt and pepper. Toss together to mix, then transfer to a serving bowl.

GREEN BEAN SALAD

o · o o

Beans are great served with a simple vinaigrette, but this dish is a little more elaborate.

INGREDIENTS
450g/1 lb green beans
15ml/1 tbsp olive oil
25g/1oz/2 tbsp butter
½ garlic clove, crushed
50g/2oz/1 cup fresh
white breadcrumbs
15ml/1 tbsp chopped fresh parsley
1 hard-boiled egg, shelled and finely chopped

FOR THE DRESSING
30ml/2 tbsp olive oil
30ml/2 tbsp sunflower oil
10ml/2 tsp white wine vinegar
½ garlic clove, crushed
1.5ml/¼ tsp Dijon mustard
pinch of sugar
pinch of salt

SERVES 4

1 Cook the beans in salted boiling water for 5–6 minutes, until tender. Drain, refresh under cold running water and place in a serving bowl.

2 To make the dressing, whisk the oils, vinegar garlic, mustard, sugar and salt in a jug (pitcher). Pour the dressing over the beans and toss.

3 Heat the oil and butter in a frying pan and cook the garlic, stirring, for 1 minute. Stir in the breadcrumbs and fry over a moderate heat, stirring frequently, for 3–4 minutes, until golden brown.

4 Remove the pan from the heat and stir in the chopped parsley and then the hard-boiled egg. Sprinkle the breadcrumb mixture over the green beans. Serve warm or at room temperature.

CORONATION SALAD

∘ ∘ ∘

The salad dressing in this dish was created for the coronation dinner of Queen Elizabeth II.

INGREDIENTS
450g/1lb new potatoes
45ml/3 tbsp French Dressing
3 spring onions
(scallions), chopped
6 eggs, hard-boiled, shelled
and halved
frisée lettuce leaves
¼ cucumber, cut into thin strips
6 large radishes, sliced
1 carton salad cress
salt and freshly ground
black pepper

FOR THE CORONATION DRESSING
30ml/2 tbsp olive oil
1 small onion, chopped
15ml/1 tbsp mild curry powder or
korma spice mix
10ml/2 tsp tomato purée (paste)
30ml/2 tbsp lemon juice
30ml/2 tbsp sherry
300ml/½ pint/1¼ cups
mayonnaise
150ml/¼ pint/⅔ cup natural
(plain) yogurt

SERVES 6

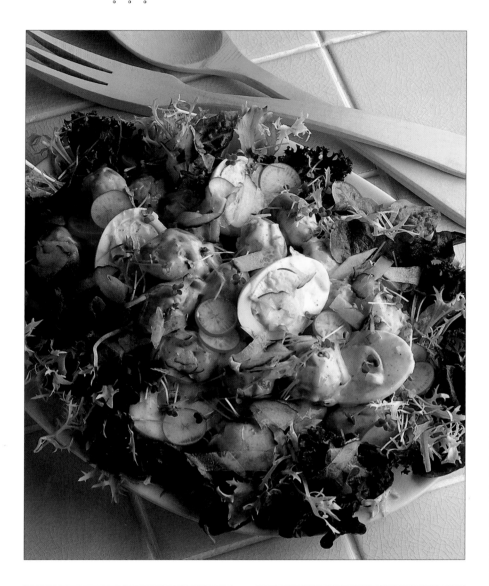

1 Boil the potatoes in salted water until tender. Drain and transfer them to a large bowl.

2 Toss the potatoes in the French dressing, stir in the spring onions, season to taste and leave to cool.

3 Meanwhile, make the coronation dressing. Heat the oil in a small pan and cook the chopped onion for 3 minutes, until soft. Stir in the curry powder or spice mix and cook for 1 minute more. Remove from the heat and mix in all the other dressing ingredients.

4 Stir the dressing into the cooled potatoes, add the eggs, then cover with clear film (plastic wrap) and chill in the refrigerator. Line a serving platter with lettuce leaves and pile the salad in the centre. Sprinkle over the cucumber strips, radishes and cress.

SWEET POTATO AND CARROT SALAD

o   o   o

This warm salad has a sweet-and-sour flavour.

INGREDIENTS

1 medium sweet potato
2 carrots, cut into thick
diagonal slices
3 medium tomatoes
8–10 iceberg lettuce leaves
75g/3oz/1/2 cup canned chickpeas,
drained and rinsed

FOR THE DRESSING
15ml/1 tbsp clear honey
90ml/6 tbsp natural (plain) yogurt
2.5ml/1/2 tsp salt
5ml/1 tsp freshly ground
black pepper

FOR THE GARNISH
15ml/1 tbsp walnuts
15ml/1 tbsp sultanas
(golden raisins)
1 small onion, cut into rings

SERVES 4

1 Peel the sweet potato and cut roughly into cubes. Boil it until it is soft but not mushy, then cover the pan and set aside.

2 Boil the carrots for just a few minutes, making sure that they remain crunchy. Add the carrots to the sweet potato.

3 Drain the water from the sweet potato and carrots and place them together in a bowl.

4 Slice the tops off the tomatoes, then scoop out the seeds with a spoon and discard. Coarsely chop the flesh. Slice the lettuce into strips across the leaves.

5 Line a salad bowl with the shredded lettuce leaves. Mix together the sweet potato, carrots, chickpeas and tomatoes and place the mixture in the centre.

6 To make the dressing, mix together all the ingredients and beat well, using a fork.

7 Garnish the salad with the walnuts, sultanas and onion rings. Pour the dressing over the top just before serving, or serve it in a separate bowl with the salad.

Cook's Tip

This salad makes an excellent light lunch or an easy family supper. Serve it with a sweet mango chutney and warm naan bread.

Variation

You can substitute other canned peas or beans for the chickpeas, such as gunga peas, also known as pigeon peas, or ful medames.

POTATO SALADS
∘ ∘ ∘

Here are two versions of a light, summery potato salad.

INGREDIENTS
900g/2lb new potatoes
5ml/1 tsp salt

FOR THE DRESSING FOR THE WARM SALAD
30ml/2 tbsp hazelnut or walnut oil
60ml/4 tbsp sunflower oil
juice of 1 lemon
15 pistachio nuts
salt and freshly ground black pepper
flat leaf parsley, to garnish

FOR THE DRESSING FOR THE COLD SALAD
75ml/5 tbsp olive oil
10ml/2 tsp white wine vinegar
1 garlic clove, crushed
90ml/6 tbsp finely chopped fresh parsley
2 large spring onions (scallions), finely chopped
salt and freshly ground black pepper

SERVES 4

1 Scrub the potatoes but don't peel them. Place them in a large pan, cover with cold water and bring to the boil over a medium heat. Add the salt, lower the heat and simmer for about 15 minutes, until tender. Drain the potatoes well and set aside to cool slightly.

2 For the warm salad, mix together the hazelnut or walnut oil with the sunflower oil and lemon juice and season well with salt and pepper.

3 Use a large, heavy knife to crush the pistachio nuts coarsely.

4 When the potatoes have cooled slightly, pour over the dressing and sprinkle with the chopped nuts. Serve immediately garnished with a sprig of parsley.

5 For the cold salad, cook the potatoes as above, drain and leave to cool completely.

6 Whisk together the olive oil, white wine vinegar, garlic, parsley and spring onions and season to taste with salt and pepper. Pour the dressing over the potatoes. Cover tightly and chill overnight. Allow to come to room temperature before serving.

POTATO SALAD WITH EGG AND LEMON DRESSING

· · ·

This recipe draws on the contrasting flavours of egg and lemon. Chopped parsley provides a fresh green finish.

INGREDIENTS
900g/2lb new potatoes
1 medium onion, finely chopped
1 hard-boiled egg
300ml/¹/₂ pint/1¹/₄ cups
mayonnaise
1 garlic clove, crushed
finely grated rind and juice of
1 lemon
60ml/4 tbsp chopped fresh parsley
salt and freshly ground
black pepper
fresh parsley sprig, to garnish

SERVES 4

1 Scrub or scrape the potatoes, place in a large pan, cover with cold water and bring to the boil over a medium heat. Add a pinch of salt, lower the heat and simmer for 15 minutes, until tender. Drain well and set aside to cool.

2 Cut the potatoes into large dice and season to taste with salt and pepper. Add the chopped onion.

3 Shell the hard-boiled egg and grate into a mixing bowl, then add the mayonnaise. Combine the garlic and lemon rind and juice in a small bowl and stir them carefully into the mayonnaise.

4 Fold the mayonnaise mixture gently, but thoroughly into the potatoes, then fold in the chopped parsley. Serve the potato salad warm or cold, garnished with sprigs of parsley.

Variation
Fresh chives make an excellent alternative to parsley.

SPICY POTATO SALAD

° ° °

This tasty and versatile salad is quick to prepare.

INGREDIENTS

900g/2lb potatoes
2 red (bell) peppers
2 celery sticks
1 shallot
2–3 spring onions (scallions)
1 fresh green chilli
1 garlic clove, crushed
10ml/2 tsp finely chopped
fresh chives, plus extra to garnish
10ml/2 tsp finely chopped
fresh basil
15ml/1 tbsp finely chopped
fresh parsley
15ml/1 tbsp single (light) cream
30ml/2 tbsp salad cream
15ml/1 tbsp mayonnaise
5ml/1 tsp prepared mild mustard
7.5ml/1½ tsp sugar
salt

SERVES 6

1 Peel the potatoes. Boil in lightly salted water for 10–12 minutes, until tender. Drain and cool, then cut into cubes and place in a large mixing bowl.

2 Halve the red peppers, cut away and discard the core and seeds and cut the flesh into small pieces. Finely chop the celery, shallot and spring onions and slice the chilli very thinly, discarding the seeds. Add all the vegetables to the potatoes together with the garlic chives, basil and parsley.

3 Blend the cream, salad cream, mayonnaise, mustard and sugar in a small bowl, stirring until the mixture is well combined.

4 Pour the dressing over the salad and stir gently, but thoroughly to coat evenly. Serve, garnished with extra chopped chives.

POTATO SALAD WITH GARLIC SAUSAGE

° ° °

*This tasty potato salad would
also make a light lunch dish.*

INGREDIENTS

*450g/1lb small waxy potatoes
30–45ml/2–3 tbsp dry white wine
2 shallots, finely chopped
15ml/1 tbsp chopped fresh parsley
15ml/1 tbsp chopped fresh tarragon
175 g/6oz cooked garlic sausage
fresh flat leaf parsley sprig,
to garnish*

FOR THE VINAIGRETTE

*10ml/2 tsp Dijon mustard
15ml/1 tbsp tarragon vinegar or
white wine vinegar
75ml/5 tbsp extra virgin olive oil
salt and freshly ground
black pepper*

SERVES 4

1 Scrub the potatoes. Boil in salted
water for 10–12 minutes, until
tender. Drain and refresh under
cold running water.

2 Peel the potatoes if you like, or
leave in their skins, and cut into
5mm/¼in slices. Sprinkle with the
wine and shallots.

Variation

The potatoes are also delicious
served on their own and
perhaps accompanied by
marinated herrings.

3 To make the vinaigrette, mix the
mustard and vinegar in a small
bowl, then whisk in the oil, 15ml/
1 tbsp at a time. Season and pour
over the potatoes.

4 Add the herbs to the potatoes
and toss until well mixed.

5 Slice the garlic sausage thinly and
toss with the potatoes. Season the
salad with salt and pepper to taste
and serve at room temperature,
garnished with a sprig of parsley.

PEPPERY BEAN SALAD

∘ ∘ ∘

INGREDIENTS

425g/15oz can red kidney beans
425g/15oz can black-eyed
beans (peas)
425g/15oz can chickpeas
¼ red (bell) pepper
¼ green (bell) pepper
6 radishes
15ml/1 tbsp chopped spring
onion (scallion)

FOR THE DRESSING

5ml/1 tsp ground cumin
15ml/1 tbsp tomato ketchup
30ml/2 tbsp extra virgin
olive oil
15ml/1 tbsp white wine vinegar
1 garlic clove, crushed
2.5ml/½ tsp hot pepper sauce

SERVES 4–6

1 Drain the red kidney beans, black-eyed beans and chickpeas and rinse under cold running water. Shake off the excess water and tip them into a large bowl.

2 Core, seed and chop the red and green peppers. Trim the radishes and slice thinly. Add the peppers, radishes and spring onion to the mixed beans.

3 Mix together the cumin, tomato ketchup, oil, vinegar and garlic in a small bowl. Add a little salt and hot pepper sauce to taste and stir again thoroughly.

4 Pour the dressing over the salad and mix gently, but thoroughly. Cover the bowl with clear film (plastic wrap) and chill the salad in the refrigerator for at least 1 hour before serving, garnished with the chopped spring onion.

SMOKED HAM AND BEAN SALAD

∘ ∘ ∘

A substantial salad that should be served in small quantities if intended as an accompaniment.

INGREDIENTS

175g/6oz dried black-eyed beans (peas)
1 onion
1 carrot
225g/8oz smoked ham, diced
3 medium tomatoes, peeled, seeded and diced
salt and freshly ground black pepper

FOR THE DRESSING
2 garlic cloves, crushed
45ml/3 tbsp olive oil
45ml/3 tbsp red wine vinegar
30ml/2 tbsp vegetable oil
15ml/1 tbsp lemon juice
15ml/1 tbsp chopped fresh basil
15ml/1 tbsp wholegrain mustard
5ml/1 tsp soy sauce
2.5 ml/¹/₂ tsp dried oregano
2.5ml/¹/₂ tsp caster (superfine) sugar
1.5ml/¹/₄ tsp Worcestershire sauce
2.5ml/¹/₂ tsp chilli sauce

SERVES 8

1 Soak the beans in cold water to cover overnight. Drain.

2 Put the beans in a large pan and add the onion and carrot. Cover with fresh cold water and bring to the boil. Boil vigorously for 15 minutes, then lower the heat and simmer for about 1 hour, until the beans are tender.

3 Drain the beans, reserving the onion and carrot. Transfer the beans to a salad bowl.

4 Finely chop the onion and carrot. Toss with the beans. Stir in the smoked ham and tomatoes.

5 For the dressing, combine all the ingredients in a small bowl and whisk to mix.

6 Pour the dressing over the ham and beans. Season to taste with salt and pepper. Toss the salad to combine, then serve.

Not just for summer, main course salads are so versatile they are

welcome all year round. This chapter includes a wonderful

range of dishes made with fish and shellfish, chicken and cheese,

nuts, noodles and, of course, salad vegetables.

MAIN COURSE
SALADS

SALADE NIÇOISE

. o o .

Served with good French bread, this regional classic makes a wonderful summer lunch or light supper dish.

INGREDIENTS

225g/8oz green beans
450g/1lb new potatoes, peeled and cut into 2.5cm/1in pieces
white wine vinegar and olive oil, for sprinkling
1 small cos (romaine) or round lettuce, torn into bitesize pieces
4 ripe plum tomatoes, quartered
1 small cucumber, peeled, seeded and diced
1 green or red (bell) pepper, seeded and thinly sliced
4 hard-boiled eggs, shelled and quartered
24 black olives
225g/8oz can tuna in brine, drained
50g/2oz can anchovy fillets in olive oil, drained
basil leaves, to garnish
garlic croûtons, to serve

FOR THE ANCHOVY VINAIGRETTE
20ml/4 tsp Dijon mustard
50g/2oz can anchovy fillets in olive oil, drained
1 garlic clove, crushed
60ml/4 tbsp lemon juice or white wine vinegar
120ml/4fl oz/½ cup sunflower oil
120ml/4fl oz/½ cup extra virgin olive oil
freshly ground black pepper

SERVES 4–6

1 First, make the anchovy vinaigrette. Place the mustard, anchovies and garlic in a bowl and mix together by pressing the garlic and anchovies against the sides of the bowl. Season generously with pepper. Using a small whisk, blend in the lemon juice or vinegar. Slowly whisk in the sunflower oil in a thin stream, followed by the olive oil, whisking until the dressing is smooth and creamy.

2 Alternatively, put all the ingredients except the oils in a food processor fitted with the metal blade and process to combine. With the machine running, slowly add the oils in a thin stream until the vinaigrette is thick and creamy.

3 Drop the green beans into a large pan of boiling water and boil for 3 minutes, until tender, but crisp. Transfer the beans to a colander with a slotted spoon, then rinse under cold running water to refresh. Drain well again and set aside until required.

4 Add the potatoes to the same boiling water, reduce the heat and simmer for 10–15 minutes, until just tender, then drain. Sprinkle with a little vinegar and olive oil and a spoonful of the vinaigrette.

5 Arrange the lettuce on a serving platter to make a bed, top with the tomatoes, cucumber and red or green pepper, then add the green beans and potatoes.

6 Arrange the eggs around the edge. Place the olives, tuna and anchovies on top and garnish with the basil leaves. Drizzle with the remaining vinaigrette and serve with garlic croûtons.

Cook's Tip

To make garlic croûtons, thinly slice a French loaf or cut a larger loaf, such as rustic country bread, into 2.5cm/1in cubes. Place the bread in a single layer on a baking sheet and cook in the oven, preheated to 180°C/350°F/ Gas 4, for 7–10 minutes, or until golden, turning once. Rub the toast with a garlic clove and serve hot, or leave to cool and store in an airtight container until needed.

MOROCCAN TUNA SALAD

∘ ∘ ∘

This salad is similar to the classic Salade Niçoise but uses tuna or swordfish steaks and fresh broad beans along with the familiar green beans.

INGREDIENTS
*about 900g/2lb fresh tuna or swordfish, sliced into 2cm/ ³/4in steaks
olive oil, for brushing*

*FOR THE SALAD
450g/1lb green beans
450g/1lb broad (fava) beans
1 cos or romaine lettuce
450g/1lb cherry tomatoes, halved, unless very tiny
30ml/2 tbsp coarsely chopped fresh coriander (cilantro)
3 hard-boiled eggs
45ml/3 tbsp olive oil
10–15ml/2–3 tsp lime or lemon juice
½ garlic clove, crushed
175–225g/6–8oz/1½–2 cups pitted black olives*

*FOR THE MARINADE
1 onion
2 garlic cloves
½ bunch fresh parsley
½ bunch fresh coriander (cilantro)
10ml/2 tsp paprika
45ml/3 tbsp olive oil
30ml/2 tbsp white wine vinegar
15ml/1 tbsp lime or lemon juice*

SERVES 6

1 To make the marinade, place all the ingredients in a food processor, add 45ml/3 tbsp water and process for 30–40 seconds.

2 Prick the fish steaks all over with a fork, place in a shallow dish and pour over the marinade, turning the fish to coat. Cover with clear film (plastic wrap) and leave in a cool place for 2–4 hours.

3 To prepare the salad, cook the green beans and broad beans in boiling salted water until tender. Drain and refresh under cold water. Discard the outer shells from the broad beans and place in a large serving bowl with the green beans.

4 Discard the outer lettuce leaves and tear the inner leaves into pieces. Add to the beans with the tomatoes and coriander. Shell the eggs and cut into eighths.

5 Mix the olive oil, lime or lemon juice and garlic to make a dressing.

6 Preheat the grill (broiler) to high and arrange the tuna or swordfish steaks in a grill pan. Brush with the marinade together with a little extra olive oil and grill (broil) for 5–6 minutes on each side, until the fish is tender and flakes easily. Brush again with marinade and more olive oil when you turn the fish over.

7 Allow the fish to cool a little, then break the steaks into large pieces. Toss into the salad with the olives and the dressing. Decorate with the eggs and serve.

Warm Fish Salad with Mango Dressing

∘ ∘ ∘

This spicy salad is best served during the summer months, preferably out of doors.

INGREDIENTS

1 French loaf
4 redfish, black bream or porgy,
each about 275g/10oz
15ml/1 tbsp vegetable oil
1 mango
1cm/½in piece of fresh root ginger
1 fresh red chilli, seeded and
finely chopped
30ml/2 tbsp lime juice
30ml/2 tbsp chopped
fresh coriander (cilantro)
175g/6oz young spinach leaves
150g/5oz pak choi (bok choy)
175g/6oz cherry tomatoes, halved

SERVES 4

1 Preheat the oven to 180°C/ 350°F/Gas 4. Cut the French loaf into 20cm/8in lengths. Slice lengthways, then cut into thick fingers. Place the bread on a baking sheet and place in the oven for 15 minutes to dry.

2 Preheat the grill (broiler) or light the barbecue and allow the embers to settle. Slash the fish deeply on both sides and brush them all over with the vegetable oil. Grill (broil) or cook the fish on the barbecue for 6 minutes, turning once.

3 Peel the mango and cut in half, discarding the stone (pit). Thinly slice one half of the flesh and set aside. Place the other half in a food processor. Peel the ginger, grate finely, then add to the mango with the red chilli, lime juice and chopped coriander. Process until smooth. Adjust to a pouring consistency by adding 30–45ml/ 2–3 tbsp water.

4 Wash the spinach and pak choi leaves in cold water and spin dry or pat them dry with kitchen paper, then distribute them among four serving plates. Place the fish on top of the leaves. Spoon the mango dressing over them and finish with the reserved slices of mango and the tomato halves. Serve immediately with the fingers of crispy French bread.

GRILLED SALMON AND SPRING VEGETABLE SALAD

. . .

Spring is the time to enjoy sweet, young vegetables. Serve with grilled salmon topped with sorrel and quail's eggs.

INGREDIENTS

350g/12oz small new potatoes, scrubbed or scraped
4 quail's eggs
115g/4oz young carrots, peeled
115g/4oz baby corn cobs
115g/4oz sugar snap peas
115g/4oz fine green beans
115g/4oz young courgettes (zucchini)
115g/4oz patty-pan squash (optional)
120ml/4fl oz/½ cup French Dressing
4 salmon fillets, each about 150g/5oz, skinned
115g/4oz sorrel, stems removed salt and freshly ground black pepper

SERVES 4

1 Bring the potatoes to the boil in lightly salted water, lower the heat and simmer for about 15 minutes, until tender. Drain well, cover and keep warm.

2 Cover the quail's eggs with boiling water and cook for 8 minutes. Refresh under cold water, shell and cut in half.

3 Bring a pan of lightly salted water to the boil, add the carrots, corn, sugar snap peas, beans, courgettes and squash, if using, and cook for 2–3 minutes, until tender-crisp. Drain well. Place the hot vegetables and potatoes in a bowl, moisten with a little of the French Dressing and set aside to cool.

4 Brush the salmon fillets with some of the French Dressing and grill (broil) for 6 minutes, turning once.

5 Place the sorrel in a stainless-steel or enamel pan with 30ml/ 2 tbsp French Dressing. Cover and soften over a gentle heat for 2 minutes. Strain in a small sieve and cool to room temperature.

6 Divide the potato and vegetable mixture among four large serving plates, then position a piece of salmon to one side of each plate. Place a spoonful of sorrel on each piece of salmon and top with two pieces of quail's egg. Season to taste with salt and pepper and serve at room temperature.

> ### *Cook's Tip*
> If sorrel is unavailable, use young spinach leaves instead. Cook it gently in the same way as the sorrel.

NOODLES WITH PINEAPPLE, GINGER AND CHILLIES
. . .

A coconut, lime and fish sauce dressing is the perfect partner to this fruity and spicy salad.

INGREDIENTS
275g/10oz dried udon noodles
½ pineapple, peeled, cored and sliced into 4 cm/1½in rings
45ml/3 tbsp light brown sugar
60ml/4 tbsp lime juice
60ml/4 tbsp coconut milk
30ml/2 tbsp Thai fish sauce
30ml/2 tbsp grated fresh root ginger
2 garlic cloves, finely chopped
1 ripe mango or 2 peaches, finely diced
freshly ground black pepper
2 spring onions (scallions), thinly sliced, 2 red chillies, seeded and finely shredded, and fresh mint leaves, to garnish

SERVES 4

1 Cook the noodles in a large pan of boiling water until tender, following the directions on the packet. Drain, refresh under cold water and drain again.

2 Place the pineapple rings in a flameproof dish, sprinkle with 30ml/2 tbsp of the sugar and grill (broil) for about 5 minutes, or until golden. Cool slightly and cut into small dice.

3 Mix the lime juice, coconut milk and fish sauce in a salad bowl. Add the remaining brown sugar with the ginger, garlic and black pepper and whisk well. Add the noodles and pineapple.

4 Add the diced mango or peaches and toss lightly to mix. Sprinkle over the sliced spring onions, shredded chillies and mint leaves before serving.

BUCKWHEAT NOODLES WITH SMOKED SALMON
. . .

Young pea sprouts are available for only a short time. You can substitute watercress, salad cress, young leeks or your favourite green vegetable or herb in this dish.

INGREDIENTS
225g/8oz buckwheat or soba noodles
15ml/1 tbsp oyster sauce
juice of ½ lemon
30–45ml/2–3 tbsp light olive oil
115g/4oz smoked salmon, cut into fine strips
115g/4oz young pea sprouts
2 ripe tomatoes, peeled, seeded and cut into strips
15ml/1 tbsp chopped chives
freshly ground black pepper

SERVES 4

1 Cook the noodles in a large pan of boiling water until tender, following the directions on the packet. Drain, then rinse under cold running water and drain well.

Cook's Tip
Soba noodles, popular in Japan, are made from a mixture of buckwheat and wheat flour.

---

2 Tip the noodles into a large bowl. Add the oyster sauce and lemon juice and season with pepper to taste. Moisten the noodles with the olive oil.

3 Add the smoked salmon, pea sprouts, tomatoes and chives. Mix well and serve immediately.

SMOKED TROUT AND NOODLE SALAD

. . .

It is important to use ripe, juicy tomatoes for this fresh-tasting salad. For a special occasion, you could use smoked salmon.

INGREDIENTS

225g/8oz somen noodles
2 smoked trout, skinned and boned
2 hard-boiled eggs, shelled and coarsely chopped
30ml/2 tbsp chopped fresh chives
lime halves, to serve (optional)

FOR THE DRESSING
6 ripe plum tomatoes
2 shallots, finely chopped
30ml/2 tbsp tiny capers, rinsed
30ml/2 tbsp chopped fresh tarragon
finely grated rind and juice of ½ orange
60ml/4 tbsp extra virgin olive oil
salt and freshly ground black pepper

SERVES 4

1 To make the dressing, halve the tomatoes, remove the cores and cut the flesh into chunks. Place in a bowl with the shallots, capers, tarragon, orange rind and juice and olive oil. Season to taste and mix well. Leave to marinate at room temperature for 1–2 hours.

2 Cook the noodles in a pan of boiling water, according to the packet instructions. Drain, rinse in cold water and drain again.

3 Toss the noodles with the dressing, then adjust the seasoning to taste. Arrange the noodles on a large serving platter or divide among four individual plates.

4 Flake the smoked trout over the noodles, then sprinkle the eggs and chives over the top. Serve, with lime halves on the side of the plate, if you like.

SMOKED TROUT AND HORSERADISH SALAD

Partner crisp lettuce leaves with smoked fish, warm potatoes and a creamy dressing.

INGREDIENTS

675g/1½ lb new potatoes
4 smoked trout fillets
115g/4oz mixed lettuce leaves
4 slices dark rye bread, cut
into fingers
salt and freshly ground
black pepper

FOR THE DRESSING
60ml/4 tbsp creamed horseradish
60ml/4 tbsp groundnut (peanut) oil
15ml/1 tbsp white wine vinegar
10ml/2 tsp caraway seeds

SERVES 4

1 Scrub the potatoes. Bring to the boil in a pan of lightly salted water and simmer for about 15 minutes, until tender. Drain well.

2 Meanwhile, remove the skin from the trout fillets and lift the flesh from the bone.

Cook's Tip

In some cases, it is better to season the leaves themselves rather than the dressing when making a salad.

---

3 To make the dressing, place all the ingredients in a screw-top jar and shake vigorously. Season the lettuce leaves and moisten them with the dressing. Distribute among four serving plates.

4 Flake the trout fillets and cut the potatoes in half. Distribute them, together with the rye bread fingers, over the salad leaves and toss to mix. Season the salad to taste with salt and pepper and serve.

THAI NOODLE SALAD

° ° °

The addition of coconut milk and sesame oil gives an unusual nutty flavour to this salad.

INGREDIENTS
*350g/12oz somen noodles
1 large carrot, cut into thin strips
1 bunch asparagus, trimmed and cut into 4cm/1¹/₂in lengths
1 red (bell) pepper, seeded and cut into fine strips
115g/4oz mangetouts (snow peas), trimmed and halved
115g/4oz baby corn cobs, halved lengthways
115g/4oz beansprouts
115g/4oz can water chestnuts, drained and thinly sliced
1 lime, cut into wedges,
50g/2oz/¹/₂ cup roasted peanuts, coarsely chopped, and fresh coriander (cilantro) leaves, to garnish*

FOR THE DRESSING
*45ml/3 tbsp torn fresh basil
75ml/5 tbsp chopped fresh mint
250ml/8fl oz/1 cup coconut milk
30ml/2 tbsp dark sesame oil
15ml/1 tbsp grated fresh root ginger
2 garlic cloves, finely chopped
juice of 1 lime
2 spring onions (scallions), chopped
salt and cayenne pepper*

SERVES 4–6

1 To make the dressing, combine all the ingredients in a bowl and mix well. Season to taste with salt and cayenne pepper.

2 Cook the noodles in a pan of boiling water, following the directions on the packet, until just tender. Drain, rinse under cold running water and drain again, then set aside until required.

3 Cook all the vegetables, except the water chestnuts, in separate pans of lightly salted boiling water until they are tender, but still crisp. Drain, plunge them immediately into cold water and drain again.

4 Toss the noodles, vegetables, water chestnuts and dressing together. Arrange on individual serving plates and garnish with the lime wedges, chopped peanuts and coriander leaves.

PRAWN NOODLE SALAD WITH FRAGRANT HERBS

∘ ∘ ∘

A light, refreshing salad with all the tangy flavour of the sea.

INGREDIENTS

*115g/4oz cellophane noodles,
soaked in hot water until soft
1 small green (bell) pepper, seeded
and cut into strips
½ cucumber, cut into strips
1 tomato, cut into strips
2 shallots, thinly sliced
16 peeled cooked prawns (shrimp)
salt and freshly ground
black pepper
fresh coriander (cilantro) leaves,
to garnish*

FOR THE DRESSING
*15ml/1 tbsp rice-wine vinegar
30ml/2 tbsp Thai fish sauce
30ml/2 tbsp lime juice
2.5ml/½ tsp grated fresh
root ginger
1 lemon grass stalk, finely chopped
1 red chilli, seeded and thinly sliced
30ml/2 tbsp coarsely chopped
fresh mint
few sprigs of tarragon, chopped
15ml/1 tbsp chopped fresh chives*

SERVES 4

1 To make the dressing, combine all the ingredients in a small bowl or jug (pitcher) and whisk well.

2 Drain the noodles, then plunge them into a pan of boiling water for 1 minute. Drain, rinse under cold running water to refresh and drain again well.

3 In a large bowl, combine the noodles with the green pepper strips, cucumber, tomato and shallots. Lightly season with salt and black pepper, then toss with the dressing.

Cook's Tip

Prawns (shrimp) are available ready-cooked and often shelled. To cook prawns, boil them for 5 minutes. Leave them to cool in the cooking liquid, then gently pull off the tail shell and twist off the head.

4 Spoon the cellophane noodles on to four individual serving plates and arrange the prawns on top of them. Garnish with a few coriander leaves and serve immediately.

EGG NOODLE SALAD WITH SESAME CHICKEN

∘ ∘ ∘

INGREDIENTS

400g/14oz fresh thin egg noodles
1 carrot, cut into long fine strips
50g/2oz mangetouts (snow peas),
trimmed, cut into fine strips
and blanched
115g/4oz/½ cup
beansprouts, blanched
30ml/2 tbsp olive oil
225g/8oz skinless, boneless chicken
breast portions, thinly sliced
30ml/2 tbsp sesame seeds, toasted
2 spring onions (scallions), thinly
sliced diagonally, and fresh
coriander (cilantro) leaves,
to garnish

FOR THE DRESSING
45ml/3 tbsp sherry vinegar
75ml/5 tbsp soy sauce
60ml/4 tbsp sesame oil
90ml/6 tbsp light olive oil
1 garlic clove, finely chopped
5ml/1 tsp grated fresh root ginger
salt and freshly ground
black pepper

SERVES 4–6

1 To make the dressing, whisk together all the ingredients in a small bowl. Season to taste.

2 Cook the noodles in a large pan of boiling water. Stir them occasionally to separate. They will take only a few minutes to cook; be careful not to overcook them. Drain the noodles, rinse under cold running water and drain well. Tip into a bowl.

3 Add the carrot, mangetouts and beansprouts to the noodles. Pour in about half the dressing, then toss the mixture well and adjust the seasoning according to taste.

4 Heat the oil in a large frying pan. Add the chicken and stir-fry for 3 minutes, or until cooked and golden. Remove from the heat. Add the sesame seeds and drizzle in some of the remaining dressing.

5 Arrange the noodle mixture on individual serving plates, making a nest on each plate. Spoon the chicken on top, dividing it equally. Sprinkle with the spring onions and coriander leaves and serve any remaining dressing separately.

CHICKEN AND PASTA SALAD

° ° °

This is a delicious way to use up left-over cooked chicken.

INGREDIENTS

225g/8oz tricolour pasta twists
30ml/2 tbsp bottled pesto sauce
15ml/1 tbsp olive oil
1 beefsteak tomato
12 pitted black olives
225g/8oz green beans, cooked
350g/12oz cooked chicken, cubed
salt and freshly ground
black pepper
fresh basil, to garnish

SERVES 4

3 Peel the beefsteak tomato by cutting a cross in the skin at the top with a sharp knife and then plunging it in boiling water for about 30 seconds. The skin will now pull off easily. Cut the tomato flesh into small cubes.

4 Add the tomato and olives to the pasta. Cut the green beans into 4cm/1½in lengths. Add the beans and chicken and season to taste with salt and pepper. Toss gently, transfer to a serving platter, garnish with basil and serve.

1 Cook the pasta in plenty of lightly salted boiling water for 10–12 minutes, until *al dente*, or as directed on the packet.

2 Drain the pasta and rinse in plenty of cold running water. Put into a bowl and stir in the pesto sauce and olive oil.

HOT AND SOUR CHICKEN SALAD

This chicken salad from Vietnam is equally delicious made with prawns.
Allow 450g/1lb fresh prawn tails to serve four people.

INGREDIENTS

2 skinless, boneless chicken
breast portions
115g/4oz beansprouts
1 head Chinese leaves (Chinese
cabbage), shredded
2 medium carrots, cut into batons
1 red onion, thinly sliced
2 large gherkins, sliced

FOR THE MARINADE
1 small fresh red chilli, seeded and
finely chopped
1cm/1/2in piece of fresh root
ginger, chopped
1 garlic clove, crushed
15ml/1 tbsp crunchy peanut butter
30ml/2 tbsp chopped fresh
coriander (cilantro)
5ml/1 tsp sugar
2.5ml/1/2 tsp salt
15ml/1 tbsp rice or white
wine vinegar
60ml/4 tbsp vegetable oil
10ml/2 tsp Thai fish sauce

SERVES 4–6

1 Slice the chicken breast portions thinly and place in a shallow bowl. Grind the chilli, ginger and garlic in a food processor or with a mortar and pestle, then add the peanut butter, chopped fresh coriander, sugar and salt.

2 Add the rice or white wine vinegar, 30ml/2 tbsp of the oil and the fish sauce to the ingredients in the food processor. Combine well. Cover the chicken with the spice mixture and marinate for at least 2–3 hours.

3 Cook the chicken in a frying pan on the hob (stovetop) or on a medium-hot barbecue for about 5 minutes, basting often and turning once. Arrange the salad ingredients on a serving dish and top with the cooked chicken.

CHICKEN SALAD WITH CORIANDER DRESSING

*Serve this salad warm to make the most of the wonderful flavour of chicken basted with a
marinade of coriander, sesame and mustard.*

INGREDIENTS

*4 medium skinless, boneless
chicken breast portions
225g/8oz mangetouts (snow peas)
2 heads decorative lettuce such as
lollo rosso or oak leaf
3 carrots, cut into batons
175g/6oz button (white)
mushrooms, sliced
175g/6oz bacon, fried and chopped*

FOR THE CORIANDER DRESSING
*120ml/4fl oz/½ cup lemon juice
30ml/2 tbsp wholegrain mustard
250ml/8fl oz/1 cup olive oil
65ml/2½ fl oz/⅓ cup sesame oil
5ml/1 tsp coriander seeds, crushed
15ml/1 tbsp chopped fresh
coriander (cilantro), to garnish*

SERVES 6

1 Mix all the dressing ingredients in a
bowl. Place the chicken in a dish and
pour over half the dressing. Cover and
marinate overnight in the refrigerator.
Chill the remaining dressing.

2 Cook the mangetouts for 2 minutes
in boiling water, then refresh in cold
water. Tear the lettuces into small
pieces and mix all the other salad
ingredients and the bacon together.
Arrange the salad on individual dishes.

3 Cook the chicken breast portions
under the grill (broiler) or on a medium
barbecue for 10–15 minutes, basting
with the marinade and turning once,
until cooked through. Thinly slice them
on the diagonal. Divide between the
bowls of salad and add some of the
dressing. Combine and sprinkle some
fresh coriander over each bowl.

CRUNCHY SALAD WITH BLACK PUDDING

· · ·

Fried until crisp, slices of black pudding are extremely good in salad, particularly with crunchy bread croûtons and sweet cherry tomatoes. Serve this salad in bowls or shallow soup plates.

INGREDIENTS

250g/9oz black pudding (blood sausage), sliced
1 focaccia loaf, plain or flavoured with sun-dried tomatoes and herbs
45ml/3 tbsp olive oil
1 cos or romaine lettuce, torn into bitesize pieces
250g/9oz cherry tomatoes, halved

FOR THE DRESSING
juice of 1 lemon
90ml/6 tbsp olive oil
10ml/2 tsp French mustard
15ml/1 tbsp clear honey
30ml/2 tbsp chopped fresh herbs, such as coriander (cilantro), chives and parsley
salt and freshly ground black pepper

SERVES 4

1 Dry-fry the black pudding in a large, non-stick frying pan for 5–10 minutes, or until browned and crisp, turning occasionally. Remove the black pudding from the pan with a slotted spoon and drain on kitchen paper.

2 Cut the focaccia into chunks. Add the oil to the juices in the frying pan and cook the focaccia cubes in two batches, turning frequently, until golden on all sides. Drain on kitchen paper.

3 Mix together the focaccia, black pudding, lettuce and cherry tomatoes in a large bowl. Mix together the dressing ingredients and season to taste with salt and pepper. Pour the dressing over the salad. Mix well and serve.

PASTA SALAD WITH SALAMI AND OLIVES

∘ ∘ ∘ ∘

Garlic and herb dressing gives a Mediterranean flavour to a few ingredients from the pantry and refrigerator, making this an excellent salad for winter.

INGREDIENTS

225g/8oz/2 cups dried gnocchi or conchiglie
50g/2oz/½ cup pitted black olives, quartered lengthways
75g/3oz thinly sliced salami, any skin removed, diced
½ small red onion, finely chopped
1 large handful fresh basil leaves

FOR THE DRESSING

60ml/4tbsp extra virgin olive oil
good pinch of sugar, to taste
juice of ½ lemon
5ml/1 tsp Dijon mustard
10ml/2 tsp dried oregano
1 garlic clove, crushed
salt and ground black pepper

SERVES 4

1 Cook the pasta in a pan of salted boiling water according to the packet instructions.

2 Meanwhile, make the herb dressing for the pasta. Put all the ingredients for the dressing in a large bowl with a little salt and ground black pepper to taste, and whisk well to mix.

3 Drain the pasta thoroughly, add it to the bowl of dressing and toss well to mix. Leave the dressed pasta to cool, stirring occasionally.

4 When the pasta is cold, add the remaining ingredients and toss well to mix again. Taste for seasoning, then serve immediately.

WALDORF HAM SALAD

Waldorf Salad first appeared at the Waldorf-Astoria Hotel, New York, in the 1890s. This modern-day version is something of a meal in itself.

INGREDIENTS

3 eating apples
15ml/1 tbsp lemon juice
2 slices cooked cured ham, each about 175g/6oz
2 celery sticks
150ml/¼ pint/⅔ cup mayonnaise
1 escarole or frisée lettuce
1 small radicchio, finely shredded
½ bunch watercress
45ml/3 tbsp walnut or olive oil
50g/2oz/½ cup broken walnuts, toasted
salt and freshly ground black pepper

SERVES 4

1 Peel, core, slice and finely shred the apples. Moisten with lemon juice to prevent them from turning brown. Cut the ham into 5cm/2in strips. Cut the celery sticks into similar-size pieces. Combine the apples, ham and celery in a bowl.

2 Add the mayonnaise and mix thoroughly.

3 Shred all the salad leaves finely, then moisten with oil. Distribute the leaves among four serving plates. Pile the mayonnaise mixture in the centre, sprinkle with toasted walnuts, season and serve.

CHICKEN LIVER, BACON AND TOMATO SALAD

∘ ∘ ∘

Warm salads are especially welcome during the cooler months of the year.

INGREDIENTS

225g/8oz young spinach, stems removed
1 frisée lettuce
105ml/7 tbsp groundnut (peanut) or sunflower oil
175g/6oz rindless unsmoked bacon, cut into strips
75g/3oz day-old bread, crusts removed and cut into short fingers
450g/1lb chicken livers
115g/4oz cherry tomatoes
salt and freshly ground black pepper

SERVES 4

1 Place the spinach and lettuce leaves in a salad bowl. Heat 60ml/ 4 tbsp of the groundnut or sunflower oil in a large, heavy frying pan, add the bacon strips and cook for 3–4 minutes, or until crisp and brown. Remove the bacon with a slotted spoon and drain on kitchen paper.

2 To make croûtons, fry the bread in the bacon-flavoured oil, tossing until crisp and golden. Drain on kitchen paper.

3 Heat the remaining oil in the frying pan, add the chicken livers and fry briskly for 2–3 minutes. Turn the chicken livers out over the salad leaves and add the bacon, croûtons and tomatoes. Season to taste with salt and pepper, toss and serve warm.

Variation

If you can't find any baby spinach leaves you can use lamb's lettuce. Watercress would make a deliciously peppery substitute, but you should use less of it and bulk the salad out with a milder leaf so that the watercress doesn't overwhelm the other flavours.

CURRY FRIED PORK AND RICE VERMICELLI SALAD

INGREDIENTS

225g/8oz lean pork
2 garlic cloves, finely chopped
2 slices fresh root ginger, peeled
and finely chopped
30–45ml/2–3 tbsp rice wine
45ml/3 tbsp vegetable oil
2 lemon grass stalks, finely chopped
10ml/2 tsp curry powder
175g/6oz/³/4 cup beansprouts
225g/8oz rice vermicelli, soaked in
warm water until soft, then drained
¹/2 lettuce, finely shredded
30ml/2 tbsp fresh mint leaves
lemon juice and Thai fish sauce,
to taste
salt and freshly ground
black pepper
2 spring onions (scallions),
chopped, 25g/1oz/¹/2 cup toasted
peanuts, chopped, and pork
crackling (optional) to garnish

SERVES 4

1 Cut the pork into thin strips. Place in a shallow dish with half the garlic and ginger. Season to taste with salt and pepper, pour over 30ml/2 tbsp rice wine and marinate for at least 1 hour.

2 Heat the vegetable oil in a frying pan or wok. Add the remaining garlic and ginger and stir-fry over a medium heat for a few seconds until fragrant and golden. Stir in the strips of pork, with the marinade, and add the lemon grass and curry powder.

3 Stir-fry over a high heat until the pork is golden and cooked through, adding more rice wine if the mixture seems too dry.

4 Place the beansprouts in a sieve. Blanch them by lowering the sieve into a pan of boiling water for 1 minute, then drain and refresh under cold running water. Drain again. Using the same water, cook the rice vermicelli for 3–5 minutes, until tender. Drain and rinse under cold running water.

5 Drain the vermicelli well and tip into a large bowl. Add the beansprouts, shredded lettuce and mint leaves. Season with lemon juice and fish sauce to taste. Toss lightly to combine the flavours.

6 Divide the vermicelli mixture among individual serving plates, making a nest on each plate. Arrange the pork mixture on top. Garnish with spring onions, toasted peanuts and pork crackling, if using. Serve.

SWEET POTATO, EGG, PORK AND BEETROOT SALAD

° ° °

This is a good way to use up leftover pork. Sweet flavours balance the bitter chicory.

INGREDIENTS
900g/2 lb sweet potatoes
4 chicory (Belgian endive) heads
5 eggs, hard-boiled
450g/1 lb pickled young beetroot (beets)
175g/6oz cold roast pork
salt

FOR THE DRESSING
75ml/5 tbsp sunflower oil
30ml/2 tbsp white wine vinegar
10ml/2 tsp Dijon mustard
5ml/1 tsp fennel seeds, crushed

SERVE 4

1 Peel the sweet potatoes and dice into equal-size pieces.

2 Add the diced sweet potatoes to a pan of salted boiling water. Bring back to the boil, then simmer for 10–15 minutes, or until the potatoes are soft. Drain and set aside to cool.

3 To make the dressing, combine the sunflower oil, vinegar, mustard and fennel seeds in a screw-top jar and shake well.

4 Separate the chicory leaves and arrange them around the edges of four serving plates.

5 Pour two thirds of the dressing over the sweet potatoes, then stir so that all the pieces of potato are coated in the dressing. Spoon the sweet potatoes on top of the chicory leaves.

6 Shell the hard-boiled eggs. Slice the eggs and beetroot and arrange to make an attractive pattern around the sweet potato.

7 Slice the pork, then cut into strips about 4 cm/1½in wide. Place in a bowl and moisten with the rest of the dressing.

8 Pile the strips of pork into the centre of each salad. Season with salt to taste and serve.

Cook's Tip
To crush the fennel seeds, grind using a mortar and pestle. If you don't have these, use two dessertspoons instead. For extra flavour try toasting the fennel seeds before crushing.

FRANKFURTER SALAD WITH MUSTARD DRESSING

° ° °

*This is a last-minute salad,
which you can make quickly.*

INGREDIENTS
*675g/1½lb small new potatoes,
scrubbed or scraped
2 eggs
350g/12oz frankfurters
1 butterhead or frisée lettuce
225g/8oz young spinach leaves,
stems removed
salt and freshly ground
black pepper*
FOR THE DRESSING

*45ml/3 tbsp safflower oil
30ml/2 tbsp olive oil
15ml/1 tbsp white wine vinegar
10ml/2 tsp mustard
5ml/1 tsp caraway seeds, crushed*

SERVES 4

1 Bring the potatoes to the boil in lightly salted water and simmer for about 15 minutes, or until tender. Drain, cover and keep warm. Hard-boil the eggs for 12 minutes. Refresh in cold water, shell and cut into quarters.

2 Score the frankfurter skins corkscrew fashion with a small knife, then cover with boiling water and simmer for about 5 minutes to heat through. Drain well, cover and keep warm.

3 To make the dressing, place all the ingredients in a screw-top jar and shake well.

4 Moisten the salad leaves with half of the dressing and distribute among four large serving plates.

5 Moisten the warm potatoes and frankfurters with the remainder of the dressing and arrange them over the salad.

6 Finish off the salad by topping with sections of hard-boiled egg, season to taste with salt and black pepper and serve warm.

Cook's Tip

This salad has a German slant to it and calls for a sweet-and-sour German-style mustard. American mustards have a similar quality.

SMOKED BACON AND GREEN BEAN PASTA SALAD

∘ ∘ ∘

INGREDIENTS

*350g/12oz/3 cups dried
wholewheat pasta twists
225g/8oz green beans
8 rashers (strips) smoked bacon
350g/12oz cherry tomatoes, halved
2 bunches spring onions
(scallions), chopped
400g/14oz can chickpeas, drained
and rinsed*

FOR THE DRESSING

*90ml/6 tbsp tomato juice
30ml/2 tbsp balsamic vinegar
5ml/1 tsp ground cumin
5ml/1 tsp ground coriander
30ml/2 tbsp chopped fresh
coriander (cilantro)
salt and freshly ground
black pepper*

SERVES 4

2 Preheat the grill (broiler) and cook the bacon for 2–3 minutes on each side, until tender. Dice the bacon and add to the beans.

3 Put the tomatoes, spring onions and chickpeas in a large bowl.

4 In smaller bowl, mix together the tomato juice, vinegar, spices, fresh coriander and seasoning.

5 Pour the dressing into a large bowl. Drain the cooked pasta thoroughly and add to the tomato mixture with the green beans and bacon. Toss all the ingredients together to mix thoroughly. Adjust the seasoning, if necessary. Serve warm or cold.

1 Cook the pasta in a large pan of lightly salted boiling water for about 8–10 minutes, until *al dente*. Meanwhile, trim and halve the green beans and cook them in boiling water for about 5 minutes, until tender. Drain thoroughly, set aside and keep warm.

Cook's Tip

Always rinse drained canned beans and pulses well before using, to remove as much of the salt solution as possible. Drain again before use.

WARM PASTA SALAD WITH ASPARAGUS

o · o o

Warm pasta, ham, eggs and Parmesan – a heavenly match.

INGREDIENTS
450g/1lb asparagus
450g/1lb dried tagliatelle
225g/8oz cooked cured ham, sliced 5mm/¼in thick, and cut into fingers
2 eggs, hard-boiled, shelled and sliced
50g/2oz piece Parmesan cheese

FOR THE DRESSING
50g/2oz cooked potato
75ml/5 tbsp olive oil
15ml/1 tbsp lemon juice
10ml/2 tsp Dijon mustard
120ml/4fl oz/½ cup vegetable stock
salt and freshly ground black pepper

SERVES 4

1 Bring a pan of lightly salted water to the boil. Trim and discard the tough, woody part of the asparagus stalks. Cut the asparagus in half and boil the thicker halves for 12 minutes, adding the asparagus tips after 6 minutes. Refresh under cold water until warm, then drain.

Cook's Tip
You can use either thin, green asparagus or the thicker blanched type with yellow or purple tips.

---

2 Finely chop 150g/5oz of the thicker asparagus pieces. Place in a food processor together with the dressing ingredients and process until smooth. Season the dressing to taste with salt and pepper.

3 Boil the pasta in a pan of salted water for 8–10 minutes, until *al dente*. Refresh under cold water.

4 Tip the pasta into a bowl and toss with the asparagus sauce. Turn out into four serving bowls. Top each pile of pasta with some of the ham, eggs and asparagus tips. Finish with shavings of Parmesan cheese and serve warm.

DEVILLED HAM AND PINEAPPLE SALAD

∘ ∘ ∘

INGREDIENTS

*225g/8oz/2 cups dried
wholewheat penne
150ml/¼ pint/⅔ cup natural
(plain) yogurt
15ml/1 tbsp cider vinegar
5ml/1 tsp wholegrain mustard
large pinch of caster
(superfine) sugar
30ml/2 tbsp hot mango chutney
115g/4oz cooked lean ham, cubed
200g/7oz can pineapple
chunks, drained
2 celery sticks, chopped
½ green (bell) pepper, seeded
and diced
15ml/1 tbsp toasted flaked (sliced)
almonds, coarsely chopped
salt and freshly ground
black pepper
crusty bread, to serve*

SERVES 4

1 Cook the pasta in a large pan of lightly salted boiling water for 8–10 minutes, until *al dente*. Drain well and rinse thoroughly. Leave to cool.

2 To make the dressing, mix the yogurt, vinegar, mustard, sugar and mango chutney together in a large bowl. Season to taste with salt and pepper. Add the pasta and toss lightly together.

3 Transfer the pasta to a serving dish. Add the ham, pineapple, celery and green pepper.

4 Sprinkle toasted almonds over the top of the salad. Serve with crusty bread.

PEAR AND PECAN NUT SALAD

○ ○ ○

Toasted pecan nuts have an affinity with crisp white pears.

INGREDIENTS

*75g/3oz/¾ cup shelled pecan
nuts, halved
3 crisp pears
175g/6oz young spinach,
stems removed
1 escarole or butterhead lettuce
1 radicchio
30ml/2 tbsp Blue Cheese and
Chive Dressing
salt and freshly ground
black pepper
crusty bread,
to serve*

SERVES 4

1 Toast the pecan nuts under a moderate grill (broiler) to bring out their flavour.

Cook's Tip
The pecan nuts will burn very quickly under the grill (broiler), so keep constant watch over them and remove them as soon as they change colour.

2 Cut the pears into even slices, leaving the skins intact but discarding the cores.

3 Place the spinach, lettuce and radicchio leaves into a large bowl. Add the pears and toasted pecans, pour over the Blue Cheese and Chive Dressing and toss well.

4 Distribute equally among four large serving plates and season to taste with salt and pepper. Serve the salad with warm crusty bread.

GOAT'S CHEESE AND FIG SALAD

o o o

Fresh figs and walnuts are perfect partners for goat's cheese and toasted buckwheat. The olive and nut oil dressing contains no vinegar, depending instead on the acidity of the goat's cheese.

INGREDIENTS

175g/6oz/1 cup couscous
30ml/2 tbsp toasted buckwheat
1 egg, hard-boiled
30ml/2 tbsp chopped fresh parsley
60ml/4 tbsp olive oil
45ml/3 tbsp walnut oil
115g/4oz rocket (arugula) leaves
1/2 frisée lettuce
175g/6oz crumbly white goat's cheese
50g/2oz/1/2 cup broken walnuts, toasted
4 ripe figs, trimmed and almost cut into four (leave the pieces joined at the base)

SERVES 4

1 Place the couscous and toasted buckwheat in a bowl, cover with boiling water and leave to soak for 15 minutes. Place in a sieve to drain off any remaining water, then spread out on a baking tray and allow to cool.

3 Toss the grated egg, parsley, couscous and buckwheat together in a bowl. Combine the olive and walnut oils using half to moisten the couscous mixture.

2 Shell the hard-boiled egg and grate finely.

4 Toss the salad leaves in the remaining oil and distribute among four large serving plates.

5 Pile the couscous mixture in the centre of each plate and crumble the goat's cheese over the top. Sprinkle with toasted walnuts, place a fig in the centre of each plate and serve immediately.

Variation

If you find the flavour of goat's cheese a little too strong, try making this salad with a milder, crumbly cheese, such as feta or Caerphilly.

Cook's Tip

Goat's cheeses vary in strength from the youngest, which are soft and mild, to strongly-flavoured, mature (sharp) cheeses, which have a firm and crumbly texture. The crumbly varieties are particularly well suited to salads.

The recipes in this chapter feature luxurious ingredients, exotic
combinations, spectacular presentations and sophisticated
flavours – truly dining in style. There is a special salad to suit
every occasion, from an *al fresco* dinner to a buffet party.

SPECIAL OCCASION SALADS

GADO GADO

∘ ∘ ∘

This classic Indonesian vegetable salad is served with a delicious hot peanut sauce.

INGREDIENTS

2 medium potatoes
175g/6oz green beans, trimmed
175g/6oz Chinese leaves (Chinese cabbage), shredded
1 iceberg lettuce
175g/6oz beansprouts
1/2 cucumber, cut into fingers
150g/5oz mooli (daikon), shredded
3 spring onions (scallions)
225g/8oz tofu, cut into large slices
3 hard-boiled eggs, shelled and quartered
1 small bunch fresh coriander (cilantro)
prawn (shrimp) crackers, to serve

FOR THE PEANUT SAUCE
150g/5oz/1 1/4 cups raw peanuts
15ml/1 tbsp vegetable oil
2 shallots or 1 small onion, finely chopped
1 garlic clove, crushed
1–2 small fresh chillies, seeded and finely chopped
1cm/1/2in square shrimp paste or 15ml/1 tbsp Thai fish sauce (optional)
30ml/2 tbsp tamarind sauce
120ml/4fl oz/1/2 cup canned coconut milk
15ml/1 tbsp clear honey

SERVES 4–6

1 Peel the potatoes. Bring to the boil in salted water and simmer for about 15 minutes, or until tender. Cook the green beans for about 3–4 minutes. Drain the potatoes and beans and refresh under cold running water.

2 To make the peanut sauce, dry-fry the peanuts in a wok, or place under a moderate grill (broiler), tossing them all the time to prevent them from burning.

3 Turn the peanuts on to a clean cloth and rub them vigorously with your hands to remove the papery skins. Place the peanuts in a food processor and process for about 2 minutes until finely crushed.

4 Heat the vegetable oil in a wok and soften the shallots or onion, garlic and chillies without letting them colour. Add the shrimp paste or fish sauce, if using, together with the tamarind sauce, coconut milk and honey.

5 Simmer briefly, add to the blended peanuts and process to form a thick sauce. Transfer to a small serving bowl and keep hot.

6 Arrange the potatoes, green beans and all the other salad ingredients on a large serving platter. Serve with the bowl of peanut sauce and prawn crackers.

Cook's Tip

Shrimp paste, also known as terasi and blachan, is widely used throughout South-east Asia. It is made from fermented shrimp, pounded to a paste with salt.

COMPOSED SALADS

. . .

A composed salad makes a perfect appetizer or light main course for a special occasion. They are light and colourful and lend themselves to endless variation – and the components can often be prepared ahead for quick assembly.

Almost any combination of ingredients can be used – let your imagination and your palate guide you. Arranged attractively on a plate or in a bowl, this type of salad offers contrasting flavours, textures and colours. Raw or cooked vegetables, fresh fruits, hard-boiled hen's or quail's eggs, smoked or cooked poultry, meat, fish or shellfish can all be used, but it is important that the dressing or other kind of seasoning unites all the varied elements harmoniously.

Unlike a more basic tossed salad in which the leaves or vegetables are tossed together with a simple vinaigrette, the components of a composed salad are kept more separate and distinctive. The ingredients might be arranged in groups, sometimes on a bed of lettuce or other salad leaves, or simply arranged in circles or rows on the serving plates.

Prawn, Avocado and Citrus Salad

INGREDIENTS

15ml/1 tbsp lemon juice
15ml/1 tbsp lime juice
15ml/1 tbsp clear honey
45ml/3 tbsp olive oil
30–45ml/2–3 tbsp walnut oil
30ml/2 tbsp chopped fresh chives
450g/1lb large cooked prawns (shrimp), peeled and deveined
1 avocado, peeled, stoned (pitted) and cut into small dice
1 pink grapefruit, peeled and segmented
1 large navel orange, peeled and segmented
30ml/2 tbsp pine nuts, toasted
salt and freshly ground black pepper

SERVES 6

1 Blend the lemon and lime juices, salt and pepper and honey in a bowl. Gradually whisk in the olive oil, then the walnut oil, to make a creamy dressing. Stir in the chives.

2 Arrange the prawns with the avocado and grapefruit and orange segments on individual serving plates. Drizzle over the dressing, sprinkle with the toasted pine nuts, and serve.

Smoked Salmon Salad with Dill

INGREDIENTS

225g/8oz smoked salmon, thinly sliced
1 fennel bulb, thinly sliced
1 medium cucumber, seeded and cut into julienne strips
30ml/2 tbsp lemon juice
120ml/4fl oz/1/2 cup olive oil
30ml/2 tbsp chopped fresh dill, plus a few sprigs to garnish
freshly ground black pepper
caviar, to garnish (optional)

SERVES 4

1 Arrange the salmon slices on four serving plates and arrange the slices of fennel alongside, together with the cucumber strips.

2 Combine the lemon juice and pepper in a small bowl. Gradually whisk in the olive oil to make a creamy vinaigrette. Stir in the dill.

3 Spoon a little vinaigrette over the fennel and cucumber. Drizzle the remaining vinaigrette over the smoked salmon and garnish with sprigs of dill. Top each salad with a spoonful of caviar, if you like, before serving.

Chicory Salad with Roquefort

INGREDIENTS

30ml/2 tbsp red wine vinegar
5ml/1 tsp Dijon mustard
50ml/2oz/1/4 cup walnut oil
15–30ml/1–2 tbsp sunflower oil
2 chicory (Belgian endive) heads
1 celery heart or 4 celery sticks, cut into julienne strips
75g/3oz/3/4 cup walnut halves, lightly toasted
115g/4oz Roquefort cheese
salt and freshly ground black pepper
fresh parsley sprigs, to garnish

SERVES 4

1 Whisk together the vinegar, mustard and salt and pepper to taste in a small bowl. Slowly whisk in the oils, to make a vinaigrette.

2 Arrange the chicory on serving plates. Sprinkle over the celery and walnuts. Crumble the Roquefort on top of each salad, drizzle over a little vinaigrette, garnish and serve.

Clockwise from far right: Prawn, Avocado and Citrus Salad; Smoked Salmon Salad with Dill; and Chicory Salad with Roquefort.

WARM MONKFISH SALAD

. . .

Monkfish has a matchless flavour and benefits from being cooked simply. Teaming it with wilted baby spinach and toasted pine nuts is inspirational.

INGREDIENTS

2 monkfish fillets, about
350g/12oz each
25g/1oz/¹/₃ cup pine nuts
15ml/1 tbsp olive oil
15g/¹/₂oz/1 tbsp butter
225g/8oz baby spinach leaves,
washed and stalks removed
salt and freshly ground
black pepper

FOR THE DRESSING

5ml/1 tsp Dijon mustard
5ml/1 tsp sherry vinegar
60ml/4 tbsp olive oil
1 garlic clove, crushed

SERVES 4

1 Holding the knife at a slight angle, cut each monkfish fillet into 12 diagonal slices. Season lightly with salt and pepper and set aside.

2 Dry-fry the pine nuts in a heavy frying pan, shaking it occasionally, until golden brown. Do not burn. Transfer to a plate; set aside.

Variation
Substitute a variety of salad leaves for the spinach.

3 Make the dressing by whisking all the ingredients together until smooth and creamy. Pour it into a small pan, season to taste with salt and pepper and heat gently.

4 Heat the oil and butter in a ridged griddle pan or frying pan until sizzling. Add the fish; sauté for 20–30 seconds on each side.

5 Put the spinach leaves in a bowl and pour over the warm dressing. Sprinkle with the toasted pine nuts, reserving a few, and toss together well. Divide the spinach leaves among four plates and arrange the monkfish slices on top. Sprinkle the reserved pine nuts on top and serve.

ASPARAGUS AND LANGOUSTINE SALAD

∘ ∘ ∘

*For a really extravagant treat,
you could make this attractive
salad with medallions of lobster.
For a more economic version,
use large prawns, allowing six
per serving.*

INGREDIENTS

*16 langoustines
16 fresh asparagus spears, trimmed
2 carrots
30ml/2 tbsp olive oil
1 garlic clove, peeled
4 fresh tarragon sprigs and some
chopped, to garnish*

FOR THE DRESSING
*30ml/2 tbsp tarragon vinegar
120ml/4fl oz/¹/₂ cup olive oil
salt and freshly ground
black pepper*

SERVES 4

1 Peel the langoustines and keep the shells for stock. Set aside.

2 Steam the asparagus over boiling salted water until just tender, but still a little crisp. Refresh under cold water, drain and place in a shallow dish.

3 Peel the carrots and cut into fine julienne shreds. Cook in a pan of lightly salted boiling water for about 3 minutes, until tender but still crunchy. Drain, refresh under cold water, then drain again. Place in the dish with the asparagus.

4 Make the dressing. Whisk the tarragon vinegar with the oil. Season to taste with salt and pepper. Pour over the vegetables and leave to marinate.

5 Heat the oil with the garlic in a frying pan until very hot. Add the langoustines and sauté until just heated through. Discard the garlic.

6 Cut the asparagus spears in half and arrange on four individual plates with the carrots. Drizzle over the dressing left in the dish and top each portion with four langoustine tails. Top with the tarragon sprigs and sprinkle the chopped tarragon on top. Serve immediately.

THAI SCENTED FISH SALAD

∘ ∘ ∘

INGREDIENTS

350g/12oz fillet of red mullet, sea
bream or snapper
1 cos or romaine lettuce
1/2 lollo biondo lettuce
1 papaya or mango, peeled
and sliced
1 pitahaya, peeled and sliced
1 large tomato, cut into wedges
1/2 cucumber, peeled and cut
into strips
3 spring onions (scallions), sliced

FOR THE MARINADE
5ml/1 tsp coriander seeds
5ml/1 tsp fennel seeds
2.5ml/1/2 tsp cumin seeds
5ml/1 tsp caster (superfine) sugar
2.5ml/1/2 tsp hot chilli sauce
30ml/2 tbsp garlic oil
salt

FOR THE DRESSING
15ml/1 tbsp creamed coconut
(coconut cream)
60ml/4 tbsp groundnut (peanut) or
safflower oil
finely grated rind and juice of
1 lime
1 fresh red chilli, seeded and
finely chopped
5ml/1 tsp sugar
45ml/3 tbsp chopped fresh
coriander (cilantro)
salt

SERVES 4

1 Cut the fish into even strips and place them on a plate or in a shallow bowl.

2 To make the marinade, crush the coriander, fennel and cumin seeds together with the caster sugar. Add the chilli sauce, garlic oil and salt and combine.

3 Spread the marinade over the fish, cover and leave to stand in a cool place for at least 20 minutes – longer if you have time.

4 To make the dressing, place the creamed coconut and salt in a screw-top jar with 45ml/3 tbsp boiling water and leave to dissolve. Add the oil, lime rind and juice, chilli, sugar and chopped coriander. Shake well and set aside.

5 Combine the lettuce leaves with the papaya or mango, pitahaya, tomato, cucumber and spring onions. Toss with the dressing, then distribute among four large serving plates.

6 Heat a large, heavy non-stick frying-pan, add the fish and cook for 5 minutes, turning once. Place the cooked fish on the salad and serve immediately.

Cook's Tip
If planning ahead, you can leave the fish in the marinade for up to 8 hours. The dressing can also be made in advance, without the fresh coriander (cilantro). Store at room temperature and add the coriander just before assembling the salad.

SAN FRANCISCO SALAD

o o o

California is a salad-maker's paradise and is renowned for the healthiness of its produce. San Francisco has become the salad capital of California.

INGREDIENTS

900g/2 lb langoustines or scampi (extra large shrimp)
50g/2oz bulb fennel, sliced
2 medium tomatoes, quartered
4 small tomatoes
30ml/2 tbsp olive oil, plus extra for moistening the salad leaves
60ml/4 tbsp brandy
150ml/¼ pint/⅔ cup dry white wine
200ml/7fl oz can lobster or crab bisque
30ml/2 tbsp chopped fresh tarragon
45ml/3 tbsp double (heavy) cream
225g/8oz green beans, trimmed
2 oranges
175g/6oz lamb's lettuce
115g/4oz rocket (arugula) leaves
½ frisée lettuce
salt and cayenne pepper

SERVES 4

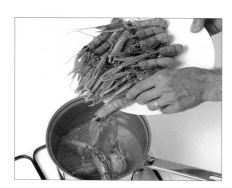

1 Bring a large pan of salted water to the boil, add the langoustines or scampi and simmer for 10 minutes. Refresh under cold running water.

2 Preheat the oven to 220°C/ 425°F/Gas 7. Twist the tails from all but four of the langoustines or scampi – reserve these to garnish the dish. Peel the outer shell from the tail meat. Put the tail peelings, carapace and claws in a heavy roasting pan with the fennel and medium tomatoes. Toss with the olive oil and roast near the top of the oven for 20 minutes to bring out the flavours.

3 Remove the roasting pan from the oven and place it over a moderate heat. Add the brandy and ignite to release the flavour of the alcohol. Add the white wine and simmer briefly.

4 Transfer the contents of the roasting pan to a food processor and reduce to a coarse purée: this will take only 10–15 seconds. Rub the purée through a fine nylon sieve into a bowl. Add the lobster or crab bisque, tarragon and cream. Season to taste with salt and a little cayenne pepper.

5 Bring a pan of salted water to the boil, add the beans and cook for 6 minutes. Drain and cool under cold running water. To segment the oranges, cut the peel from the top and bottom, and then from the sides, with a serrated knife. Loosen the segments by cutting between the membranes and the flesh with a small knife.

6 Moisten the salad leaves with olive oil and distribute among four serving plates. Fold the langoustine tails or scampi into the dressing and distribute among the plates. Add the beans, orange segments and small tomatoes. Garnish each plate with a whole langoustine or scampi and serve warm.

MILLIONAIRE'S LOBSTER SALAD

When money is no object and you're in a decadent mood, this salad is the perfect choice.

INGREDIENTS

1 medium lobster, live or cooked
1 bay leaf
1 fresh thyme sprig
675g/1½ lb new potatoes
2 ripe tomatoes
4 oranges
½ frisée lettuce
175g/6oz lamb's lettuce leaves
60ml/4 tbsp extra virgin olive oil
200g/7oz can young artichokes in brine, quartered
1 small bunch fresh tarragon, chervil or flat leaf parsley
salt

FOR THE DRESSING

30ml/2 tbsp frozen concentrated orange juice, thawed
75g/3oz/6 tbsp unsalted (sweet) butter, diced
salt and cayenne pepper

SERVES 4

1 If the lobster needs cooking, add it whole to a large pan of cold salted water with the bay leaf and thyme. Bring to the boil and simmer for 15 minutes. Cool under running water.

2 Twist off the legs and claws, and separate the tail from the body. Break the claws with a hammer and remove the meat. Cut the tail piece open, slice the meat and set aside.

3 Bring the potatoes to the boil in salted water and simmer for about 15 minutes, until tender. Drain, cover and keep warm.

4 Cut a cross in the skin of the tomatoes, cover with boiling water and leave for 30 seconds. Cool under cold running water and slip off the skins. Halve the tomatoes, discard the seeds, then cut the flesh into large dice.

5 To segment the oranges, remove the peel from the top, bottom and sides with a serrated knife. With a small paring knife, loosen the orange segments by cutting carefully between the flesh and the membranes, holding the fruit over a small bowl.

Variation

This dish is also delicious prepared in exactly the same way with crawfish, which is also known as langouste or rock lobster.

6 To make the dressing, pour the orange juice into a heatproof bowl and set it over a pan containing about 2.5cm/1in gently simmering water. Heat the juice for 1 minute, turn off the heat, then add the butter, a little at a time, whisking constantly, until the dressing reaches a coating consistency.

7 Season to taste with salt and a pinch of cayenne pepper, cover and keep warm.

8 Dress the salad leaves with olive oil, then divide among four large serving plates. Moisten the potatoes, artichokes and orange segments with olive oil and distribute among the leaves.

9 Lay the sliced lobster over the salad, spoon on the warm dressing, add the diced tomato and decorate with the fresh herbs. Serve the salad at room temperature.

GENOESE SQUID SALAD

. . .

INGREDIENTS

450g/1lb prepared squid,
cut into rings
4 garlic cloves, coarsely chopped
300ml/½ pint/1¼ cups Italian
red wine
450g/1lb waxy new
potatoes, scrubbed
225g/8oz green beans, trimmed
and cut into short lengths
2–3 sun-dried tomatoes in oil,
drained and thinly
sliced lengthways
60ml/4 tbsp extra virgin olive oil
15ml/1 tbsp red wine vinegar
salt and freshly ground
black pepper

SERVES 4–6

1 Preheat the oven to 180°C/
350°F/Gas 4. Put the squid rings in
an earthenware dish with half the
garlic, the wine and pepper to taste.
Cover and bake for 45 minutes, or
until the squid is tender.

2 Put the potatoes in a pan, cover
with cold water and add a good
pinch of salt. Bring to the boil,
cover and simmer over a low heat
for about 15 minutes, until tender.
Using a slotted spoon, lift out the
potatoes and set aside. Add the
beans to the boiling water and
cook for 3 minutes. Drain.

3 When the potatoes are cool
enough to handle, slice them
thickly on the diagonal and place
them in a bowl with the warm
beans and sun-dried tomatoes.
Whisk the oil, vinegar and the
remaining garlic in a jug (pitcher)
and add salt and pepper to taste.
Pour over the potato mixture.

4 Drain the squid and discard the
liquid. Add the squid to the potato
mixture and mix very gently.
Arrange on individual plates and
season liberally with pepper.

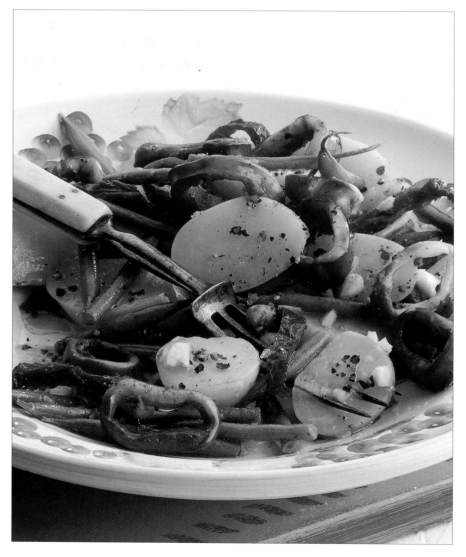

Cook's Tip

The French potato called
Charlotte is perfect for this
salad because it retains its
shape when boiled.
Prepared squid can be bought
from supermarkets with
fresh fish counters, and
from fishmongers.

TUNA CARPACCIO

° ° °

Fillet of beef is most often used for carpaccio, but meaty fish, such as tuna and swordfish, make a change. The secret is to slice the fish wafer thin.

INGREDIENTS

2 fresh tuna steaks, about 450g/1lb total weight
60ml/4 tbsp extra virgin olive oil
15ml/1 tbsp balsamic vinegar
5ml/1 tsp caster (superfine) sugar
30ml/2 tbsp bottled green peppercorns or capers, drained
salt and freshly ground black pepper
lemon wedges and green salad, to serve

SERVES 4

1 Remove the skin from each tuna steak and place each steak between two sheets of clear film (plastic wrap) or baking parchment. Pound with the side of a rolling pin or the flat side of a meat mallet until the steak is flattened slightly.

2 Roll up the tuna steaks as tightly as possible, then wrap tightly in clear film. Place the tuna steaks in the freezer for about 4 hours, or until firm.

Cook's Tip
Don't skimp the freezing, as this makes it possible to cut wafer-thin slices of tuna.

3 Unwrap the tuna and cut crossways into the thinnest possible slices. Arrange the slices on four individual serving plates.

4 Whisk together the oil, vinegar, sugar and peppercorns or capers, season to taste with salt and pepper and pour over the tuna. Cover and allow to come to room temperature for 30 minutes before serving with lemon wedges and green salad.

Cook's Tip
Raw fish is safe to eat as long as it is very fresh, so check with your fishmonger before purchase and make and serve the carpaccio the same day. Do not buy fish that has been frozen and thawed.

SALADE MOUCLADE

° ° ° °

Mouclade is a famous dish from La Rochelle in South-west France. It consists of mussels in a light curry cream sauce. Here the flavours appear in a salad of warm lentils and spinach.

INGREDIENTS

45ml/3 tbsp olive oil
1 onion, finely chopped
350g/12oz/1½ cups Puy or green lentils
900ml/1½ pints/3¾ cups vegetable stock
2 kg/4½lb fresh mussels in their shells
75ml/5 tbsp white wine
2.5ml/½ tsp curry paste
pinch of saffron
30ml/2 tbsp double (heavy) cream
2 large carrots, peeled
4 celery sticks
900g/2lb young spinach, stalks removed
15ml/1 tbsp garlic oil
salt and cayenne pepper

SERVES 4

1 Heat the oil in a heavy pan and cook the onion for 6–8 minutes, until soft, but not coloured. Add the lentils and vegetable stock, bring to the boil, lower the heat and simmer for 45 minutes, until tender. Remove from the heat and set aside to cool.

2 Clean the mussels thoroughly, discarding any that are damaged. Any that are open should close if given a sharp tap; if they fail to do so, discard these too.

3 Place the mussels in a large pan, add the wine, cover and steam over a high heat, shaking the pan occasionally, for 12 minutes. Strain the mussels in a colander, reserving the cooking liquid. Discard any that have not opened during the cooking. Take all but four of the mussels out of their shells.

4 Strain the mussel liquid through a fine sieve or muslin (cheesecloth) into a wide, shallow pan to remove any grit or sand.

5 Add the curry paste and saffron to the pan, then reduce the liquid over a high heat until the pan is almost dry. Remove from the heat, stir in the cream, season to taste with salt and pepper and combine with the mussels.

6 Cut the carrot and celery into 5cm/2in batons and cook in lightly salted boiling water for 3 minutes. Drain well, cool and moisten with olive oil.

7 Wash the spinach, put the wet leaves into a large pan, cover and steam for 30 seconds. Immerse in cold water, then press the leaves dry in a colander. Moisten with garlic oil and season.

8 Spoon the lentils into the centre of four plates. Place heaps of spinach around the edge, with some carrot and celery on top. Spoon over the mussels and garnish with the reserved mussels in their shells.

HOT COCONUT, PRAWN AND PAPAYA SALAD

Transport yourself to the Far East with this wonderful dish.

INGREDIENTS

225g/8oz raw or cooked prawn (shrimp) tails, peeled and deveined
2 ripe papayas
225g/8oz cos or romaine or iceberg lettuce leaves, Chinese leaves (Chinese cabbage) and young spinach leaves
1 firm tomato, peeled, seeded and coarsely chopped
3 spring onions (scallions), shredded
1 small bunch fresh coriander (cilantro), shredded, and 1 large chilli, sliced, to garnish

FOR THE DRESSING
15ml/1 tbsp creamed coconut (coconut cream)
90ml/6 tbsp vegetable oil
juice of 1 lime
2.5ml/1/2 tsp hot chilli sauce
10ml/2 tsp Thai fish sauce
5ml/1 tsp sugar

SERVES 4–6

2 If using raw prawn tails, cover with cold water in a pan, bring to the boil and simmer for no longer than 2 minutes. Drain thoroughly and set aside. If using cooked prawns, pat dry with kitchen paper.

3 Cut the papayas in half from top to bottom and remove the black seeds. Peel off the skin and cut the flesh into equal-size pieces.

4 Place the salad leaves in a bowl. Add the prawn tails, papayas, tomato and spring onions. Pour over the dressing, garnish with the coriander and chilli, and serve.

1 To make the dressing, place the creamed coconut in a screw-top jar and add 30ml/2 tbsp boiling water to soften it. Add the oil, lime juice, chilli sauce, fish sauce and sugar. Shake well to mix and set aside. Do not chill.

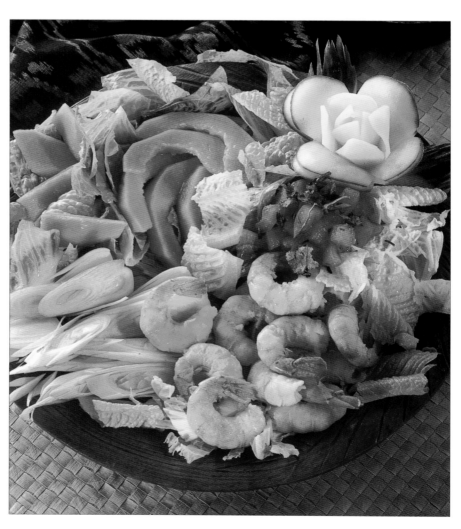

Roasted Chicken and Walnut Salad

The chickens may be cooked the day before eating and the salad finished on the day itself.

INGREDIENTS

4 fresh tarragon or rosemary sprigs
2 x 1.75kg/4–4¹/₂lb chickens
65g/2¹/₂oz/5 tbsp softened butter
150ml/¹/₄ pint/²/₃ cup chicken stock
150ml/¹/₄ pint/²/₃ cup white wine
115g/4oz/1 cup walnut pieces
1 small cantaloupe melon
lettuce leaves
450g/1 lb seedless grapes or pitted cherries
salt and freshly ground black pepper

FOR THE DRESSING
30ml/2 tbsp tarragon vinegar
120ml/4fl oz/¹/₂ cup light olive oil
30ml/2 tbsp chopped fresh mixed herbs such as parsley, mint, tarragon

SERVES 8

1 Preheat the oven to 200°C/ 400°F/Gas 6. Put the herb sprigs inside the chickens and season with salt and pepper.

2 Spread the chickens with 50g/ 2oz/4 tbsp of the softened butter, place in a roasting pan and pour the stock around them. Cover loosely with foil and roast for about 1¹/₂ hours, basting twice, until browned and the juices run clear. Remove from the roasting pan and leave to cool.

3 Add the wine to the roasting pan. Bring to the boil over a medium heat and cook until syrupy. Strain and leave to cool. Heat the remaining butter in a frying pan and gently fry the walnuts until lightly browned. Scoop the melon flesh into balls or cut into cubes.

4 To make the dressing, whisk the vinegar and olive oil together with a little salt and pepper to taste. Skim off the fat from the chicken juices and add the juices to the dressing with the herbs. Adjust the seasoning to taste.

5 Cut the chicken into serving portions and arrange them on a bed of lettuce leaves. Sprinkle over the grapes or cherries and melon balls or cubes and spoon over the dressing. Sprinkle with the toasted walnuts and serve.

CHICKEN LIVER SALAD

. . .

This delicious salad may be served as a main course for a summer lunch party, or as a tasty first course served on individual plates.

INGREDIENTS

mixed salad leaves, such as frisée, oak leaf lettuce, radicchio, rocket (arugula)
1 avocado
30ml/2 tbsp lemon or lime juice
2 pink grapefruit
350g/12oz chicken livers
30ml/2 tbsp olive oil
1 garlic clove, crushed
salt and freshly ground black pepper
whole fresh chives, to garnish

FOR THE DRESSING
30ml/2 tbsp lemon juice
60ml/4 tbsp olive oil
2.5ml/½ tsp wholegrain mustard
2.5ml/½ tsp clear honey
15ml/1 tbsp chopped fresh chives
salt and freshly ground black pepper

SERVES 4

1 To make the dressing, put the lemon juice, olive oil, wholegrain mustard, honey and fresh chives into a screw-top jar, and shake vigorously. Season to taste with salt and freshly ground black pepper.

2 Arrange the mixed salad leaves attractively on a large serving plate.

3 Peel and stone (pit) the avocado, dice the flesh and mix with the lemon or lime juice to prevent it from browning. Add to the plate of mixed leaves.

4 Peel the grapefruit with a small serrated knife, removing as much of the white pith as possible. Split into segments and arrange with the salad leaves and avocado on the serving plate.

5 Pat dry the chicken livers on kitchen paper and remove any unwanted pieces.

6 Using a sharp knife, cut the larger chicken livers in half. Leave the smaller ones whole.

> ### Cook's Tip
> If using frozen chicken livers, thaw them thoroughly first.

7 Heat the oil in a large frying pan. Stir-fry the chicken livers and garlic briskly until the livers are brown all over (they should be slightly pink inside).

8 Season the chicken livers to taste with salt and black pepper, remove from the pan and drain well on kitchen paper.

9 Place the chicken livers, while still warm, on the salad leaves and spoon over the dressing. Garnish with the whole chives and serve the salad immediately.

GRILLED CHICKEN SALAD WITH LAVENDER

Lavender may seem an odd ingredient, but its delightful scent has a natural affinity with garlic, orange and other herbs.

INGREDIENTS

4 boneless, skinless chicken breast portions
900ml/1½ pints/3¾ cups light chicken stock
175g/6oz/1 cup fine polenta or cornmeal
50g/2oz/4 tbsp butter
450g/1 lb young spinach leaves
175g/6oz lamb's lettuce leaves
8 small tomatoes, halved
salt and ground black pepper
8 fresh lavender sprigs, to garnish

FOR THE LAVENDER MARINADE
6 fresh lavender flowers
10ml/2 tsp finely grated orange rind
2 garlic cloves, crushed
10ml/2 tsp clear honey
30ml/2 tbsp olive oil
10ml/2 tsp chopped fresh thyme
10ml/2 tsp chopped fresh marjoram
salt

SERVES 4

2 To prepare the polenta, bring the chicken stock to the boil in a large, heavy pan. Add the polenta or cornmeal in a slow, steady stream, stirring constantly, until thick: this will take 2–3 minutes. Turn the cooked polenta out on to a 2.5cm/1in deep buttered tray and leave to cool.

3 Heat the grill (broiler) to a moderate temperature. If using a barbecue, let the embers settle to a steady glow. Grill (broil) the chicken breast portions for about 15 minutes, turning them once.

4 Cut the cooled polenta into 2.5cm/1in cubes with a wet knife. Heat the remaining butter in a large frying pan and fry the polenta cubes until golden brown.

5 Divide the salad leaves and tomatoes among four large serving plates. Slice each chicken breast portion and lay over the salad. Place the polenta cubes among the salad and season to taste with salt and pepper. Garnish with the sprigs of lavender and serve.

1 To make the marinade, strip the lavender flowers from their stems and combine with the orange rind, garlic, honey and a pinch of salt. Add the olive oil, thyme and marjoram. Slash the chicken deeply, spread over the mixture and leave to marinate in a cool place for at least 20 minutes.

Cook's Tip
This lavender marinade is a delicious flavouring for salt-water fish as well as chicken. Try it spread over grilled cod, haddock, halibut, sea bass or bream.

DIJON CHICKEN SALAD

° ° °

This attractive and classical dish is ideal to serve for a simple but tasty and elegant lunch.

INGREDIENTS

4 skinless, boneless chicken breast portions
mixed salad leaves such as frisée, oakleaf lettuce and radicchio

FOR THE MARINADE
30ml/2 tbsp tarragon wine vinegar
5ml/1 tsp Dijon mustard
5ml/1 tsp clear honey
90ml/6 tbsp olive oil
salt and freshly ground black pepper

FOR THE MUSTARD DRESSING
30ml/2 tbsp Dijon mustard
3 garlic cloves, crushed
15ml/1 tbsp grated onion
60ml/4 tbsp white wine

SERVES 4

3 Turn the chicken over in the marinade to coat completely, cover with clear film (plastic wrap) and chill in the refrigerator overnight.

4 Preheat the oven to 190°C/375°F/Gas 5. Transfer the chicken and the marinade into an ovenproof dish, cover with kitchen foil and bake for about 35 minutes, or until tender. Leave the chicken to cool in the liquid.

6 Thinly slice the chicken and fan out the slices.

7 Arrange the chicken slices on a serving dish with the salad leaves. Spoon over some of the mustard dressing and serve. Serve the rest of the dressing separately in a bowl or jug (pitcher).

1 To make the marinade mix the vinegar, mustard, honey and olive oil, together in a shallow glass or earthenware dish that is large enough to hold the chicken breasts in a single layer. Season to taste with salt and pepper.

2 Add the chicken breast portions to the dish, making sure they do not overlap each other.

5 To make the mustard dressing, put all the ingredients into a screw-top jar and shake vigorously.

Cook's Tip
The dressing can be made several days in advance and stored in the refrigerator.

DUCK AND PASTA SALAD

° ° °

The acidity of fruit is a very good accompaniment to a rich meat, such as duck, as it adds a tartness that makes the meat more digestible. This luxurious salad includes apple, orange and, in the dressing, dried cherries. The rigatoni adds a welcome element of carbohydrate and makes the dish a complete meal.

INGREDIENTS

2 boneless duck breast fillets
5ml/1 tsp coriander seeds, crushed
350g/12oz dried rigatoni
1 eating apple, diced
2 oranges, segmented
salt and freshly ground black pepper
fresh chopped coriander (cilantro) and mint, to garnish

FOR THE DRESSING

150ml/¼ pint/⅔ cup orange juice
15ml/1 tbsp lemon juice
10ml/2 tsp clear honey
1 shallot, finely chopped
1 garlic clove, crushed
1 celery stick, chopped
75g/3oz/¾ cup dried cherries
45ml/3 tbsp port
15ml/1 tbsp chopped fresh mint
30ml/2 tbsp chopped fresh coriander (cilantro)

SERVES 6

1 Preheat the grill (broiler). Remove the skin and fat from the duck breast fillets, season with salt and pepper and rub with the crushed coriander seeds.

2 Grill (broil) the duck fillets for 7–10 minutes (depending on the size). Wrap the duck fillets in foil and leave for 20 minutes.

3 Cook the pasta in a large pan of lightly salted, boiling water for 8–10 minutes, until *al dente*. Drain thoroughly and rinse under cold running water. Set the pasta aside to cool.

4 To make the dressing, put the orange juice, lemon juice, honey, shallot, garlic, celery, cherries, port, mint and fresh coriander into a small bowl. Whisk together, cover with clear film (plastic wrap) and leave to marinate for 30 minutes.

5 Unwrap the duck fillets from the foil and, using a very sharp carving knife, slice the duck very thinly. (It should still be slightly pink in the centre.)

6 Put the pasta into a large mixing bowl, add the dressing, diced apple and segments of orange. Toss well to coat the pasta.

7 Transfer the salad to a serving plate with the duck slices and garnish with the chopped coriander and mint.

DUCK SALAD WITH ORANGE SAUCE

° ° °

The rich, gamey flavour of duck provides the foundation for this delicious salad.

INGREDIENTS

1 small orange
2 boneless duck breast fillets
150ml/¼ pint/⅔ cup dry white wine
5ml/1 tsp ground coriander seeds
2.5ml/½ tsp ground cumin or fennel seeds
30ml/2 tbsp caster (superfine) sugar
juice of ½ small lime or lemon
75g/3oz day-old bread, thickly sliced
45ml/3 tbsp garlic oil
½ escarole lettuce
½ frisée lettuce
30ml/2 tbsp sunflower oil
salt and cayenne pepper
4 sprigs fresh coriander (cilantro), to garnish

SERVES 4

1 Halve the orange and slice thickly. Discard any seeds and place the slices in a small pan. Cover with water, bring to the boil and simmer for 5 minutes. Drain the orange slices and set aside.

2 Pierce the skin of the duck fillets diagonally with a small knife (this will help release the fat). Rub the skin with salt.

3 Place a steel or cast-iron frying pan over a steady heat and cook the fillets for 20 minutes, turning once, until they are medium-rare. Transfer to a warm plate, cover and keep warm.

4 Heat the sediment in the frying pan until it begins to darken and caramelize. Add the dry white wine and stir constantly to loosen the sediment. Add the ground coriander, cumin or fennel seeds, sugar and orange slices.

5 Boil quickly and reduce to a coating consistency. Sharpen with the lime or lemon juice and season to taste with salt and cayenne pepper. Transfer the orange sauce to a bowl, cover and keep warm.

6 Remove the crusts from the bread and cut the bread into short fingers. Heat the garlic oil in a heavy frying pan and brown the croûtons. Season with salt, then turn out on to kitchen paper.

7 Moisten the salad leaves with a little sunflower oil and distribute them equally among four large serving plates.

8 Slice the duck diagonally with a carving knife. Divide the meat into four and lift on to each salad plate. Spoon on the orange sauce, sprinkle the salad with croûtons, decorate with a sprig of fresh coriander and serve warm.

APRICOT DUCK WITH BEANSPROUT SALAD

*Duck is rich in fat, so it stays beautifully moist when cooked on a barbecue,
while any excess fat drains away.*

INGREDIENTS

4 duck breast fillets, with skin
1 small red onion, thinly sliced
115g/4oz/³⁄4 cup ready-to-eat
dried apricots
15ml/1 tbsp clear honey
5ml/1 tsp sesame oil
10ml/2 tsp ground star anise
salt and freshly ground
black pepper

FOR THE SALAD

2 spring onions (scallions)
½ head Chinese leaves (Chinese
cabbage), finely shredded
150g/5oz/2 cups beansprouts
15ml/1 tbsp light soy sauce
15ml/1 tbsp groundnut (peanut) oil
5ml/1 tsp sesame oil
5ml/1 tsp clear honey

SERVES 4

1 Place the duck breast fillets, skin side down, on a chopping board or clean work surface and cut a long slit down one side of each one with a sharp kitchen knife, cutting almost through, to form a large pocket.

2 Tuck the slices of onion and the apricots inside the pocket and press the breast firmly back into shape. Secure with metal skewers.

3 Mix together the clear honey and sesame oil and brush generously over the duck, particularly the skin. Sprinkle over the star anise and season with plenty of salt and fresh black pepper.

4 To make the salad, shred the spring onions, then mix together with the shredded Chinese leaves and beansprouts in a large bowl.

5 Shake together all the salad dressing ingredients in a screw-topped jar. Season to taste with salt and pepper. Toss into the salad.

6 Cook the duck under a medium-hot grill (broiler) or on a barbecue for 12–15 minutes, turning once, until golden brown on the outside.

Cook's Tip

If you prefer not to eat the beansprouts raw, they can be blanched by plunging them into boiling water for 1 minute. Drain and refresh in cold water.

SESAME DUCK AND NOODLE SALAD

° ° °

This salad is a complete meal in itself and makes a wonderful summer lunch. The marinade is a marvellous blend of South-east Asian flavours.

INGREDIENTS

2 duck breast fillets
15ml/1 tbsp sunflower oil
150g/5oz sugar snap peas
2 carrots, cut into 7.5cm/3in sticks
225g/8oz medium egg noodles
6 spring onions (scallions), sliced
salt
30ml/2 tbsp fresh coriander
(cilantro) leaves,
to garnish

FOR THE MARINADE
15ml/1 tbsp sesame oil
5ml/1 tsp ground coriander
5ml/1 tsp Chinese five-
spice powder

FOR THE DRESSING
15ml/1 tbsp vinegar
5ml/1 tsp soft light brown sugar
5ml/1 tsp soy sauce
1 garlic clove, crushed
15ml/1 tbsp sesame seeds, toasted
45ml/3 tbsp sunflower oil
30ml/2 tbsp sesame oil
freshly ground black pepper

SERVES 4

1 Slice the duck breast fillets thinly across and place in a shallow dish. Mix together all the ingredients for the marinade, pour over the duck and turn well to coat thoroughly. Cover with clear film (plastic wrap) and leave in a cool place for about 30 minutes.

2 Heat the oil in a frying pan, add the slices of duck and stir-fry for 3–4 minutes, until cooked. Remove from the pan and set aside.

3 Bring a pan of lightly salted water to the boil. Place the sugar snap peas and carrots in a steamer that will fit on top of the pan. When the water boils, add the noodles. Place the steamer on top and steam the vegetables while cooking the noodles.

4 Set the steamed vegetables aside. Drain the noodles, refresh under cold running water and drain again. Place them in a large serving bowl.

5 To make the dressing, mix the vinegar, sugar, soy sauce, garlic and sesame seeds in a bowl. Add a generous grinding of pepper, then whisk in the oils.

6 Pour the dressing over the egg noodles and toss well to mix. Add the sugar snap peas, carrots, spring onions and duck slices and toss again to mix. Sprinkle the fresh coriander leaves over the top and serve immediately.

GRILLED SPICED QUAIL WITH MIXED LEAF AND MUSHROOM SALAD

· · ·

This is a perfect supper dish for autumnal entertaining. Quail is at its best when the breast meat is removed from the carcass, so that it cooks quickly and can be served rare.

INGREDIENTS

8 quail breast portions
50g/2oz/¼ cup butter
5ml/1 tsp paprika
salt and freshly ground
black pepper

FOR THE SALAD
60ml/4 tbsp walnut oil
30ml/2 tbsp olive oil
45ml/3 tbsp balsamic vinegar
25g/1oz/2 tbsp butter
75g/3oz/generous 1 cup chanterelle
mushrooms, sliced if large
25g/1oz/3 tbsp walnut
halves, toasted
115g/4oz mixed salad leaves

SERVES 4

1 Preheat the grill (broiler). Arrange the quail portions on the grill rack, skin sides up. Dot with half the butter and sprinkle with half the paprika and a little salt.

2 Grill (broil) the quail portions for 3 minutes. Turn and dot with the remaining butter and sprinkle with the remaining paprika and a little salt. Grill for a further 3 minutes, or until cooked. Transfer to a warmed dish, cover and set aside.

3 To make the dressing, whisk the oils with the balsamic vinegar, then season to taste with salt and pepper.

Cook's Tip
Take care when toasting the walnuts as they scorch quickly. The best way to toast them is to heat a non-stick frying pan until hot. Add the walnuts and cook for 3–5 minutes, or until golden, turning them frequently.

4 Melt the butter in a frying pan. Cook the chanterelles for about 3 minutes, or until just beginning to soften. Add the walnuts and heat through. Remove from the heat.

5 Thinly slice the cooked quail portions and arrange them on four individual serving plates with the chanterelles, walnuts and mixed salad leaves. Drizzle the oil and vinegar dressing over the salad and serve warm.

PROSCIUTTO SALAD WITH AN AVOCADO FAN

Avocados are amazingly versatile, but they are at their most elegant when sliced thinly and fanned on a plate.

INGREDIENTS

3 avocados
150g/5oz prosciutto
75–115g/3–4oz rocket
(arugula) leaves
24 marinated black olives, drained

FOR THE DRESSING

15ml/1 tbsp balsamic vinegar
5ml/1 tsp lemon juice
5ml/1 tsp prepared English
(hot) mustard
5ml/1 tsp sugar
75ml/5 tbsp olive oil
salt and freshly ground
black pepper

SERVES 4

1 To make the dressing, combine the balsamic vinegar, lemon juice, mustard and sugar in a bowl. Gradually whisk in the olive oil, season to taste with salt and pepper and set aside.

2 Cut two of the avocados in half. Remove and discard the stones (pits) and skins, and cut the flesh into 1cm/½in thick slices. Gently toss with half the dressing. Place the prosciutto, avocado slices and rocket leaves on four serving plates. Sprinkle the olives and the remaining dressing over the top.

3 Halve, stone (pit) and peel the remaining avocado. Slice each half lengthways into eighths. Gently draw a cannelle knife across the quarters at 1cm/½in intervals to create regular stripes.

4 Using a sharp knife, make four cuts lengthways down each avocado eighth, leaving 1cm/½in intact at the end. Carefully fan out the slices and arrange one fan on the side of each plate.

MELON AND PROSCIUTTO SALAD

Sections of cool, fragrant melon covered with thin slices of air-dried ham – a classic appetizer.

INGREDIENTS

1 large melon (cantaloupe or Charentais)
175g/6oz prosciutto, thinly sliced

FOR THE SALSA
225g/8oz strawberries
5ml/1 tsp caster (superfine) sugar
30ml/2 tbsp sunflower oil
15ml/1 tbsp orange juice
2.5ml/½ tsp finely grated orange rind
2.5ml/½ tsp grated fresh root ginger
salt and freshly ground black pepper

SERVES 4

1 Halve the melon and take the seeds out with a spoon. Cut the rind away with a paring knife, then slice the melon flesh thickly. Cover with clear film (plastic wrap) and chill until ready to serve.

2 To make the salsa, hull the strawberries and cut them into large dice. Place in a small mixing bowl with the sugar and crush lightly to release the juices. Add the sunflower oil, orange juice and rind and ginger. Season with salt and a generous twist of pepper.

3 Arrange the melon slices on a serving plate and lay the prosciutto over the top. Serve the salsa separately in a small bowl.

WILD MUSHROOM SALAD WITH PROSCIUTTO

· ○ ○

Autumn provides a wealth of ingredients for the salad maker. Most treasured of all are wild mushrooms, found mainly in deciduous woodland. If you are not familiar with edible species, larger supermarkets and specialist delicatessens often sell a wide range.

INGREDIENTS
175g/6oz prosciutto, thickly sliced
½ oak leaf lettuce
½ frisée lettuce
15ml/1 tbsp walnut oil
40g/1½oz/3 tbsp butter
450g/1lb wild or cultivated mushrooms such as chanterelles, field blewits, oyster mushrooms, champignons de Paris, sliced
60ml/4 tbsp brandy
salt and freshly ground black pepper

FOR THE HERB PANCAKE
45ml/3 tbsp plain (all-purpose) flour
75ml/5 tbsp milk
1 egg, plus 1 egg yolk
60ml/4 tbsp grated Parmesan cheese
45ml/3 tbsp chopped fresh mixed herbs such as parsley, thyme, tarragon, marjoram, chives

SERVES 4

1 To make the pancakes, combine the flour with the milk in a jug (pitcher). Beat in the egg and egg yolk with the Parmesan and herbs. Season with salt and pepper. Place a non-stick frying pan over a steady heat. Pour in enough batter to coat the base of the pan.

2 When the batter has set, turn the pancake over and cook briefly on the other side. Turn the pancake out and leave to cool. Continue until you have used all the batter.

3 Roll the pancakes together and cut into 1cm/½in ribbons. Cut the prosciutto into ribbons and toss with the pancake ribbons.

4 Moisten the salad leaves with the walnut oil and divide among four plates. Place the pancake and prosciutto ribbons in the centre.

5 Melt the butter in a heavy frying pan. Add the mushrooms and cook for 6–8 minutes. Add the brandy and ignite with a match or taper. When the flames have subsided, spoon the mushrooms on to the salad, season to taste with salt and pepper and serve immediately while still warm.

WARM SALAD OF BAYONNE HAM AND NEW POTATOES

○   ○   ○

INGREDIENTS

*225g/8oz new potatoes, halved
if large
50g/2oz green beans
115g/4oz young spinach leaves
2 spring onions (scallions), sliced
4 eggs, hard-boiled, shelled
and quartered
50g/2oz Bayonne ham, cut
into strips
juice of ¹/₂ lemon
salt and freshly ground
black pepper*

FOR THE DRESSING

*60ml/4 tbsp olive oil
5ml/1 tsp ground turmeric
5ml/1 tsp ground cumin
50g/2oz/¹/₂ cup shelled hazelnuts*

SERVES 4

1 Cook the potatoes in salted boiling water for 10–15 minutes, or until tender, then drain well. Cook the beans in salted boiling water for 2 minutes, then drain.

2 Toss the potatoes and green beans with the spinach and spring onions in a bowl.

3 Arrange the egg quarters on the salad and sprinkle the strips of ham over the top. Sprinkle with the lemon juice and season with plenty of salt and pepper.

4 Heat the dressing ingredients in a large frying pan and cook, stirring frequently, until the nuts turn golden. Pour the hot, nutty dressing over the salad and serve before the leaves wilt.

Variation

Replace the potatoes with a 400g/14oz can drained and rinsed mixed beans and peas.

PERUVIAN SALAD

° ° °

This really is a spectacular-looking salad. It could be served as a side dish or would make a delicious light lunch. In Peru, white rice would be used, but brown rice adds an interesting texture and flavour.

INGREDIENTS

*225g/8oz/2 cups cooked long grain brown or white rice
15ml/1 tbsp chopped fresh parsley
1 red (bell) pepper, halved and seeded
1 small onion, sliced into rings
olive oil, for sprinkling
115g/4oz green beans, halved
50g/2oz/½ cup baby corn cobs
4 quail's eggs, hard-boiled
25–50g/1–2oz Spanish ham, cut into thin slices (optional)
1 small avocado
lemon juice, for sprinkling
75g/3oz mixed salad leaves
15ml/1 tbsp capers
about 10 stuffed olives, halved*

FOR THE DRESSING

*1 garlic clove, crushed
60ml/4 tbsp olive oil
45ml/3 tbsp sunflower oil
30ml/2 tbsp lemon juice
45ml/3 tbsp natural (plain) yogurt
2.5ml/½ tsp mustard
2.5ml/½ tsp sugar
salt and freshly ground black pepper*

SERVES 4

1 To make the dressing, whisk all the ingredients in a bowl with a fork until smooth.

2 Put the rice in a large salad bowl and spoon in half the dressing. Stir in the parsley and set aside.

3 Place the pepper, cut side down, in a small roasting pan. Add the onion rings. Sprinkle the onion with a little olive oil and place the pan under a hot grill (broiler) for 5–6 minutes until the pepper blackens and blisters and the onion turns golden. Stir the onion once or twice so that it cooks evenly.

4 Stir the sliced onion into the rice. Put the pepper in a plastic bag and knot the bag. When cool enough to handle, peel the pepper halves and cut the flesh into thin strips.

5 Cook the green beans in boiling water for 2 minutes, then add the corn and cook for 1–2 minutes more, until tender. Drain, refresh under cold water, then drain again. Place the vegetables in a mixing bowl and add the pepper strips, quail's eggs and ham, if using.

6 Peel the avocado, remove the stone (pit) and cut the flesh into slices or chunks. Sprinkle with the lemon juice. Put the salad leaves in a separate mixing bowl, add the avocado and mix lightly. Arrange the mixture on top of the rice.

7 Stir about 45ml/3 tbsp of the remaining dressing into the green bean and pepper mixture. Pile this on top of the avocado mixture.

8 Sprinkle the capers and stuffed olives on top and serve the salad with the remaining dressing.

BEEF AND HERBY PASTA SALAD

° ° °

Marinated beef is grilled and served warm with pasta salad.

INGREDIENTS
450g/1lb beef fillet
450 g/1 lb fresh tagliatelle with
sun-dried tomatoes and herbs
115g/4oz cherry tomatoes
½ cucumber

FOR THE MARINADE
15ml/1 tbsp soy sauce
15ml/1 tbsp sherry
5ml/1 tsp grated fresh root ginger
1 garlic clove, crushed

FOR THE HERB DRESSING
30ml/2 tbsp horseradish sauce
150ml/¼ pint/⅔ cup natural
(plain) yogurt
1 garlic clove, crushed
30–45ml/2–3 tbsp chopped fresh
mixed herbs such as chives,
parsley, thyme
salt and freshly ground
black pepper

SERVES 6

1 To make the marinade, mix all the ingredients together in a shallow dish. Add the beef fillet and turn to coat well. Cover with clear film (plastic wrap) and leave in a cool place for 30 minutes to allow the flavours to penetrate the meat.

2 Preheat the grill (broiler). Lift the fillet out of the marinade and pat it dry with kitchen paper. Place the fillet on a grill (broiler) rack and grill (broil) for 8 minutes on each side, basting with the marinade.

3 Transfer the fillet to a plate, cover with foil and leave to stand for 20 minutes.

4 To make the herb dressing, put all the ingredients into a bowl and mix thoroughly. Cook the pasta in a large pan of lightly salted boiling water according to the packet instructions until it is *al dente*. Drain thoroughly, rinse under cold water and leave to dry.

5 Halve the cherry tomatoes. Cut the cucumber in half lengthways, scoop out the seeds with a teaspoon and slice the flesh thinly into crescents.

6 Put the tagliatelle, tomato halves, cucumber and dressing into a mixing bowl and toss to coat. Slice the beef and arrange on individual serving plates with the pasta salad. Serve warm.

ROCKBURGER SALAD WITH SESAME CROÛTONS

° ° °

This salad plays on the ingredients that make up the all-American beefburger.

INGREDIENTS

900g/2 lb lean minced (ground) beef
1 egg
1 medium onion, finely chopped
10ml/2 tsp Dijon mustard
2.5ml/½ tsp celery salt
115g/4oz Roquefort or other blue cheese
1 large sesame seed loaf
45ml/3 tbsp olive oil
1 small iceberg lettuce
50g/2oz rocket (arugula) leaves
120ml/4fl oz/½ cup French Dressing
4 ripe tomatoes, quartered
4 spring onions (scallions), sliced
freshly ground black pepper

SERVES 4

2 Flatten the pieces between two sheets of plastic or waxed paper to form 13cm/5in rounds.

5 Grill (broil) the burgers at the same temperature for 10 minutes, turning once.

3 Place 15g/½oz of the blue cheese on eight of the burgers. Sandwich with the remaining burgers and press the edges firmly. Stack the burgers between sheets of plastic or waxed paper and chill until ready to cook.

6 Toss the salad leaves with the French Dressing, then distribute among four large serving plates. Place two rockburgers in the centre of each plate and arrange the tomatoes, spring onions and sesame croûtons around the edge.

1 Place the minced beef, egg, onion, mustard, celery salt and pepper in a mixing bowl. Combine thoroughly. Divide the mixture into 16 equal portions.

4 To make the sesame croûtons, preheat the grill (broiler) to a moderate temperature. Remove the sesame seed crust from the loaf, then cut the crust into short fingers. Moisten with olive oil and toast evenly for 10–15 minutes.

Cook's Tip

If you can't find a sesame seed loaf, use a French stick. Cut the stick into slices of about 1cm/½in, brush with olive oil and place on a baking sheet. Bake in the oven on a low heat for about 15 minutes until the bread rounds are crisp and golden.

THAI BEEF SALAD

A hearty salad of beef and crunchy vegetables, laced with a tangy chilli and lime dressing.
Cooking the meat on the barbecue would give a truly delicious flavour to the salad.

INGREDIENTS

2 sirloin steaks, about
225g/8oz each
1 red onion, thinly sliced
1/2 cucumber, thinly sliced
into batons
1 lemon grass stalk, finely chopped
30ml/2 tbsp chopped spring
onions (scallions)
juice of 2 limes
15–30ml/1–2 tbsp Thai fish sauce
2–4 red chillies, thinly sliced, fresh
coriander (cilantro), Chinese
mustard cress and mint, to garnish

SERVES 4

1 Pan-fry the beef steaks or cook on the barbecue until medium-rare. Leave the steaks to rest for 10–15 minutes.

2 When the steaks have cooled slightly, slice them thinly, using a heavy knife, and put the slices into a large bowl.

3 Add the sliced onion, cucumber batons and chopped lemon grass.

4 Add the spring onions. Toss and season with lime juice and Thai fish sauce. Serve at room temperature or chilled, garnished with the chillies, coriander, mustard cress and mint.

NEW ORLEANS STEAK SALAD

The New Orleans "Poor Boy" started life in the Italian Creole community, as a sandwich filled with leftover scraps. This salad, made with tender beef steak, is a variation on the sandwich.

INGREDIENTS

4 sirloin or rump (round) steaks,
about 175g/6oz each
1 escarole lettuce
1 bunch watercress
4 tomatoes, quartered
4 large gherkins, sliced
4 spring onions (scallions), sliced
4 canned artichoke hearts, halved
175g/6oz button (white)
mushrooms, sliced
12 green olives
120ml/4fl oz French dressing
salt and freshly ground
black pepper

SERVES 4

1 Season the steaks with plenty of black pepper and cook under a preheated hot grill (broiler) or on a hot barbecue, for 4–6 minutes, turning once, until they are medium-rare. Transfer them to a plate, cover with foil and leave the steaks to rest in a warm place.

2 Combine the salad leaves with all the ingredients except the steak, and toss with the French dressing.

3 Divide the salad between four plates. Slice each steak diagonally and arrange the slices over the salad. Season with salt and fresh black pepper and serve.

The perfect end to a summer lunch, *al fresco* supper, a barbecue

or picnic, fruit salad is a favourite with young and old alike. The

recipes in this chapter make full use of the massive range of

fruits available, from familiar to exotic and from fresh to dried.

FRUIT SALADS

FRESH FRUIT SALAD

This basic fruit salad is always welcome, especially after a rich main course. It is endlessly adaptable – when peaches and strawberries are out of season, use bananas and grapes, or any other fruit.

INGREDIENTS

*2 eating apples
2 oranges
2 peaches
16–20 strawberries
30ml/2 tbsp lemon juice
15–30ml/1–2 tbsp orange
flower water
icing (confectioners') sugar
a few fresh mint leaves, to decorate*

SERVES 6

1 Peel and core the apples and cut into thin slices. Peel the oranges with a sharp knife, removing all the pith, and segment them, catching the juice in a bowl.

2 Plunge the peaches for 1 minute into boiling water, peel off the skin and cut the flesh into thick slices, discarding the stone (pit).

3 Hull the strawberries and halve or quarter if larger. Place all the fruit in a large serving bowl.

4 Blend together the lemon juice, orange flower water and orange juice. Taste and add a little icing sugar to sweeten. Pour the fruit juice mixture over the salad and serve decorated with mint leaves.

DRIED FRUIT SALAD

This wonderful combination of fresh and dried fruit makes an excellent dessert throughout the year. You can use frozen raspberries and blackberries during the winter months.

INGREDIENTS

*115g/4oz/½ cup dried apricots
115g/4oz/½ cup dried peaches
1 pear
1 eating apple
1 orange
115g/4oz/⅔ cup mixed raspberries
and blackberries
1 cinnamon stick
50g/2oz/¼ cup caster
(superfine) sugar
15ml/1 tbsp clear honey
15ml/1 tbsp lemon juice*

SERVES 4

1 Soak the dried apricots and peaches in water for 1–2 hours, until plump, then drain and halve or quarter. Peel and core the pear and apple and cut into cubes.

2 Peel the orange with a sharp knife, removing all the pith, and cut into wedges. Place all the fruit in a large pan with the raspberries and blackberries.

3 Add 600ml/1 pint/2½ cups water, the cinnamon stick, sugar and honey and bring to the boil. Cover and simmer very gently for 10–12 minutes, then remove the pan from the heat.

4 Stir in the lemon juice. Leave to cool, then transfer to a bowl and chill in the refrigerator for about 1–2 hours before serving.

COOL GREEN FRUIT SALAD
. . .

A sophisticated, simple fruit salad for any time of the year.

INGREDIENTS
3 Ogen or Galia melons
115g/4oz seedless green grapes
2 kiwi fruit
1 star fruit
1 green-skinned eating apple
1 lime
175ml/6fl oz/³/4 cup sparkling grape juice

SERVES 6

1 Halve the melons and remove the seeds. Keeping the shells intact, scoop out the flesh with a melon baller or use a spoon, then cut into cubes. Reserve the melon shells.

2 Remove any stems from the grapes and, if they are large, cut them in half. Peel and chop the kiwi fruit. Thinly slice the star fruit. Core and thinly slice the apple and place in a mixing bowl with the melon, grapes, kiwi fruit and star fruit.

3 Thinly pare the rind from the lime and cut it in fine strips. Blanch the lime strips in boiling water for 30 seconds, drain and rinse in cold water. Squeeze the juice from the lime and toss the juice into the bowl of fruit.

4 Spoon the prepared fruit into the reserved melon shells and chill the shells in the refrigerator until required. Just before serving, spoon the sparkling grape juice over the fruit and sprinkle with the strips of lime rind.

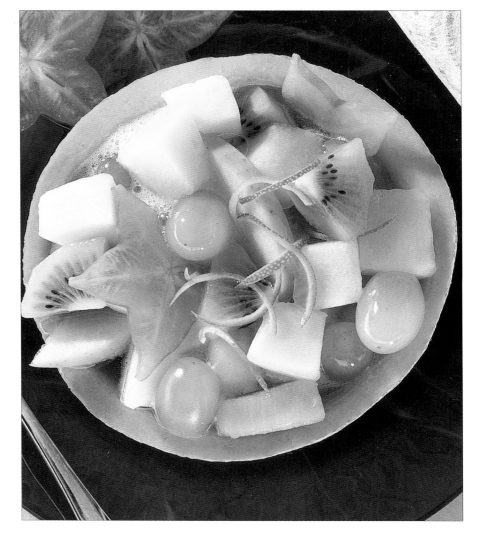

Cook's Tip

On a hot summer's day, serve the filled melon shells nestling on a platter of crushed ice to keep them beautifully cool.

WINTER FRUIT SALAD

∘ ⟋ ∘

INGREDIENTS

225g/8oz can pineapple cubes in
fruit juice
200ml/7fl oz/scant 1 cup freshly
squeezed orange juice
200ml/7fl oz/scant 1 cup
unsweetened apple juice
30ml/2 tbsp orange or apple liqueur
30ml/2 tbsp clear
honey (optional)
2 oranges, peeled
2 green-skinned eating
apples, chopped
2 pears, chopped
4 plums, stoned (pitted)
and chopped
12 fresh dates, stoned (pitted)
and chopped
115g/4oz/½ cup ready-to-eat
dried apricots
fresh mint sprigs, to decorate

SERVES 6

1 Drain the pineapple, reserving the juice. Put the pineapple juice, orange juice, apple juice, liqueur and honey, if using, in a large serving bowl and stir.

Cook's Tip

Use other unsweetened fruit juices, such as pink grapefruit and pineapple juice, in place of the orange and apple juice.

---

2 Using a small sharp knife, segment the oranges, catching any juice in the bowl. Put the orange segments and pineapple in the fruit juice mixture.

3 Add the chopped apples and pears to the bowl.

4 Stir in the plums, dates and dried apricots, cover with clear film (plastic wrap) and chill in the refrigerator for several hours. Decorate with fresh mint sprigs before serving.

ITALIAN FRUIT SALAD AND ICE CREAM

In the summer in Italy, little pavement fruit stores sell small dishes of macerated soft fruits. Delectable on their own, they also make wonderful ice cream.

INGREDIENTS

900g/2lb mixed summer fruits such as strawberries, raspberries, blueberries, peaches, apricots, plums, melons
juice of 3–4 oranges
juice of 1 lemon
15ml/1 tbsp liquid pear and apple concentrate
60ml/4 tbsp whipping cream
30ml/2 tbsp orange liqueur (optional)
fresh mint sprigs, to decorate

SERVES 6

1 Prepare all the fruit according to type and then cut it into fairly small pieces.

2 Put the fruit into a serving bowl and pour over enough orange juice to cover. Add the lemon juice and chill for 2 hours.

3 Set half the macerated fruit aside to serve as it is. Process the rest in a blender or food processor to a smooth purée.

4 Gently warm the pear and apple concentrate and stir into the fruit purée. Whip the cream and fold it in, then add the liqueur, if using.

5 Churn the mixture in an ice-cream maker, following the manufacturer's instructions, or place it in a freezerproof container. Freeze until ice crystals form around the edge, then beat the mixture until smooth.

6 Repeat the process once or twice, then freeze until firm.

7 Transfer the ice cream to the refrigerator to soften slightly before serving in scoops, with the fruit, decorated with sprigs of mint.

> ### Cook's Tip
> The macerated fruit also makes a delicious drink. Purée in a blender or food processor, then press through a sieve.

WATERMELON, GINGER AND GRAPEFRUIT SALAD

∘ ∘ ∘

This pretty, pink combination is very light and refreshing for any summer meal.

INGREDIENTS

*450g/1lb/2 cups watermelon flesh
2 ruby or pink grapefruit
2 pieces preserved stem ginger and
30ml/2 tbsp of the syrup*

SERVES 4

1 Remove any seeds from the watermelon and cut the flesh into bitesize chunks.

2 Using a small, sharp knife, cut away all the peel and white pith from the grapefruit. Carefully cut between the membranes and lift out the segments, catching any juice in a bowl.

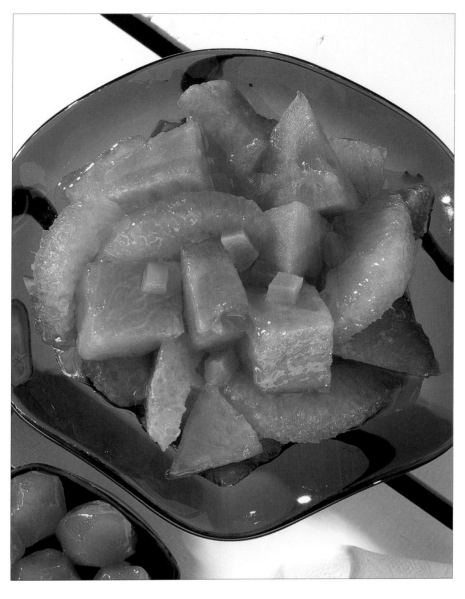

Cook's Tip

Toss the fruits gently – grapefruit segments will break up easily and the appearance of the dish will be spoiled.

3 Finely chop the stem ginger and place in a serving bowl with the melon cubes and grapefruit segments, adding the reserved juice.

4 Spoon over the ginger syrup and toss the fruits lightly to mix. Cover with clear film (plastic wrap) and chill before serving.

479

FRESH FRUIT WITH MANGO COULIS

. . .

This bright, flavourful sauce is easy to prepare and ideal for making a simple fruit salad seem special.

INGREDIENTS

*1 large ripe mango, peeled, stoned (pitted) and chopped
rind of 1 unwaxed orange
juice of 3 oranges
caster (superfine) sugar, to taste
2 peaches
2 nectarines
1 small mango, peeled
2 plums
1 pear or 1/2 small melon
juice of 1 lemon
25–50g/1–2oz/heaped tbsp wild strawberries (optional)
25–50g/1–2oz/
heaped tbsp raspberries
25–50g/1–2oz/
heaped tbsp blueberries
small fresh mint sprigs, to decorate*

SERVES 6

1 In a food processor fitted with a metal blade, process the large mango until smooth. Add the orange rind and juice and sugar to taste and process again until very smooth. Press through a sieve into a bowl and chill.

2 Slice and stone (pit) the peaches, nectarines, small mango and plums. Quarter the pear and remove the core or, if using, slice the melon thinly and remove the skin.

3 Place the sliced fruits on a large plate, sprinkle with the lemon juice, cover with clear film (plastic wrap) and chill in the refrigerator for up to 3 hours before serving. (Some fruits discolour if cut too far ahead of time.)

4 To serve, arrange the sliced fruits attractively on serving plates, spoon the berries on top, drizzle with a little mango coulis and decorate with mint sprigs. Serve the remaining coulis separately.

PINEAPPLE CRUSH WITH STRAWBERRIES AND LYCHEES

∘ ∘ ∘

The sweet, tropical flavours of pineapple and lychees combine well with aromatic strawberries.

INGREDIENTS
2 small pineapples
450g/1lb/4 cups strawberries
400g/14oz can lychees
45ml/3 tbsp kirsch or white rum
30ml/2 tbsp icing (confectioners') sugar

SERVES 4

1 Remove the crowns from both pineapples by twisting sharply. Reserve the leaves for decoration.

2 Cut both pineapples in half diagonally using a long-bladed, serrated knife.

3 Cut around the flesh inside the skin of all the pineapple halves with a small, sharp, serrated knife, keeping the skin intact. Remove the core from the pineapple and discard. Chop the flesh. Reserve the skins.

4 Hull the strawberries and gently combine with the pineapple and lychees, taking care not to damage the fruit.

5 Mix the kirsch or rum with the icing sugar, pour over the fruit and freeze for 45 minutes.

6 Turn out the fruit into the pineapple skins, decorate with the reserved pineapple leaves and serve immediately.

Variation
Try using sapodillas instead of lychees in this recipe. Make sure that they are really ripe or they will be horrible.

Cook's Tip
A ripe pineapple will resist pressure when squeezed and will have a sweet, fragrant smell. In winter freezing conditions can cause the flesh to blacken.

MUSCAT GRAPE FRAPPÉ
◦ ◦ ◦

The flavour and perfume of the Muscat grape is rarely more enticing than when captured in this sophisticated, icy-cool salad. Because of its alcohol content this dish is not suitable for young children.

INGREDIENTS

½ bottle Muscat wine, Beaumes de Venise, Frontignan or Rivesaltes
450g/1lb Muscat grapes

SERVES 4

1 Pour the wine into a stainless-steel or enamel tray, add 150ml/¼ pint/⅔ cup water, mix well and freeze for for about 3 hours, or until the wine is completely solid.

2 Remove the seeds from the grapes with a pair of tweezers. If you have time, you can also peel the grapes. Scrape across the frozen wine with a tablespoon to make a fine ice. Combine the grapes with the ice, spoon into four shallow glasses and serve immediately.

GRAPEFRUIT SALAD WITH CAMPARI AND ORANGE

The bitter-sweet flavour of Campari combines especially well with citrus fruit, such as grapefruit and oranges. Because of its alcohol content, this dish is not suitable for young children.

INGREDIENTS

45ml/3 tbsp caster
(superfine) sugar
60ml/4 tbsp Campari
30ml/2 tbsp lemon juice
4 grapefruit
5 oranges
4 fresh mint sprigs, to decorate

SERVES 4

1 Bring 150ml/¼ pint/⅔ cup water to the boil in a small pan, add the sugar and simmer until dissolved. Transfer to a bowl; leave to cool.

2 Add the Campari and lemon juice to the syrup and stir well to mix. Cut the peel from the top, bottom and sides of the grapefruit and oranges with a serrated knife. Segment the fruit into a bowl by slipping a small paring knife between the flesh and the membranes. Combine the fruit with the Campari syrup, cover with clear film (plastic wrap) and chill until ready to serve.

3 Spoon the salad into four dishes, decorate with a sprig of fresh mint and serve.

Cook's Tip
When buying citrus fruit, choose brightly coloured varieties that feel heavy for their size.

DRESSED STRAWBERRIES

∘ ∘ ∘

INGREDIENTS

350g/12oz/2 cups raspberries or
tayberries, fresh
or frozen
45ml/3 tbsp caster
(superfine) sugar
1 passion fruit
675g/1½lb/6 cups small
fresh strawberries
8 plain finger
biscuits (cookies),
to serve

SERVES 4

4 Pass the blended fruit sauce through a fine nylon sieve to remove the seeds, pressing it through with the back of a spoon.

5 Fold the strawberries into the sauce, then spoon into four stemmed glasses. Serve with plain finger biscuits.

1 Place the raspberries or tayberries and sugar in a stain-resistant pan and soften over a gentle heat to release the juices. Simmer for 5 minutes. Leave to cool.

2 Halve the passion fruit and scoop out the seeds and juice.

3 Turn the raspberries or tayberries into a food processor or blender, add the passion fruit and process until a smooth purée forms.

MIXED MELON SALAD WITH WILD STRAWBERRIES

Ice-cold melon is a delicious way to end a meal. Here several varieties are combined with strongly flavoured wild or woodland strawberries.

INGREDIENTS

*1 Charentais melon
1 cantaloupe melon
900g/2lb watermelon
175g/6oz/1½ cups wild
strawberries
4 fresh mint sprigs, to decorate*

SERVES 4

1 Cut all the melons in half using a large knife.

2 Remove the seeds from the Charentais and cantaloupe melons with a spoon.

3 With a melon baller, take out as many balls as you can from all three melons. Combine in a large bowl, cover with clear film (plastic wrap) and chill in the refrigerator until ready to serve.

4 Add the wild strawberries to the melon balls and turn out into four stemmed glass dishes.

5 Decorate with sprigs of fresh mint and serve while still very cold and refreshing.

FRUIT KEBABS WITH MANGO AND YOGURT SAUCE

° ° °

*This colourful dessert is ideal
for a party.*

INGREDIENTS
*½ pineapple, peeled, cored
and cubed
2 kiwi fruit, peeled and cubed
150g/5oz/scant 1 cup strawberries,
hulled and cut in half lengthways
½ mango, peeled, stoned (pitted)
and cubed*

FOR THE SAUCE
*120ml/4fl oz/½ cup fresh
mango purée
120ml/4fl oz/½ cup thick natural
(plain) yogurt
5ml/1 tsp sugar
few drops of vanilla
essence (extract)
15ml/1 tbsp finely shredded fresh
mint leaves
1 fresh mint sprig, to decorate*

SERVES 4

1 To make the sauce, beat together
the mango purée, natural yogurt,
sugar and vanilla with an electric
hand mixer.

2 Stir in the shredded mint. Cover
the sauce and chill until required.

Cook's Tip
Use 1–1½ peeled and stoned
(pitted) mangoes for the purée.

---

3 Thread the fruit on to twelve
15cm/6in wooden skewers,
alternating the pineapple, kiwi
fruit, strawberries and mango.

4 Transfer the mango and yogurt
sauce to an attractive bowl,
decorate with a mint sprig and
place in the centre of a large
serving platter. Surround with the
kebabs and serve.

TROPICAL FRUITS IN CINNAMON SYRUP

° ° °

*These glistening fruits are best
prepared a day in advance to
allow the flavours to develop
and mingle.*

INGREDIENTS
*450g/1lb/2¼ cups caster
(superfine) sugar
1 cinnamon stick
1 large or 2 medium papayas
(about 675g/1½lb), peeled, seeded
and cut lengthways into thin pieces
1 large or 2 medium mangoes
(about 675 g/1½lb) peeled, stoned
(pitted) and cut lengthways into
thin pieces
1 large or 2 small star fruit (about
225g/8oz) thinly sliced*

SERVES 6

1 Sprinkle about one-third of the
sugar over the base of a large,
heavy pan. Add the cinnamon stick
and half of the papaya, mango and
star fruit pieces.

2 Sprinkle half of the remaining
sugar over the fruit pieces in the
pan. Add the remaining papaya,
mango and star fruit and sprinkle
with the remaining sugar.

3 Cover the pan and cook the
fruit over medium heat for about
35–45 minutes, until the sugar
dissolves completely. Gently shake
the pan occasionally, but do not
stir or the fruit will collapse and
become soggy.

4 Uncover the pan and simmer for
about 10 minutes, until the fruit
becomes translucent. Remove the
pan from the heat and leave to
cool. Discard the cinnamon stick.

5 Transfer the fruit and syrup to
a bowl, cover and chill overnight
before serving.

BANANA AND MASCARPONE

If you are a fan of cold banana custard, you'll love this recipe. It is an adult version of an old favourite. No one will guess that the secret is ready-made custard sauce.

INGREDIENTS
250g/9oz/generous 1 cup mascarpone cheese
300ml/½ pint/1¼ cups fresh ready-made custard sauce
150ml/¼ pint/⅔ cup Greek (US strained plain) yogurt
4 bananas
juice of 1 lime
50 g/2oz/½ cup pecan nuts, coarsely chopped
120ml/4fl oz/½ cup maple syrup

SERVES 4–6

1 Combine the mascarpone, custard sauce and yogurt in a large bowl and beat together with a wooden spoon until smooth. Make this mixture up to several hours ahead, if you like. Cover and chill, then stir before using.

2 Slice the bananas diagonally and place in a separate bowl. Pour over the lime juice and toss together until the bananas are coated.

3 Divide half the custard mixture among four to six dessert glasses and top each portion with a spoonful of the banana mixture.

4 Spoon the remaining custard mixture into the glasses and top with the rest of the bananas. Sprinkle the nuts over the top. Drizzle maple syrup over each dessert and chill for 30 minutes before serving.

BANANAS WITH LIME AND CARDAMOM

Cardamom and bananas go together perfectly, and this luxurious dessert makes an original treat.

INGREDIENTS
6 small bananas
50g/2oz/¼ cup butter
seeds from 4 cardamom pods, crushed
50g/2oz/½ cup flaked (sliced) almonds
thinly pared rind and juice of 2 limes
50g/2oz/⅓ cup light muscovado (brown) sugar
30ml/2 tbsp dark rum
vanilla ice cream, to serve

SERVES 4

1 Peel and halve the bananas lengthways. Heat half the butter in a frying pan. Add half the bananas and cook until the undersides are golden. Turn carefully, using a fish slice (metal spatula). Cook until golden all over.

2 Once cooked, transfer the bananas to a heatproof serving dish. Cook the remaining bananas in the same way.

3 Melt the remaining butter, then add the cardamom seeds and almonds. Cook, stirring until the almonds are golden.

4 Stir in the lime rind and juice, then the sugar. Cook, stirring, until the mixture is smooth, bubbling and slightly reduced. Stir in the rum. Pour the sauce over the bananas and serve immediately, with vanilla ice cream.

MELON TRIO WITH GINGER BISCUITS
° ° °

INGREDIENTS

¼ watermelon
½ honeydew melon
½ charentais melon
60ml/4 tbsp preserved stem
ginger syrup

FOR THE BISCUITS (COOKIES)
25g/1oz/2 tbsp unsalted
(sweet) butter
25g/1oz/2 tbsp caster
(superfine) sugar
5ml/1 tsp clear honey
25g/1oz/¼ cup plain (all-
purpose) flour
25g/1oz/¼ cup luxury glacé
(candied) mixed fruit,
finely chopped
1 piece of preserved stem ginger in
syrup, drained and
finely chopped
30ml/2 tbsp flaked
(sliced) almonds

SERVES 4

3 Line a baking sheet with baking parchment. Space four spoonfuls of the biscuit mixture on the parchment at regular intervals, leaving plenty of room for spreading. Flatten the mixture slightly into rounds and bake for 15 minutes or until the tops are golden brown.

4 Let the biscuits cool on the baking sheet for 1 minute, then lift each one in turn, using a fish slice (metal spatula), and drape over a rolling pin to cool and harden. Repeat with the remaining ginger mixture to make eight biscuits.

5 Serve the chilled melon chunks with some of the syrup and the ginger biscuits.

Cook's Tip

For an even prettier effect, scoop the melon flesh into balls with the large end of a melon baller.

---

1 Using a spoon, remove the seeds from the melons and discard. Cut them into wedges, then slice off the rind. Cut all the flesh into chunks and mix in a bowl. Stir in the ginger syrup, cover with clear film (plastic wrap) and chill until ready to serve.

2 Meanwhile, make the biscuits. Preheat the oven to 180°C/ 350°F/Gas 4. Heat the butter, sugar and honey in a pan until melted. Remove from the heat and stir in the remaining ingredients.

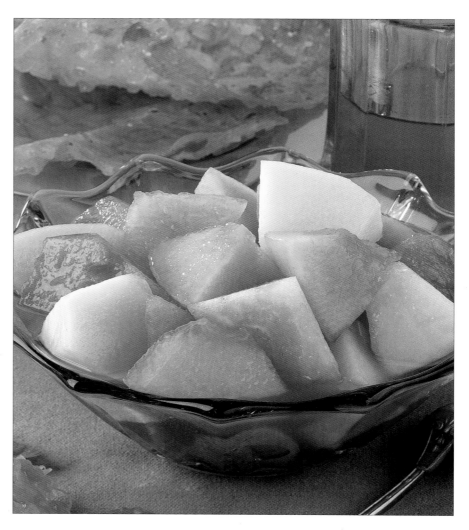

JAMAICAN FRUIT TRIFLE

∘ ∘ ∘

INGREDIENTS

*1 large sweet pineapple,
peeled and cored,
about 350g/12oz
300ml/½ pint/1¼ cups double
(heavy) cream
200ml/7fl oz/scant 1 cup
crème fraîche
60ml/4 tbsp icing (confectioners')
sugar, sifted
10ml/2 tsp pure vanilla
essence (extract)
30ml/2 tbsp white or coconut rum
3 papayas, peeled, seeded
and chopped
3 mangoes, peeled, stoned (pitted)
and chopped
thinly pared rind and juice
of 1 lime
25g/1oz/⅓ cup coarsely shredded
or flaked coconut, toasted*

SERVES 8

1 Cut the pineapple into large chunks, place in a food processor or blender and process briefly until chopped. Tip into a sieve placed over a bowl and leave for about 5 minutes so that most of the juice drains from the fruit.

2 Whip the double cream to very soft peaks, then lightly, but thoroughly fold in the crème fraîche, sifted icing sugar, vanilla essence and rum.

3 Fold the drained, chopped pineapple into the cream mixture. Place the chopped papayas and mangoes in a large bowl and pour over the lime juice. Gently stir the fruit mixture to combine. Cut the pared lime rind into thin shreds and add it to the bowl.

4 Divide the fruit mixture and the pineapple cream among eight dessert plates. Decorate with the lime shreds, toasted coconut and a few small pineapple leaves, if you like, and serve immediately.

Cook's Tip

It is important to let the pineapple purée drain thoroughly, otherwise the pineapple cream will be watery. Don't throw away the drained pineapple juice – mix it with sparkling mineral water for a refreshing drink.

TROPICAL FRUIT GRATIN

∘ ∘ ∘

This out-of-the-ordinary gratin is strictly for adults. A colourful combination of fruit is topped with a simple sabayon before being flashed under the grill.

INGREDIENTS
2 tamarillos
½ sweet pineapple
1 ripe mango
175g/6oz/1½ cups blackberries
120ml/4fl oz/½ cup sparkling white wine
115g/4oz/½ cup caster (superfine) sugar
6 egg yolks

SERVES 4

1 Cut each tamarillo in half lengthways and then into thick slices. Cut the rind and core from the pineapple and take spiral slices off the outside to remove the eyes. Cut the flesh into chunks. Peel the mango, cut it in half and cut the flesh away from the central stone (pit) in slices.

2 Divide all the fruit, including the blackberries, among four 14cm/5½in gratin dishes set on a baking sheet and set aside. Heat the wine and sugar in a pan until the sugar has dissolved. Bring to the boil and cook for 5 minutes.

3 Put the egg yolks in a heatproof bowl. Set the bowl over a pan of simmering water and whisk until pale. Gradually pour in the hot sugar syrup, whisking constantly, until the mixture has thickened. Preheat the grill (broiler).

4 Spoon the mixture over the fruit. Place the baking sheet on a low shelf under the hot grill until the topping is golden. Serve hot.

GRILLED PINEAPPLE WITH PAPAYA SAUCE

∘ ∘ ∘

Pineapple cooked this way takes on a superb flavour and is sensational when served with the papaya sauce.

INGREDIENTS
1 sweet pineapple
melted butter, for greasing and brushing
2 pieces drained preserved stem ginger in syrup, cut into fine batons, plus 30ml/2 tbsp of the syrup from the jar
30ml/2 tbsp demerara (raw) sugar
pinch of ground cinnamon
fresh mint sprigs, to decorate

FOR THE SAUCE
1 ripe papaya, peeled and seeded
175ml/6fl oz/¾ cup apple juice

SERVES 6

1 Peel the pineapple and take spiral slices off the outside to remove the eyes. Cut it crossways into six slices, each 2.5cm/1in thick. Line a baking sheet with a sheet of foil, rolling up the sides to make a rim. Grease the foil with melted butter. Preheat the grill (broiler).

2 Arrange the pineapple slices on the lined baking sheet. Brush with butter, then top with the ginger batons, sugar and cinnamon. Drizzle over the stem ginger syrup. Grill (broil) for 5–7 minutes or until the slices are golden and lightly charred on top.

3 Meanwhile, make the sauce. Cut a few slices from the papaya and set aside, then purée the remainder with the apple juice in a blender or food processor.

4 Press the purée through a sieve placed over a bowl, then stir in any juices from cooking the pineapple.

5 Serve the pineapple slices with a little sauce drizzled around each plate. Decorate with the reserved papaya slices and the mint sprigs.

CITRUS FRUIT FLAMBÉ

∘ ∘ ∘

*A fruit flambé is a dramatic
finale for a dinner party.*

INGREDIENTS

4 oranges
2 ruby grapefruit
2 limes
50g/2oz/¼ cup butter
50g/2oz/⅓ cup light muscovado
(brown) sugar
45ml/3 tbsp Cointreau
fresh mint sprigs, to decorate

FOR THE PRALINE
oil, for greasing
115g/4oz/½ cup caster
(superfine) sugar
50g/2oz/½ cup shelled
pistachio nuts

SERVES 4

1 First, make the pistachio praline.
Brush a baking sheet lightly with
oil. Place the caster sugar and nuts
in a small heavy pan and cook over
a low heat, gently swirling the pan
occasionally until the sugar has
completely melted.

2 Continue to cook over a fairly
low heat until the nuts start to pop
and the sugar has turned a dark
golden colour. Pour on to the oiled
baking sheet and set aside to cool.
Using a sharp knife, chop the
praline into coarse chunks.

3 Cut all the rind and pith from
the citrus fruits. Holding each fruit
in turn over a large bowl, cut
between the membranes with a
paring knife so that the segments
fall into the bowl, with any juice.

4 Heat the butter and muscovado
sugar together in a heavy frying
pan until the sugar has melted and
the mixture is golden. Strain the
orange, grapefruit and lime juices
into the pan and continue to cook,
stirring occasionally, until the juice
has reduced and is syrupy.

5 Add the fruit segments and warm
through without stirring. Pour over
the Cointreau and set it alight. As
soon as the flames die down, spoon
the fruit flambé into serving dishes.
Sprinkle some praline over each
portion and decorate with mint.

> *Cook's Tip*
> Cointreau is the best-known
> brand name of an orange-
> flavoured liqueur, generically
> known as triple sec.

EXOTIC TROPICAL FRUIT SALAD
∘ ∘ ∘

Passion fruit makes a superb dressing for any kinds of fruit, but really brings out the flavour of exotic varieties.

INGREDIENTS
1 mango
1 papaya
2 kiwi fruit
coconut or vanilla ice cream, to serve

FOR THE DRESSING
3 passion fruit
thinly pared rind and juice of 1 lime
5ml/1 tsp hazelnut or walnut oil
15ml/1 tbsp clear honey

SERVES 6

1 Peel the mango, cut it into three slices, then cut the flesh into chunks and place it in a large bowl. Peel the papaya and cut it in half. Scoop and discard out the seeds, then chop the flesh.

Cook's Tip
A clear golden honey scented with orange blossom or acacia blossom would be perfect for the dressing.

2 Cut both ends off each kiwi fruit, then stand them on a board. Using a small sharp knife, cut off the skin from top to bottom. Cut each kiwi fruit in half lengthways, then cut into thick slices. Combine all the fruit in a large bowl.

3 Make the dressing. Cut each passion fruit in half and scoop the seeds out into a sieve set over a small bowl. Press the seeds well to extract all their juices. Lightly whisk the remaining dressing ingredients into the passion fruit juice, then pour the dressing over the fruit. Mix gently to combine. Cover and chill for 1 hour before serving with scoops of coconut or vanilla ice cream.

INDEX